Whispers of Grace-Filled Blessings from the Mercy Seat

A Coaching Odyssey for a Princess of Great Destiny...

Now, Treasured Princess, Get Ready to Walk Out

Your Destiny Journey,

One Joy-Filled Footprint After

the Next..

Jan Gantos

WESTBOW
PRESS®
A DIVISION OF THOMAS NELSON
& ZONDERVAN

Scripture quotations taken from the Holy Bible, New Living Translation, Copyright © 1996, 2004. Used by permission of Tyndale House Publishers, Inc., Wheaton, Illinois 60189. All rights reserved.

Scripture taken from the Holy Bible, NEW INTERNATIONAL VERSION®. Copyright © 1973, 1978, 1984 by Biblica, Inc. All rights reserved worldwide. Used by permission. NEW INTERNATIONAL VERSION® and NIV® are registered trademarks of Biblica, Inc. Use of either trademark for the offering of goods or services requires the prior written consent of Biblica US, Inc.

Scripture taken from the New King James Version. Copyright © 1979, 1980, 1982 by Thomas Nelson, Inc. Used by permission. All rights reserved.

Some Scripture quotations in this publication are from The Message. Copyright © by Eugene H. Peterson 1993, 1994, 1995, 1996, 2000, 2001, 2002. Used by permission of NavPress Publishing Group.

WestBow Press books may be ordered through booksellers or by contacting:

WestBow Press
A Division of Thomas Nelson & Zondervan
1663 Liberty Drive
Bloomington, IN 47403
www.westbowpress.com
1 (866) 928-1240

Because of the dynamic nature of the Internet, any web addresses or links contained in this book may have changed since publication and may no longer be valid. The views expressed in this work are solely those of the author and do not necessarily reflect the views of the publisher, and the publisher hereby disclaims any responsibility for them.

Any people depicted in stock imagery provided by Getty Images are models, and such images are being used for illustrative purposes only. Certain stock imagery © Getty Images.

ISBN: 978-1-4908-5623-0 (sc)
ISBN: 978-1-4908-5624-7 (hc)
ISBN: 978-1-4908-5622-3 (e)

Library of Congress Control Number: 2014918276

Print information available on the last page.

WestBow Press rev. date: 07/12/2019

In loving memory of our son, Jeremiah Gantos

To all six children of our blended family, their spouses, and fiancees: Adam & Denise, Anita & Chris, Curtis & Brittany & her three children: Adrionna, Gary, and Skyler, Matthew & Krystol, Lawrence Jr. & Keila, and Danielle & Kevin

CONTENTS

Part Three: Feeling Kind of Insecure?
Become God's "Anchor Throwing" Princess

Part Four: Feeling a Tinge of Rejection?
Become a "Balcony Coach" Princess

Part Five: Feeling a Slight Bit Unforgiving?
Become a "Grace Planting" Princess

Part Six: Feeling a Smidgen Down?
Become a "Heart Lifting" Princess

Part Seven: Feeling an "Attitude" Issue Rising Up?
Become a "Kindness Extending" Princess

A NEVER-ENDING LOVE STORY FOR A PRINCESS OF GREAT DESTINY...

Every Princess of our Messiah is a *Princess of Great Destiny*. The destiny odyssey of each Princess is one that is waiting to be filled with His richest blessings, His joy, and His never-ending love... The fascinating thing is that, while every odyssey bears some similarities, no two are identical.

As an organizational life coach, for a *Princess of Great Destiny*, I work with my client to present strategies, based on her long and short-term goals-strategies that will help streamline her "to-do" lists, and weekly schedules. Realistic expectations, focus, and healthy boundaries are a key part of the coaching process. If applicable, we include her educational and career planning aspirations. A special emphasis of the coaching process is placed on creating room for more great "God Time." The objective is simply this:

To introduce ways a Princess can "DE-STRESS" from her overloaded,
over-committed, energy depleted, overwhelming,
too busy, busy, busy, burned-out,
I need a gallon of that "Calgon Bath Time Take Me Away" Stuff... life.

As an inspirational life coach for a *Princess Of Great Destiny*, I customize a plan to fit her dreams, personality type, areas of giftedness... The coaching approach I favor is an interactive exchange of creative ideas, techniques, and strategies, that lead to a personalized action plan. This coaching tool is designed to help you identify and explore your spiritual gifts, in greater depth. It is also designed to introduce creative ways for you to develop those gifts that run parallel to God's plan and purpose for your life.

I have been honored and blessed by insightful words, spoken into my life, by teachers, life coaches, writers, pastors, friends... My prayer is that I will speak into your life, throughout the pages of this book.

As a life coach, it's such a delight to applaud the efforts of each Princess. It's so awesome to celebrate her for who she is-God's treasured Princess. And, it's my pleasure to recognize her for what she has worked so hard to accomplish. What a joy it is to encourage her, as she begins to fulfill her vision, her dreams, her goals... some of which she has held in her heart for a very long time. I love to lean over the balcony of her life, celebrating with her, as she brings God glory, with each footstep of her odyssey-one that is designed exclusively for her, by the God who just adores her!

The goal is to pass along a generous dose of God's extraordinarily calming balm, to the next Princess. Just what Dr. Jesus prescribes as the Rx "De-Stressor" of choice, formulated for the benefit of those of us who could use a handful of His peace and tranquility.

How Can I Benefit from Organizational and Time-Management Life Coaching?

As a life coach, the questions I seem to be asked most often, sound something like this: "How can I make life work without getting stressed to the max?" "When I have such a full plate already, how can I remain flexible, just in case God may need to interrupt my agenda, at any given time?" "I want to be able to step outside of my circumstances that may be presenting some challenges, so that I can come alongside and encourage the next Princess. How do I accomplish this goal?" I need help strengthening my boundaries. Where would you suggest that I begin?"

Life Coaching, no matter the niche, becomes an essential ingredient for a Princess of Great Destiny, who desires to suceed at reaching her goals, realizing her dreams, and living out the call God has on her life. Even when confronted with stressful personal scenarios, or tapped out energy levels, implementing specific coaching tools and techniques, coupled with applying God's Wisdom, in order to help make healthy life choices, she can greatly benefit from the coaching process.

Life Coaching is key to having a meaningful, intentional, and purposeful God-focused life. Organizational and Time Management Life Coaching are instrumental in providing ways to help alleviate some of the stressors we might frequently face; some of the challenges that may be standing in the way of our ability to stay focused.

The following is an introductory outline of the focus formula I developed, to begin moving things in the right direction for the "stressed-out" Princess. Perhaps your heart is intent upon growing more intimate with the God who calls you His Jewel. It's my prayer that the following formula, though only an outline, will be of benefit:

FOCUS + ORGANIZATION + TIME MANAGEMENT SKILLS + FLEXIBILITY = MORE GREAT GOD TIME!

As your life coach, one of the first priorities we'll focus on is to empower you with tools that will assist you in implementing the positive changes you want to make in your life. The importance of setting realistic goals is the first priority. In individual coaching sessions, I pass along insight and ideas on how to organize time efficiently and effectively. The sessions are structured so that the coaching experience becomes a continuous flow of ideas between the two of us.

So, how do we maximize our time and minimize those time-consuming distractions-distractions that tend to drive us, as females, up a veritable wall, (without mentioning any names, other than my own, of course)? When utilized properly, these skills can become instrumental in freeing up quality time, precious time, uninterrupted time, sacred time-time to spend sitting ever so quietly at His feet...

Hmmm... Just imagine... Imagine sitting so still that you can feel Messiah's breath on your face... Sitting so quietly that you can hear the rhythm of His heartbeat, sense His love, and capture His enthusiasm regarding creative ways you, as a Princess of Great Destiny, can become a balcony coach for the next Princess... Imagine encouraging her to reach, even higher, for a goal or dream she has all but given up on ever reaching. Imagine passing on the legacy of affirmation and encouragement, to the next generation. Hmmm... Just imagine...

An Organizational And Time Management Blueprint: The Wow Paradigm

The *Organizational And Time Management Blueprint,* or, the *Wow Paradigm,* for short, is one I use most often when working with coaching clients who are pre-teens, teens, students preparing for college, newly engaged, newly married, or first-time moms and nanas. Once we have established a *Personalized Action Plan,* she can catch a glimpse into how mom, nana, grammy, auntie, mimi... is able to do all the things she does, and make it look like a cake-walk. There are times, in the life of every Princess, when we know that life is anything but a stroll in the park on a Sunday afternoon. We become keenly aware that real life rarely looks like the epitomy of a fairy tale. The good news is that God is available, 24/7, to help us through each time crunch, so we can avoid fatigue at the thought of one more commitment. Maintaining good boundaries is key!

From a Christian life coaching perspective, your schedule, on a day-to-day basis, will need to be flexible enough so that God can alter it, and take you in another direction. It's wise to maintain a degree of flexibility so that God, at any given time, can interrupt our plans. These interruptions are sometimes referred to as "God" moments, or as a "God" thing. Had we not have remained adaptable to changes in our agendas, to the extent to which that's possible, we may have missed some awesome God moments.

The following is the *WOW* formula that can be instrumental in helping my client and I work together at customizing it, changing it, or modifying it to fit her busy lifestyle. It has become foundational for the first seven coaching sessions, and is what I find helpful to put the process of flexibility into action. It also works well in helping to bring about a more balanced, focused, and intentional atmosphere, to the sometimes "beyond crazy" life of a cherished Princess:

*PERSEVERENCE + PROTECTION OF
YOUR PERSONAL BIBLE STUDY
TIME...CONTEMPLATIVE PRAYER TIME...
DEVOTIONAL PRAYER TIME...PRAISE AND
WORSHIP TIME...INTERCESSORY PRAYER
TIME...FAMILY TIME & LEISURE TIME...
EQUALS
MORE GREAT GOD TIME!*

THANKS TO MY FAMILY AND LIFELONG BALCONY COACHES

Whispers of Grace-Filled Blessings From The Mercy Seat... is dedicated to my Messiah Jesus, the Author and Finisher of my faith. I give You all the praise, all the honor, and all the glory! Lord, You are my original Balcony

Coach. Thank You for never giving up on me. Thank You for Your Everlasting Love; a love that is truly amazing...

When I was young, my daddy would lean over the balcony of my life whispering, "Whatever you decide to do, put your heart into it, and just do your best. I love you." Daddy has been gone for several years now, but it's almost as if I can still hear his whispers in my ear. This book, in part, is the result of his balcony coaching.

My husband, also known as "Honey", and I have been married for twenty-seven years. He has been my writing coach for the last twenty years. "Thank you bunches, Honey, for encouraging me to be forever joyful, praise God, and trust Him through every trial, instead of whining like the "Princess-In-Training" that, at times, we both know I can be. And, for a first-born who is married to a first-born, that is quite a challenge! You deserve a huge medal of perseverance for putting up with me. And while I'm hard at work, practicing the art of becoming a recovering perfectionist, I'll be sure to order that medal A.S.A.P!"

Thank you, Adam and Danielle, for being children who have impacted my life in such a positive and powerful way. A huge thanks, Adam, for challenging me to never give up. Thank you so much for being so faithful, and for sticking by my side, no matter what. Thank you for your wisdom, Adam, that seemed so often to surpass your age.

Danielle, thank you for reminding me to "stop and smell the roses" when life, as a single mom, presented some really tough challenges, hard choices, and truly difficult decisions. No matter how arduous a process that life appeared to be, you could always make me laugh. What a sense of humor you seem to have been born with! You are both indelibly imprinted on my heart and permanently etched in my soul. I love you both so much!

Their spouses and fiancees: Adam & Denise, Anita & Chris, Jeremy & Jessica, Curtis & Brittany & her three children: Adrionna, Gary, and Skyler, Matthew & Krystol, Lawrence Jr. & Keila, and Danielle & Kevin. Thank you for touching our lives with so many blessings, laughter, and pretty wild, yet always great "memory-making moments" together! I laugh every time I think of the occassions, over the past twenty-seven years, when you changed addresses almost as often as people change their socks-or so it seems. I finally gave up trying to memorize new addresses, states, zip codes, and area codes. As a last resort, I began making that fabulous invention, otherwise known as a pencil eraser, a mandatory requirement for my address book. I love you!

To our thirteen GrandSugars: Charlotte, Alexander, Isaiah, Alisa Grace, Liberty, Ezra, Jonathan, Ashton, B. G. Grace, Eli, Adriana, Skyler, Gary, and number fourteen who's on her way. You guys and dolls are the absolute best! I love you to the moon and back!

To the following women I so deeply admire, appreciate, and will be forever grateful for: Sherry, (Sher), Lenora, Diane, Linda Sue, Marg, Ruth, Judy, Nancy S., Mindy, Margie, Nancy G., Mary Lou & Mary S. I am so appreciative for hours upon hours of impromptu coaching, and for all the prayers, the encouragement, and the incredible grace you extended me as I worked on this book. Each of you are so special! I love you, my forever friends.

My thanks to Sherry P., a free-lance editor, for her critique of the third re-write. Thank you, Sherry, for gently prompting me to wrap cellophane around my heart and place it on display to be seen by each reader.

To Sher: For all the really late night/early morning chats, for interceding on my behalf, and that of my family; for all the times you sharpened me, like iron, thank you, Sher. You're a special friend and an amazing woman of God!

Larry and I are so appreciative of the following couples who have touched our hearts, and impacted our lives, in so many ways:

Pastor Duane and Diane McLaughlin

Pastor Bob and Lenora DeLemos

Ed and Susan Kravitz

Mark and Nancy Riechle - Inkeepers:

Dr. Gary and Barb Rosberg

Pastor Mike & JoEllen Welte

Linda Sue and Greg Lambert

Margaret and Dennis Wilson

Pastor Don & Helen Sanders

Southmoreland B & B

America's Family Coaches

Calvary Chapel Meadow Mesa (CCMM)

My thanks to the following coaching professors of the International Christian Coaching Association (ICCA), of Light University: To Dwight Bain, Executive Director BCLC-Board of Christian Life Coaching, Dr. Catherine Hart Weber, Dr. Katie Brazelton, Dr. Georgia Shaffer, Dr. Sylvia Frejd, Sandra Dopf Lee, Dr. Richard Eley, and Jeff Jernigan. Thank you so much for modeling godly integrity, as you instill, in the students of Light University, coaching tools and techniques that are instrumental in adding to our coaching toolbox. These tools contain a literal plethora of coaching gems designed to inspire, encourage, empower, train, and challenge to excel!

To Dr. Tim Clinton, President of American Association of Christian Counselors, (AACC), and co-founder of Light Counseling, Inc. And, to Julie Clinton, President of Extraordinary Women, host of EWomen conferences, and author of Extraordinary Women. Thank you both for inspiring so many, and for modeling His love and grace, with excellence, for our lives!

The following is a letter addressed to you, a Princess of Great Destiny. Personalize it with your first name and make a copy to refer to it whenever you need a *Refreshing Hug!*

Precious Princess _____,

Please take a sacred moment and pause, as the Spirit of God breathes His breath of fresh anointing into your soul. He is preparing your heart and empowering you, His Jewel, to spend time at His feet, every day and every step of the way toward becoming the...

BEAUTIFUL, LOVING, POISED, PASSIONATE, FOCUSED,

RESULT-ORIENTED, INSPIRING, ENCOURAGING, ENTHUSIASTIC,

CHERISHED PRINCESS
OF
OUR MESSIAH!

As you delve deeply into the Word of God, it is my desire to lean over the balcony of your life and challenge you to do your best. It's just what the Lord had in mind when He inscribed your soul on the palms of His hands, (see: Isaiah 49:16 NKJV). I would consider it a privilege, and my pleasure, to come alongside you and encourage you, as you live your life purposefully and intentionally for His Glory! What a blessing it becomes to realize that God's Word, His Ways, His Precepts, and His Wisdom are continually being imparted to you, by the Spirit of God.

Please join me, as we turn our focus to passing this amazing legacy on to the next Princess; on to the next generation. Let's purpose to uncover the nuggets of truth found in His Word. It is the legacy your Abba Daddy has implanted in your heart and soul. It is a legacy filled with His richest blessings, nestled among His Covenant Promises, like priceless gifts just waiting to be opened, one after another, by you, God's highly favored Princess...

SHOWERS OF BLESSING FOR HIS TREASURED PRINCESS...

May God bless you, His treasured Princess, with His Blanket of Grace, His Canopy of Protection, and His Banner of Loving Promises over your life. May He bless you with His unending favor for your odyssey, one inspiring moment after the next. May Messiah bless every gift of encouragement, every impartation of hope, and every bouquet of grace-filled blessings you present to those He brings into your life. As He waltzes you out of your own challenges, may God equip you to empower those He places along your odyssey trail, with the necessary ingredients to cultivate a heart intent upon being a blessing to others.

May your Abba bless you with the desire to come alongside the next Princess, and offer words of hope, enthusiasm, encouragement, and blessing... May He give you a passion to partner with, and be supportive of those He intends to place in your sphere of influence. May He instill in your heart a willingness to use the gifts He has so graciously bestowed upon you, for the benefit of others.

May you intentionally and purposefully practice the waltz of encouragement, focusing on helping others to become all that the Lord so longs for them to become. And, may the waltz go on and on and on... between you and the God who holds you in His arms, and promises to never let you go...

The Lover of your soul desires to leave His tender and grace-filled footprints upon the fertile soil of your heart; nurturing footprints that only the God of unparalleled compassion, grace, and loving kindness, can give.

Father God, draw Your Princess straight into Your "Now Time" for her life. Thank You, Lord, for crowning her with Your favor, Your grace-filled blessings, and Your forever love...

Be Drenched in His Showers of Blessings!

Jan

PART ONE: FEELING JUST A LITTLE DISCOURAGED? BECOME A "HOPE-INSPIRING" PRINCESS

"Encouragers have been called 'balcony people,' ...they always seem to be found leaning over the balcony of our lives saying, 'You can do it...I believe in you.' Encouragers are conveyors of God's blessing because God Himself is a balcony person..."

-H. Norman Wright
Your Tomorrows Can Be Different Than Your Yesterdays
Fleming H. Revel, A division of Baker Book House Company

BOUQUETS OF GRACE-FILLED BLESSINGS

"You crown the year with Your goodness, and
Your paths drip with abundance."
Psalm 65:11 NKJV

The never-ending love story of a Princess of Great Destiny, is filled with precious moments, each day, to become immersed in the richness of God's Word, His Wisdom, and His Grace... From the opening Scripture passage of: *Whispers of Grace-filled Blessings...* through *Heart Whispers, Bouquets of Grace-Filled Blessings, Gems of Wisdom,* and *Refreshing Hugs,* it's my prayer that you will feel His love, as He so lavishly pours it over your life; it's also my prayer that your destiny odyssey be crowned with God's goodness and His richest blessings...

Each new day dawns as a blank page, filled with endless possibilities that stretch across the canvas of your life. And here's some great news: God is plum crazy about you, treasured Princess. He wants to be included in your first thoughts of the morning, and throughout your entire day, as it stretches far into the evening...

Deuteronomy 6:5, in the contemporary Bible version, The Message, poignantly expresses the love we're to have for our Savior. It reads, "Love God, your God, with your whole heart: love him with all that's in you, love him with all you've got."

The following verses are found in Psalm 85:10-11, and, would be easy to commit to memory. They poetically express the relationship among God's love, truth, righteousness, and peace:

"Unfailing love and truth have met together.
Righteousness and peace have kissed!
Truth springs up from the earth,
and righteousness smiles down from heaven."

The verses in Psalm 25:4-5, speak volumes about consulting with God concerning our plans for each day. Regardless of the Scripture verse or Bible version you choose, try personalizing a passage by inserting your first name.

These are examples of ways I have personally found helpful in growing closer to God through prayer. My hope is that you may be able to learn from these examples by using your own style and personality, as you pray God's Word back to Him.

The next thing I do, each morning, is to relinquish my agenda. I hand over my "to do" list for God to alter, delete, or use in any way that's pleasing to Him. I end this time by asking some questions: "Father God, whose life can I bless today? To whom can I speak words of encouragement-words filled with Your joy, peace, and grace?" It's so beautiful to watch, as God reveals His answers. He may answer differently than expected, but that's because He is God of the unexpected.

I hope you'll join me in committing to spend as much time as possible, each day, at the feet of our Lord. I can't think of anything more nourishing than to develop a deeper walk with the Lover of your soul, and mine. Here are a few questions to ponder during your quiet time each morning: Do you long to fill your dance card by dancing every dance with Jesus? Can you envision yourself, gliding along your odyssey, with your King leading every step of the way? Are you intentional about seeking His passion, heartbeat, and destiny for your life?

May God shower you, His Jewel, with His custom-designed blessings for your journey. May He grace you with a longing to encourage those He places on the doorstep of your heart!

Heart Whispers...

Dear God, You hold our heart, hopes, and dreams in the palms of Your hands,

Please show Your Princess the path You have personally blueprinted for her life. As she seeks You with her whole heart, teach her Your will, Your ways, and Your truth. Shower her with Your richest blessings. In the name of the God who personally designs the individualized odyssey He has created, for each cherished Bride of His, to follow. Amen.

Bouquets of Grace-Filled Blessings...

"Extraordinary woman, let the gentle Holy Spirit nurture you in love and truth today. Look to the sky-not wanting more from God, but more of God."

-Julie Clinton
Living God's Dream for You
An Extraordinary Women Devotional
Harvest House Publishers

Gems of Wisdom...

Isaiah 49:15-16
Psalm 25:4-5
Proverbs 13:12
John 16:13

Refreshing Hugs...

Proverbs 13:12 is a great "hope booster" to pray back to God. I'll use the New Living Translation as an example: God, Your Word tells me that: "Hope deferred makes the heart sick, but when dreams come true, there is life and joy."

In your quiet time today, give God thanks for crowning your life with His goodness, His grace, and His truth.

A creative way to make tomorrow a special day for a friend-someone who would welcome a special blessing, would be to give them a box of chocolates and a single rose.

If possible, keep the gift anonymous by using a computer generated message. Place it on her doorstep, ring the doorbell, and quickly leave. May God bless you for being intentional about encouraging the next Princess you meet on your journey...

FROM BURN-OUT TO HOPE INSPIRING

"So there is a special rest still waiting for the people of God.
For all who enter into God's rest will find rest from their
labors, just as God rested after creating the world."
Hebrews 4:9-10

Are you operating on overload? Are the stresses and pressures of life standing in the way of living the intentional life God has custom designed just for you? Are you dealing with issues of people pleasing? Are you fighting to keep your feet on the ground and your head above water? I can relate. Here's some great news: We serve a God who understands each and every struggle we face. He knows the challenges and the vast amount of patience we will need to overcome those challenges. He is the only One who can fit the pieces together perfectly, planting our footprints firmly upon His.

Here's a personal scenario of burn-out that occured more than twenty-five years ago. I had recently met my husband, who had five children; I had two. Fast forward. He proposed shortly after we met. We married a few months later. Realistically, combining a family of seven children, (five boys and two girls), could have its moments, and prove to be a bit challenging. I must have blinked, because our family grew from seven children to include six spouses and eight GrandSugars, with the ninth one almost here.

My expectations were staggering. My perception of super wife, super mom, super nana, speaker, and life coach, daughter, care giver...

Hmmm, the opportunity I had been waiting for had finally arrived. It was an opportunity of a lifetime for a recovering perfectionist. The timing was perfect, (no pun intended). It was time to burn that Superwoman cape. We'll come back to that cape-burning thing later.

I need to clarify a point: I take full responsibility for not only attempting to please everyone in my immediate world, but taking that goal to the next level, as well. I was over the top. I was convinced that every special occasion, and the gift to go with it, had to be just perfect. Every holiday had to be a major event, with all the bells and whistles I could possibly create. Seriously? I was simply beyond exhausted, and I was the only one to blame.

Our precious Savior invites us to come to Him for a respite-a rest from our weariness and a rejuvenation for our just plain tuckered out souls. Nestled among His tender words, we find, in Matthew 11:28, this great Rx: "Come to Me, all you who are weary and carry heavy burdens, and I will give you rest."

Do you need refreshment for your soul?	*Come to Jesus...*
Do you need a break from constant stressors?	*Come to Jesus...*
Do you need an Rx for burn-out?	*Come to Jesus...*
Do you need help setting healthy boundaries?	*Come to Jesus...*
Do you need a fresh action plan for your life?	*Come to Jesus...*

I would be remiss if I led you to believe that once you've surrendered to the Lord, giving Him permission to do whatever it takes so that your character will look more like His, that life is going to be smooth sailing, from that point on. From my perspective, asking the Lord for an added dose of perseverance, a new outlook on priorities (what's really important and what's really not), would be a good start. In addition, admitting that Superwoman is a myth of epic proportions is huge!

Ultimately, those of us who have bought into the myth will come to the point where we need to give the Holy Spirit permission to do what He does perfectly: guide and instruct us, and help us establish realistic expectations of ourselves and others.

God stands ready to pour His refreshing balm over your life. The Spirit of God comes to the rescue to help us transition from exhausted, battle-scarred warriors, to "wounded healers," as Henri Nouwen simply phrases it, in his insightful book *The Wounded Healer*. There's hope and there's help. It may take lots of work, but, the end result will be worth it all...

Heart Whispers...

Dear God, You gift us with a refreshing for our weariness and exchange Your calming balm for our stressed out lives,

You are such a good God! You have equipped Your Princess with all the necessary things she will need for her odyssey. In Your infinite Wisdom, You strategically place those who have a passion for empowering and inspiring others, into the life of Your cherished Daughter... So, Holy Spirit, I ask that You fill Your Princess with Your love, peace, and "Bubbling-Over Joy!" In the name of the God who is the lifter of our heads and our hearts! Amen.

Bouquets of Grace-Filled Blessings...

"Are you are overloaded, your hands filled with heavy cares? Be faithful... keep trusting in God. He will take away your heavy cares and place a harp in your grasp, so you may sing glory and honor to God for all He has done."

-Anita Corrine Donahue
When I Am Praising God
Barbour Publishing

Gems of Wisdom...

Exodus 17: 10-13; Exodus 18:14-24
Psalm 3:3
Philemon 1:20
Romans 1:7

Refreshing Hugs...

Plan a "Calgon...Take Me Away" day, all by your lonesome. Treat wonderful you to a stress-free, rest and relaxation day!

OUR HERO

"But we see Jesus, who... for the suffering of death... by
the grace of God, might taste death for everyone."
Hebrews 2:9 NKJV

Breaking News: "Suddenly, we see him struggling to reach the eight year old girl, pulling her up from underneath the icy cold rushing waters, before they envelope her in their freezing clutches…" From time to time, we witness a newscast account similar to the one just described. I deeply admire someone who would risk their own life for the sake of another. We call them heroes. But there is no one like our Hero Jesus; no one who would give their life like He gave His, for all mankind. There is no one, like our Messiah, who freely chose to suffer the throes of death, so that He could give us life. There is no one like our Savior, who arrived supernaturally, on the scene of humanity, offering, as the NKJV of John 10:10, so strikingly expresses it, so we could "have life, and…have it abundantly." What an amazing God we serve!

Here's a thought-provoking question-one I have often pondered: If our Savior faced a horrific death, on a wooden cross, after being tortured beyond recognition, would He have done it solely for my sake? For yours? Would Jesus die an unspeakable, tormented death just to save me? To save you? I believe you would answer that question with a resounding yes! So would I. Praise God, He would, and He did… and death could not hold Him in the ground. As precious Daughters of our Risen Lord, let's remind each other often to give Him highest praise, for we serve the Risen Savior.

If we truly want to please God, our top priority will be to give Him our best. When we give the Lord our whole heart, soul, mind, and strength-when we worship Him, and give Him praise, our King is delighted. There are so many creative ways to demonstrate love for our awesome Hero.

King David provides an excellent role model. As Israel's worship leader, he proclaims this truth in Psalm 119:164, "I will praise You seven times a day because all Your laws are just." Just as praise and worship give honor and glory to God, they also serve to usher the believer into His Presence. It is there, in His Holy Presence, that we feel so alive, so blessed, as we worship our King, from the depths of our soul.

Heart Whispers...

Dear God, You are the great "I AM." You are He who died and rose again, so we might live an abundant life,

You sacrificed everything-Your very life, Lord Jesus, to give us our salvation... You have given us a truly abundant and joyful life. You are our Hero. And, while the world has honored many heroes, and rightfully so, You are the only perfect Hero for all mankind. Bless Your treasured Princess with Your Presence, as she seeks Your face daily.

According to Revelation 22:13, You are the only One who can make this claim, "I am the Alpha and the Omega, the First and the Last, the Beginning and the End." In the name of our Lord, our Savior, our Messiah Jesus. Amen.

Bouquets of Grace-Filled Blessings...

"...want to know the coolest thing about the One who gave up the crown of heaven for a crown of thorns? He did it just for you."

-Max Lucado
He Chose The Nails
Word Publishing

Gems of Wisdom...

Galatians 3:13-14
Hebrews 12:2

Refreshing Hugs...

I can sense His unending love, kindness, and grace. My prayer is that you can sense it too!

GRACE IN THE MIDST OF FIRE

"He heals the broken hearted, binding up their wounds."
Psalm 147:3

Feeling bruised by life's disappointments?	*Seek His Grace...*
Energy level running on low?	*Seek His Grace...*
Feeling emotionally tapped?	*Seek His Grace...*
Feeling discouraged?	*Seek His Grace...*

God reassures us that, while we may get hurt again, He stands ready to take our hand and walk with us through the rising waters, the raging flames, the stormy winds; situations which seem, at times, as if they might overwhelm us. Let's listen to His words from Isaiah 43:2, that form a promise only God can make:

"When you go through deep waters and great trouble, I will be with you.
When you go through rivers of difficulty, you will not drown!
When you walk through the fire of oppression, you will not be burned up;
the flames will not consume you. For I am the Lord, your God, the Holy
One of Israel, Your Savior."

When the Lord makes a promise, it is irrevocable. When He says, "I will be with you," He is giving us His 100% guarantee! Daniel 3:25, using the NKJV, describes the account from King Nebuchadnezzar's first hand report. The king sees four men in the midst of a fiery furnace. "Look!...I see four men loose, walking in the midst of the fire; and they are not hurt, and the form of the fourth is like the Son of God." Jesus had come to the rescue by providing Shadrach, Meshach, and Abednego His supernatural protection. Their example of God's miracle-working power, before a heathen king, was nothing short of awe-inspiring. Our God is such an amazing God!

Please remember this: There will be times, in each of our lives, when we are so wounded and broken... times when we may be experiencing great loss, that Jesus will need to use our example, including our response to those circumstances. God can use these times for the benefit of unbelievers who are witnessing events, like the one described in Daniel 3:25, with their own eyes.

While the Lord did not throw Shadrach, Meshach, and Abednego into the fire; that action was perpetrated at the command of the unbelieving, wicked and arrogant king; God used this very scary scenario to display His miraculous wonders to Nebuchadnezzar. Indeed, the God of Shadrach, Meshach, and Abednego, could not be messed with; He is the God of deliverance, no matter how hot the flames from the fiery furnace of life are turned up...

We do not know if the king ever became a believer. What we do know is this: God used the incident to stand as a beautiful testimony of the unfathomable grace He spreads, like a magnificent blanket, over our lives. He sends help by alerting our friends that we need their prayers and encouragement. There may also be times when we will need a supernatural hand, like that of an angel, to help us through what has often been referred to as: "The Dark Night Of The Soul," experienced by the Apostle John.

Should we be undergoing what may seem like an onslaught of trials, may we be mindful of staying so connected to the Father that we do not miss the importance of what He longs to teach us, through those volatile times. Let's purpose to trust the God whose grace is sufficient for any "fiery circumstance" we may encounter. A stunning example of just how special we are to the Lord, can be found in Ephesians 2:10, "For we are God's masterpiece. He has created us anew in Christ Jesus, so that we can do the good things He planned for us long ago." Your destiny, cherished Princess, is sealed by the Spirit of God. His Promises to you are guaranteed!

Heart Whispers...

Dear God, You are the One who brings us through our trials with Your caring, compassionate, and strength empowering love,

Your compassion reaches past our deepest struggles. With eyes that adore us, You are able to touch and minister to us, Holy Spirit, by pouring Your healing balm of grace into the midst of our harshest wounds. You are the Balm of Gilead. Give Your Princess the much needed assurance that, by Your grace, she will be able to persevere, and be a victorious overcomer. In the name of the God who provides us with an endless measure of His matchless grace. Amen.

Bouquets of Grace-Filled Blessings...

"He hears our cry and knows our sorrows... The Lord always comes to us in the midst of the storm. He uses the very thing that is threatening to overwhelm us as a highway into our hearts and lives."

-Richard Exley
Strength for the Storm
Thomas Nelson Publishing

Gems of Wisdom...

Psalm 37:39-40
Deuteronomy 31:6
Isaiah 43:1-4
Psalm 27:5

Refreshing Hugs...

If God has put someone on your heart, don't delay; begin praying for them and continue interceding until He lifts the burden. If you keep a prayer journal, you may want to include a short progress report and the date of each answered prayer.

FROM STRESSED TO A "REJUVENATED" YOU

"...a certain woman named Martha welcomed Him into her house. And
she had a sister called Mary, who also sat at Jesus' feet and heard His
word. But Martha was distracted with much serving, and...said, "Lord, do
You not care that my sister has left me to serve alone? Therefore tell her
to help me." ...Jesus answered and said to her, "Martha, Martha, you are
worried and troubled about many things. But one thing is needed, and
Mary has chosen that good part, which will not be taken away from her."
Luke 10:38-42 NKJV

God never intended us to feel we have failed if we have not accomplished
everything on our "To Do" list by the end of each day. No, rather, I am
convinced that He would want us to take several mini "rest breaks" throughout
the day. To rest in the Lord is to open wide the door of "Rejuvenation" for
our stressed-out lives. That's why I suggest a daily "Refreshing Time" with
the Lord.

To value His Divine Wisdom is a way of showing God our love for Him.
He knows we need a daily kitty cat nap, whatever that may look like for each
of us. King David expressed this break as a "Selah" in the Book of Psalms.
If we hit the pause button, for a few minutes during our day, about fifteen
minutes, three times a day, if possible, that would be great!

Tranquil stillness can provide us with an opportunity to sit at the feet
of our Messiah and just listen, like Mary did... When we do that, instead of
being distracted by all kinds of external influences, even ones that are noble,
like Martha's hospitality was, Jesus has an opportunity to whisper songs of
peace and well-being to our hearts. Should you work outside your home, many
companies give their employees a "break time." If you work at home, you will
need to become disciplined at incorporating a break into your routine, a few
times a day. Part of living intentionally is to use times like these to allow the
Holy Spirit to refresh and restore you... body, heart, mind, and soul.

Pausing from work, for a few minutes during our daily work schedule,
does not come naturally for some of us, particularly if our personality falls
into the "Type A" classification. Unfortunately, in the early stages of my
odyssey adventure, I was highly qualified for this category. There were many

times, in the past, that I failed to give myself the much needed break time necessary, to function effectively, as we were designed to do. King David used the term "Selah" as a musical notation signifying a pause. David, in the KJV of the Book of Psalms, used the term approximately seventy-five times. Selah was a time to pause and reflect. I began referring to these break times as "Selah Breaks." As I incorporated these breaks into my daily regimen, things began to change. It wasn't long before I felt refreshed and relaxed, once again.

It's an easy thing to fall back into a continual work cycle. I have worked from home for many years now. Once in awhile, I still find it necessary to remind myself to take mini breaks, several times a day. For example, if I am working on a large project like forming *Kitchen Klasses For Kool Kids...* for young Princesses... pause breaks are necessary to maintain my focus. Whether you're home schooling, working from home, working at the office... you can greatly benefit by fitting in several mini breaks, throughout your day.

Several of my coaching clients have expressed the same type of experience-not taking a much needed break time, during work hours. It usually looks something like this: Miss Type A allows herself to become so caught up with constant, ceaseless activity, that she soon finds herself teetering on the brink of exhaustion. She seems to have developed some kind of aversion to hitting the pause button, a few times, throughout her day. And, no, I am not mentioning any names, other than my own, of course.

While serving the Lord is what we should be doing, there needs to be a healthy balance. Let's take Martha, in the tenth chapter of the Book of Luke, as an example. Martha was "Miss Hospitality Plus," as she welcomed Jesus into her home and proceeded to insure that He was comfortable and well fed. Mary, her sister, chose to worship the Messiah in a different way. Mary decided to sit at the Lord's feet, listening to the Wisdom He wanted to impart through His teaching. Let's take one more look at what Messiah Jesus had to say regarding Mary's choice of worship that very same day; this time using the NLT of Luke 10:42, "...there is really only one thing worth being concerned about. Mary has discovered it-and I won't take it away from her."

So, the choices we are presented with tend to look something like the following... Choice #1: We can become receptacles for worry and anxiety, and frequently become stressed to the max... Choice #2: We can become so busy that we race through our days as if we had on a pair of roller blades, collapsing into bed at night, but are too wound up to sleep restfully... Choice #3: We can choose to take fifteen minutes, several times a day, for Selah Breaks. Choice #3 affords us the chance to feel relaxed and refreshed, throughout the evening. And, we'll be in a better position to get that REM sleep, every Princess needs, in order to function the way God designed us to.

Just an aside: When I thought I had finally gotten the hang of this "break" thing, I blew it. I worked throughout each designated rest break, for several days. So, to take it to the next level, I put a daily reminder, in big red ink letters marked "Rest," on my calender. There it was... I could not miss it... "Jan, take a break" Now!!!...

Okay, this is the point at which you are suppose to show such compassion for your frazzled friend by saying something like, "Poor Baby! She's exhausted from working so hard and doesn't even have time for a break." Seriously, though, we do need to set healthy boundaries, and stick to them. So, whatever it looks like in order for you to function well, and spend a little extra quality time with Jesus, on any given day... Just do it!

The next step was to figure out what to do with this new found truth. I was just clueless about what to do with my totally unrealistic daily lists. Well, long story short, I grabbed my "To-Do" notepad. And, well, I just had the best time shreading that little puppy to pieces. The list of things I need to get done, each day, has become far more realistic. The expectations I have of myself have also become more reasonable. It took awhile, but in the end, with a sigh of relief, I whispered, "Gee, this really works for me."

During Selah Breaks, allow yourself a built-in margin with no structured activity; extra blocks of time, to just relax. This suggestion may help alleviate the frustration of unfinished "To Do" lists at the end of each day. Your list will have become shorter and, consequently, far more realistic. Now, you can just plop down at the Lord's feet and enjoy His Presence...

I began working on this personal action plan fourteen years ago. I found it necessary to revise, several times, before I began working with coaching clients who needed help in making life work for them. What a difference it has made to me, personally, and to my clients. My attitude, not to mention what it has added to my energy level, have been really positive. I no longer whine about the lack of time I have to "get it all done," because, I have appointed Jesus as my personal Agenda Maker and Time Management Life Coach Consultant... He is just the absolute best!

Heart Whispers...

Dear God, You are our Perfect Time Management and Organizational Life Coach,

You have apportioned the same twenty-four hours every day, for each of us. You call each Princess to enjoy whatever type of work she may do. You call her to maintain her family responsibilities; to witness and spread the Good News about Your Kingdom; to fellowship; to minister to the needs of others through You love and grace. It soon becomes apparent, Lord, that taking time out of our busy schedules, to recline in Your loving arms for a daily refreshing, is important to our well-being. It is particularly necessary, if Your precious Princess is committed to maintaining a balanced perspective, and healthy personal boundaries. Thank You for providing her with opportunities to indulge in mini breaks, throughout the course of her busy work day.

Thank You, God, for so lavishly pouring Your love and grace over our lives. In the name of the God who offers each Princess, tranquil moments, each day, to sit at His feet... quietly resting and listening... just listening for His Whispers... Amen.

Bouquets of Grace-Filled Blessings...

"Felllowship with Him is a matter of priorities and a matter of choice. It's the better part of the meal life has to offer...in fact, the main course... And what did Mary do? All she did was sit. It is where she sat that made the difference."

-Ken Gire
Intimate Moments With The Savior
Zondervan Publishing House

Gems of Wisdom...

Isaiah 32:18
Psalm 90:12
Song of Songs 2:10

Refreshing Hugs...

Suggestion: On your calendar block out time for a few mini breaks daily. If you're at home, working, hang a "Do Not Disturb" sign on the door and cover the doorbell with duck tape. This method also works well if you happen to be home, but have had a hectic morning or afternoon, and just need a little breathing room. Either way, get ready to be blessed and refreshed, as you indulge in a few break times-guilt-free, of course!

THE CHOICEST PEARL

"Getting Wisdom is the most important thing you can
do! And whatever else you do, get good judgment."
Proverbs 4:7

"...the Kingdom of Heaven is like a pearl merchant on the lookout for choice pearls. When he discovered a pearl of great value, he sold everything he owned and bought it!" What was the cost of this precious pearl? Proverbs 4:7 tells us this about God's Wisdom, "Getting Wisdom is the most important thing you can do! ...whatever else you do, get good judgment." Let's substitute, for the moment, "the choicest pearl" for Wisdom. What Proverbs 4:7 is saying is that Wisdom is so important, though it cost us everything we have, we are to give it all up in order to gain this pearl of great price. In Proverbs 9:10, we are told this, "Fear of the Lord is the beginning of wisdom. Knowlege of the Holy One results in understanding."

In order to gain an intimate relationship with the Lord, we must value Him above all. The merchant, in the parable Jesus tells, symbolically represents every child of God. Now, this merchant sold everything he had for something that was far more valuable than anything he owned. So, I'd like to pose the same question to you, that I have asked myself: Wouldn't knowledge of the Holy One be worth everything you or I possess?

As we peruse through the pages of God's Word, we soon discover that it offers a veritable storehouse of what I like to refer to as "Spiritual Manna" for our odyssey. The characteristic of "good judgment," referred to in Proverbs 4:7, stems from asking for God's Wisdom. Good judgment comes from getting close to our Master by studying His character... Knowing God also comes by studying the men and women in His Word, who exemplify His character, through their words, their core values, and their actions. When we take what we learn about our Lord, and begin to apply it to our own circumstances or issues, we begin to act more like Him...

Here's one more thought to ponder: If we hand over all of our unmet goals and aspirations, along with any future expectations, to God, so that we might be unencumbered... free to spread the Good News of His Kingdom, and to work on fulfilling God's call on our lives, what result might we expect?

A part of practicing God's Wisdom, instead of relying on our own, is to learn the art of saying no. I will address the busyness syndrome in another segment. For now, I would just like to reinforce the issue of healthy boundaries. If we truly want to pattern our character after His, we will need to copy His Wisdom Principles. We will assuredly come to the point where we will need to say no to those expectations others may have of us. The great news, however, is the fact that the little "no" word will enable us to be free to please God, and to say yes to His plans for our present and our future...

We, as believers, know that God is the only One who can turn our dreams and longings, when they fit into His Will and His unique plans for each of us, into beautiful dreams realized, and fulfilling goals successfully accomplished!

2 Peter 1:3 tells us this, in respect to our growth when it comes to knowing God more... "As we know Jesus better, His divine power gives us everything we need for living a godly life." What Princess could ask for anything more?

When we discover the spiritual bounty contained in God's Word, we will want to give Him thanks for each gem the Holy Spirit desires to reveal to us along the way. The ultimate goal will be to pass along these gems of God's Wisdom and Knowledge, and to encourage the next precious one to search and study His Word for more of these spiritual treasures to pass on to the next Princess...

The Apostle Paul, in Philippians 3:8, makes this bold proclamation, "Yes, everything else is worthless when compared with the priceless gain of knowing Christ Jesus my Lord... I have discarded everything else...so that I may have Christ and become one with Him." God's Wisdom and Good Judgment is truly our great reward. It is, indeed, the choicest pearl of all!

Heart Whispers...

Dear God, You are the God of wisdom and sound judgment,

Please help Your Beloved Princess, as she travels along her journey in search of the spiritual treasures contained within the pages of Your Word. As she studies, may she grow closer to you, Messiah Jesus. May she seek the fellowship of others through Bible studies, church, church events... Bless her, God, with a heartfelt desire to take a shawl of encouragement along the way, ready to gently place it over the shoulders of the next Princess... In the name of the

God whose treasures are filled to overflowing with His wisdom and good judgment, that are His good pleasure to give, in abundance... Amen.

Bouquets of Grace-Filled Blessings...

"We can easily drift aimlessly in the direction of others' plans for us...and not respecting God's plans for us... Saying no may well be the most powerful and most valuable tool in a woman's tool box."

-Linda Andersen
the too-busy book
Waterbrook Press

Gems of Wisdom...

Proverbs 3:6
Jeremiah 29:10-11
Isaiah 30:21

Refreshing Hugs...

In a journal or notepad, make a list of five blessings that come to mind when you think about what you have learned through the wisdom and knowledge you have discovered in God's Word. Now might be the perfect opportunity to give God the highest praise, for imparting awesome gifts to you, His esteemed Princess.

LOVING GOD WITH A PASSION

"And you must love the Lord your God with all your heart, all your soul,
all your mind, and all your strength... 'Love your neighbor as yourself.'"
Mark 12:30-31

The words of Mark 12:30, with the exception of the phrase, "all your mind," initially appeared in the Old Testament in verse 6:5 of the Book of Deuteronomy. God wants us to love Him with passion. Clearly, the Lord wants us to be completely, totally, unequivocally His, and His alone. This is why the adjective "all" is used four times in this short passage. God wants to make sure that we get it! He wants 100% of our devotion, 100% of the time!

The Apostle Paul, in 2 Corinthians 11:2, reminds us that we are to be jealous people when it comes to our personal relationship with the Lord, "I am jealous for you with the jealousy of God Himself. For I promised you as a pure bride to one husband, Christ." So, what Paul is saying is that with every fiber of our being, we are to belong to God. Exodus 20:5, speaks about this same jealousy when God forbids the worship of idols or anything else besides Himself; in fact, it becomes the fifth commandment, "...for I, the Lord your God, am a jealous God who will not share your affection with any other god!"

The following questions are ones we can ponder. Once again, I'll use myself as an example: "Do I, Jan, love the Lord with everything that is within me? Do I, Jan, love Him with a fervent love? An all-consuming love? Do I, Jan, love my God with a love that permeates my whole being: heart, soul, body, mind and strength?" Take some time to think over your response. You may also find it helpful to journal your thoughts.

Jesus teaches His disciples to develop, cultivate, and apply to daily living. One of the disciplines Jesus teaches, by example, has to do with how we learn to build relationships with others. We begin with the most important relationship-that of our relationship with God. It takes precedence over all other relationships we will ever form. Mark 12:30-31, tells us that we must love Him, "...with all [our] heart...soul...mind, and...strength," [emphasis mine]. Genesis 19:5, tells us that when we obey God, and keep His covenant, as the NKJV phrases it, "then you shall be a special treasure to Me."

Will you join me in committing to give God your all? Will you commit to holding nothing back? Treasured Princess, one of the innumerable gifts our Savior gives, to every believer, is this: He fills us to overflowing with His love, grace, promises, protection, and provisions. God's supply never runs out. The more we love Him, the more love He gives us to love Him. God's love is endless. His love stretches into eternity... Amazing Love! Fabulous Love! Forever Love!

Heart Whispers...

Dear God, You are the Author of love, grace, promises, protection, provision... and every spiritual discipline,

Your endless reservoir of love is beyond incredible! Thank You, Holy Spirit, for filling us with Your gifts. In Mark 12:31, You tell us to do this, "...Love your neighbor as yourself." Help Your Precious Princess to do just that! May she give Your agape love sacrificially and unselfishly, asking nothing in return. In the name of the God who multiplies our love for Him, causing it to grow and grow and grow... And who gives us His love so we may give it away to precious souls throughout our world. Amen.

Bouquets of Grace-Filled Blessings...

"The Jesus habit of love is choosing consistently to do something that is beneficial, kind, and encouraging for someone, before considering your own needs and being willing...to sacrifice for the sake of others."

-Jay Dennis
The Jesus Habits
Broadman & Holman Publishers

Gems of Wisdom...

Colossians 1:9-10
John 13:34-35
John 15:12
Romans 13:8

Refreshing Hugs...

I have kept a spiritual journal for God, in the form of an inspirational devotional, for the past twenty plus years. Eventually, that journal became an idea, and ultimately, a paradigm, for this book. I have also incorporated many of these disciplines into my life coaching practice.

My friend, Nancy, was also keeping a spiritual journal, long before the two of us met. About a year after Nancy and I became sisters in Jesus, we were asked to teach a session on this subject, and its benefits, for a women's retreat.

Nancy and I learned many valuable life lessons during the time we spent together, preparing for that retreat. As a result, we were able to give life application examples, from some of the disciplines.

Should you wish to explore spiritual journaling, in greater depth, please refer to my contact information at the back of this book. It would be my pleasure to help you discover this type of journaling as a model of practical application, when practicing spiritual disciplines.

IT'S TIME TO SURRENDER

"You have charged us to keep Your commandments carefully. Oh,
that my actions would consistently reflect Your principles!... When
I learn Your righteous laws, I will thank You by living as I should.
I will obey Your principles. Please don't give up on me! ...don't let
me wander from Your commands. I have hidden Your Word in my
heart that I might not sin against You. Blessed are You, O Lord;
teach me Your principles... I have rejoiced in Your decrees as much
as in riches. I will study Your commandments and reflect on Your
ways. I will delight in Your principles and not forget Your Word."
Psalm 119:4-16

King David was all too acquainted with periods of downspiraling
compromise, when he temporarily forgot to whom he belonged. He paid
a high price for his ungodly behavior. Eventually, David did make a one
hundred and eighty degree turn. With great intentionality, he purposed in
his heart to praise God, no matter what! Psalm 34:1, as it reads in the NKJV,
describes David's passion for his God, "I will bless the Lord at all times; His
praise shall continually be in my mouth."

If Jesus is our Lord, He is Lord over all. He becomes Lord of our circumstances,
Lord of our time, our gifts, our possessions, (and, yes, that also includes our
Princess shoe collection), our talents, our resources... He becomes Lord over our
finances, and Lord over our body, which He refers to as His temple.

To truly make Jesus the Lord over our life, a surrender is required-
surrender of anything that would stand in the way of modeling the character
of our Messiah. Something to reflect upon... Are you ready to surrender
yourself totally so you can walk out God's Will for your life? The following
description is what Contemplative Prayer looks like for me. It provides a good
way to position myself to surrender my will to His Will, and to conform
my ways to His Ways. My hope is that the following description of what
Contemplative Prayer might look like, will help you view your time with God
as sacred time... just you and your Messiah...

> Contemplative Prayer is basically quiet prayer. It is a sacred
> prayer time between God and us. We just show up in our
> jeans and sweatshirt. There's no need for make-up... No frills

no fluff, no glitz, no glitter. We just show up, in our quiet place, to lounge at His feet. The sole requirement is to bring our deepest desire, which is to seek His face and love Him. We want to love and serve our Master, regardless of where He sends us. We want to love and serve Him with every drop of passion we have within us...

When we were toddlers and had just started learning how to walk, our mom or dad or nana or papa purposely let go of our hand, and we would seemingly float, suspended in mid air for just a brief second, followed by a plop down to earth, landing on our padded bottom. While most of us are not able to remember, at such a tender age, what we were actually doing was learning how to put our well-being into someone else's hands. It's called trust! As toddlers, we learned to trust that someone would be there to keep us from really getting hurt. Trust. The mere sound of the word brings with it a feeling of comfort and a sense of security.

If we are ready to surrender all, every attitude that is not Christ-like, every attempt to control, then we are ready to forge ahead to trust and obey God. We know that He is the epitome of trust, and that's a really awesome thing! Actually, if you stop and think about it, trust and obedience are the only solution, since they are the prerequisites for our complete surrender to God. And, like the toddler scenario, our Papa God can be completely trusted to catch us, should we start to tumble.

God knows our struggles. He is keenly aware of our temptation to take matters into our own hands. Let me be totally transparent with you. While it was many years ago, it wasn't pretty when I thought I needed to take control of the reigns of my life. I blew it big time. But, God is faithful, all the time! He will never let go of your hand or mine... Never!

Let's take one more glance at forgiving others for wounding us, betraying us, or hurting us in any way. We need to surrender. We've talked about forgiving others, several times. If forgiveness is not an issue with you, please fast forward. However, if you are still struggling with unforgiveness, please keep reading. Surrendering unforgiveness in our hearts is not optional. We can't just give lip service to forgiving... We must surrender all of it. In order to accomplish this, we are going to need: Contemplative Prayer Time, Sacred

Prayer Time, Alone Time... just you and God... just me and God. Pursue Him, pour out your heart to Him. Surrender...

To me, Contemplative Prayer is a beautiful way to shut out the rest of the immediate world so we can focus on Him. We run to God, just as we are. We bring our tendency to try to maintain control of our life. Conflicted, maybe, because we know it's going to be challenging, but at the same time, we truly want to hand it over to Him, once and for all. We need to completely surrender...despite wanting to hold on to whatever it is that we still want to retain a measure of control over. Psalm 119:5 reads, "Oh that my actions would consistently reflect Your principles."

When, at last, we surrender all those areas that need the touch of our Master Potter's hand; when we surrender all those attitudes we felt we were justified in clinging to, He meets us exactly where we are. And, in exchange, God hands us a magnificent gift, tied with a bow made out of His Never-Ending Grace. We open the gift to find something beautiful...sacred time... all the time we could ever ask for... It's God's gift of Sacred Moments...

Try to imagine the Lord setting aside time to listen to your prayers, your cries for help, and, yes, your ultimate surrender. And that's not all. God carves out time to listen to your adoration, your praise, your gratitude... His gift of time is, indeed, sacred. God's desire is to commune with you in those sacred moments... The King of the Universe chisels out time, with the express purpose of spending it with you. The finale occurs when the Lord offers to exchange your surrender, and mine, with His Matchless Grace...

May God richly bless you as you follow King David's example from Psalm 119:4-5. Set your sights solely on Him. Line up your will with His Perfect Will for your life. As for me, what I think I need to do right now is to run, not walk, to the Mercy Seat, to ask for His incredible grace, once again...

Heart Whispers...

Dear God, Your Grace is Stunning,

You understand our struggles to forgive, just as You know all about our attempt to control situations, or, other people. You also understand our ultimate desire to surrender all of it, to You. You are well aware of the relief we feel when we have totally surrendered our will, asking that You conform it to Your Will for us.

Please instill in our hearts, God, the courage to surrender everything we may still want to cling to, ever so tightly. You know our hearts. You know that we sincerely want to release all our frailties, weaknesses, and sin, to You, God. Please replace any desire to control, with the courage, and the empowerment, to walk out Your destiny plan for each of our lives.

Please help Your devoted Princess to keep her eyes focused upon You, and to align her priorities to match Your priorities for her life. Give her the courage to overcome the challenges she may encounter, as she surrenders those things she may still be holding onto. Bless her, God, as she purposes to make her actions consistently reflect the principles You model in Your Word. In the name of the God who throws us His life raft, every time we begin to drift... Amen.

Bouquets of Grace-Filled Blessings...

"In His sight we are not what we feel, but what we will. Let us...not live in the summerhouse of emotion, but in the central citadel of the will, wholly yielded and devoted to the will of God."

-F.B. Meyer
The Secret of Guidance
Moody Press-Updated Edition

Gems of Wisdom...

Romans 12:2
Hebrews 13:20-21
Colossians 1:9

Refreshing Hugs...

Let's purpose to get ever so still before Him, surrendering anything we still need to relinquish, and turn those things over to Him. Once we have given God permission to take over the Lordship of our life, we position ourselves to do some Contemplative Prayer Time with Jesus. I'm looking so forward to it. I hope you are, as well...

A CHANGE OF PERSPECTIVE

"Can you solve the mysteries of God? Can you discover
everything there is to know about the Almighty?"
Job 11:7

Following numerous afflictions-stripped of nearly everything of immense value to him, especially his children, Job's friends began to question his righteousness. Bombarded by so many calamities, Job began to exhibit signs of bitterness. He imagined that God must be angry with him to allow such devastating scenarios to take place in his life.

Have you ever felt like Job? I have to admit that I have felt a little like him. I came to the point that I knew, in my own case, I had to give up the spirit of resentment that was robbing me of the pure joy of appreciating the blessing of God's incomprehensible Grace and Mercy, for starters. God spoke through my friend Sher, who brought a balanced perspective to my concern over really trivial "stuff." She reminded me to focus on blessings, instead of worrying over situations that, in the scheme of things, really weren't very important at all.

One of several object lessons that can be learned from the Book of Job, is that God reminded Job, through his friend, that none of us can understand "...the mysteries of God." God's mysteries are far more complex than our finite minds are capable of fathoming. At the end of Job's story the scene changes; we see our merciful and loving God restore to Job ten-fold, the losses he had incurred. The lesson I learned is that negative emotions, of any nature, stand in the way of God's desire to provide for, and bless, His sheep; to guide us back to Him when we allow our heart to wander from our core values, one of which is gratefulness.

The Lord desires to restore, ten-fold, the losses that we incur. If we remain transparent, God can use our example to gently correct those who are caught up in the "poor me" trap. God is just waiting to pour out His Correcting Balm upon those of us, myself included, who are guilty of indulging in major pity-parties... The bottom line is that the "victim mentality" has to go, in the name of Jesus. And, while I haven't indulged in one of those for decades, thank goodness, what took their place are the memories of His Loving Kindness and His Promises, spoken through my special friend, that resonate, like a beautiful melody, ministering to my soul.

It is my prayer that God's Word will bathe you in His Wisdom and His Love, as He teaches you new perspectives that will add balance to your life, daily...

Heart Whispers...

Dear God, You are the Master of Renewal,

You have breathed Your very Breath into us to give us the abundant life You have created for each Highly Esteemed Princess. Thank You for every provision that You give, with such lavish generosity. I ask, Lord, that You restore, tenfold, the losses Your Precious Daughter may have suffered; restore them, God, regardless of whether they are physical, relational, material, emotional... Help each Princess to use her time and her spiritual gifts to empower others toward seeking a balanced perspective and a grateful heart. In the name of the God who freely hands us His Gifts of Restoration, Renewal, and Revitalization... Amen.

Bouquets of Grace-Filled Blessings...

"When we are grieving, we tend to feel as if nothing makes sense. It is difficult to remember the good days. Job struggled deeply with perspective... the gift of perspective to the sufferer is a much needed blessing."

-Shelley Chapin
Counselors, Comforters and Friends
Victor Books

Gems of Wisdom...

Jeremiah 30:17
Jeremiah 31:13

Refreshing Hugs...

Ask God how you might best extend the gift of a balanced perspective, coupled with grace, to someone who has recently experienced a loss for which they are grieving.

WINGS OF PROTECTION

"Do not touch my anointed ones, and do my prophets no harm."
1 Chronicles 16:22 NKJV

Believers are God's "anointed ones." We dwell under the wings of His Divine
Protection. Psalm 91:1-4 and 91:9-16, contain a few of my favorite passages. They
serve as a reminder of God's provision of protection: "Those who live in the shelter
of the Most High will find rest in the shadow of the Almighty. This I declare
of the Lord: He alone is my refuge, my place of safety; He is my God, and I am
trusting Him... He will shield you with His wings. He will shelter you with His
feathers. His faithful promises are your armor and protection."

The Lord appoints His angels to guard our steps. He reassures us with
this promise in Psalm 91:11-12, "For He orders His angels to protect you
wherever you go. They will hold you with their hands to keep you from
striking your foot on a stone."

The following is a perfect example of God's protection. My children were
quite young. I had taken a position as an assistant office manager for a CPA
firm. It was part of my job to remove old inserts in heavy bound notebooks,
and replace them with the current rules and regulations governing accounting
practices. One morning, I went into the firm's library. I reached for a book
toward the top of one of the shelves. These accounting books were quite heavy.

Same story, part two: I began to pull out the book I needed, and, before
I knew it, I was on the floor, at the back of the opposite wall, with many
books scattered all over the room. There were a few books that came within
inches of my feet. Had any one of those books hit my head, well, I try not to
think about what the repercussions might have been. Totally unaware of the
underlying danger that lurked within those shelves, because of the weight of
so many heavy books, I thanked God for His angels that He sends to minister
to us and keep us out of harms way.

God wants us to take His promises to heart, as we pray over our loved
ones. When my children were young, I would pray Psalm 91:1-4 and 9-16,
over them. When Honey and I combined our family, I began praying this
Psalm over each of the seven children, Honey, and myself. As each daughter-
in-love and son-in-law were added, they became part of my Psalms 91 prayers.

I have begun a personalized devotional prayer time for each of them, as I lift their needs up to God.

Anointed Princess, the Lord is your high tower. When you pray His Word back to Him, for yourself, your family, your friends, your co-workers, military, country, foreign lands, missionaries... it delights Him. Let's remember to thank Him as He watches over us, and those who are dear to us, with His loving care... Now would be a great time to praise and thank Him for His promises of protection, even when you may be unaware of harm, to you, or those who are so very special to you... God is such a Great God! Always...

Heart Whispers...

Dear God, You are our Protector, Defender, and Deliverer,

You always make us feel so loved, protected, watched over, and cared for... Thank You for the angels You have assigned to protect Your Treasured Ones. We want to "...live in the shelter of the Most High," to seek refuge from the perils that might affect us, or those we love.

Lord Jesus, please place Your angels over Your Beautiful Princess, and over her loved ones... 24/7. If there is someone who is reading this *Heart Whisper*, but is still feeling insecure, please chase away all of her doubts! Reassure her, as only You can, Lord, that, as she becomes able to trust You completely, she can face each day, knowing that Your peace surrounds her, because You are ever present to watch over her... In the name of the God who watches over us, continually; the God who dispatches His angels to protect and deliver us by keeping us out of harms way... Amen.

Bouquets of Grace-Filled Blessings...

"An innumerable company of angels watch and protect God's royal children... We are well defended, since all the twenty-thousand chariots of God are armed for our deliverance."

-Charles Spurgeon
Morning and Evening
Thomas Nelson Publishing

Gems of Wisdom...

Read Psalm 91 in your favorite Bible verse
Deuteronomy 33:27
Psalm 121:5-8
Psalm 34:7

Refreshing Hugs...

If you do not have children of your own, but may have neices, nephews, or close friends who have children, set aside time each day to pray Psalm 91:1-4, 9-16, over each of them. May God bless your time with Him as you intercede for others.

RETRACING HIS FOOTPRINTS...
ONE PRINT AT A TIME

"And now, just as you accepted Christ Jesus as your Lord, you
must continue to live in obedience to Him. Let your roots grow
down into Him and draw up nourishment from Him, so you will
grow in faith, strong and vigorous in the truth you were taught.
Let your lives overflow with thanksgiving for all He has done."
Colossians 2:6-7

The Book of Colossians reads like God's Prayer Book for every believer.
In Romans 8:34, paraphrased, Jesus tells us that He is seated at the right
hand of God and is continually interceding on our behalf. In I Thessalonians
5:16-18, we can almost picture, in our mind, what our life with the Lord will
begin to look like, when we grow to look more and more like our Savior with
each passing day. We are to, "Always be joyful. Keep on praying. No matter
what happens, always be thankful, for this is God's will for you who belong
to Christ Jesus."

The NKJV of Colossians 2:6-7, tells us to be "...abounding...with
thanksgiving." The KJV elaborates: "Rejoice evermore. Pray without ceasing.
In everything give thanks: for this is the will of God in Christ Jesus concerning
you." The powerful message that appears in Colossians 1:27-29, as it reads
in the NLT, is one that every believer needs to carry in their heart... it is a
message delivered by the Apostle Paul to remind the Church that God is
pleased when we know that Christ lives in each of us; and God assures us
that we will partake in Christ's glory as we share the message of the Gospel,
everywhere we go...

"For it has pleased God to tell His people that the riches and glory
of Christ are for you Gentiles, too. For this is the secret: Christ lives
in you, and this is your assurance that you will share in His glory.
So, everywhere we go, we tell everyone about Christ. We warn them
and teach them with all the wisdom God has given us, for we want
to present them to God, perfect in their relationship to Christ..."

Every day, we are to work on rejoicing, making our very breath one continuous prayer, and giving thanks to our Redeemer for all He does for His Precious Bride. And wherever we go we need to share with others about our Messiah Jesus, and the message of the Gospel... Do I fail to carry out His will, one hundred percent of every step of the way I have taken, to this point, along my odyssey travels? Yes, there have been many times when I have fallen short. But, I am trying. I am trying to follow God's will for my life by putting my heart, soul, mind, and strength into patterning my walk after His footprints... I want to share the Gospel with others so they will be "perfect in their relationship to Christ" as well.

You know, Princess of Messiah Jesus, I so long to hear the Lord's voice, as He whispers those beautiful words of affirmation, in Matthew 25:21, "...Well done, My good and faithful servant..." I believe that you want to hear those words, too. I often find myself praying this prayer: "Lord God, please help me to stay faithful to the end...which is, in fact, just the beginning!" Please know that while I probably haven't met you personally, I will be praying that prayer, whenever the Holy Spirit prompts my heart for you, my "sis" in Jesus.

My forever friend, Sher, is an amazing woman of God. She stays so close to our Messiah, you can almost see His dust on her face. When Sherry prays, it's almost as if the words come tumbling, ever so spontaneously, out of her mouth. "Sher, I dedicate this segment to you, with a grateful heart, because, for the last seventeen years, you have modeled what it looks like to live and to walk out our prayers for ourselves, those we love, and all of our brothers and sisters in the Lord. Thank you for being a truly great inspiration and blessing to me, Sher!".

I will close with these words, spoken by Pastor Charles Stanley, in one of his radio broadcasts, "Pray daily that you may be an extension of His life, an expression of His love, and an exhibition of His power."

Heart Whispers...

Dear God, You leave Your footprints for us to follow as we walk out our destiny, one footprint at a time,

We want to walk in Your footprints, Messiah Jesus. We want to be so close to You that we can feel Your breath on our face, as You whisper Your design for our lives.

May Your Princess become all that You have called her to be. May she walk out that example to family, friends, co-workers, "sisters," neighbors... In the name of our soon coming King, who adorns us with His favor as we follow His leading daily... Amen.

Bouquets of Grace-Filled Blessings...

"...Know that God is pleased when he sees the effort you are making. He will be applauding you for your improvements, not waiting in the wings to berate you for your shortcomings."

-Katie Brazelton and Shelley Leith
Character Makeover
Zondervan

Gems of Wisdom...

Psalm 17:15
Matthew 25:21
Zephaniah 3:17

Refreshing Hugs...

I have just one brief word for now, and that is: "You Are So Special!" Be blessed beyond measure!

A GENUINE "REAL DEAL" KIND OF LOVE

"I have loved you even as the Father has loved Me. Remain in My love."
John 15:9

Love! Love! Love! A genuine love for our Precious God is the secret that unlocks the floodgates of heaven, saturating us in His Goodness, His Kindness, His Grace... God tells us that we must share His kind of love, that genuine, sincere love for mankind. It is the most precious gift we, as a Princess of the Most High God, have to share-the gift of salvation; the gift of our Savior, Messiah Jesus. Our Father God loves us and has blessed us so we can abide, stay, tarry, rest, dwell, reside...in His love. He has equipped us to share His gift of eternal life with others. The NKJV of 2 Timothy 4:2, phrases it this way, "Preach the word! Be ready in season and out of season..."

I encourage you to allow the love of God to flow through you. Love those you serve, and those who serve you. Since the word "love" is an action word, we can put into action the love God gives us by illustrating that love to those He places along our odyssey road. One of the wonderful attributes of the love of God is that there are a multitude of ways to demonstrate it...

When we learn to love, as Jesus loves, in an unconditional way, people will begin to respond to us. Even the most difficult people, those who exhibit a "hard heart," for example, or display a stubborn spirit, are no match for God's Incredible Love. I have witnessed a few people, with the hardest of hearts, so utterly resistant that they would not budge. But they began to melt, like an ice-packed mountain pass as warmer temperatures and sunshine begin to thaw its frozen glaze. After a while, as the Spirit of God begins to minister to them, their icy cold heart becomes pliable in the hand of the Master Heart-Melter.

It never ceases to amaze me as I witness God prune away at the stain that sin has left on a heart. He snips away at all the dross and stubborn crustiness. The Lord cuts away at all our issues, down to the bare roots. His work is meticulous and He will not stop until He reshapes the intent of our heart causing it to match the intent of His. He will not cease until we begin to cultivate a heart filled with goodness, mercy, and grace. He will not quit until our heart looks a whole lot more like His. He will not be satisfied until He is able to declare us fit laborers for His Harvest. And, part of being "fit" and cultivating a heart like His, also has to do with forgiving others, just as Christ has forgiven us.

If we truly are committed to being "fit " as a laborer for His Harvest, we must be cleansed of our unwillingness to forgive those who have hurt us. Listen to Beth Moore's words, in her book, *Praying God's Word.* She begins by gently confronting her readers, in her own personal teaching style, as she skillfully drives home God's "primary agenda." Beth addresses God's ultimate goal; that every believer be confomed into Christ's likeness, "No other word sums up His character in relationship to us like the word *forgiving.* We never look more like Christ," she continues, "than when we forgive; since that's God's goal..." Hmmm, that means that the reverse is also true; we look less and less like Jesus when we refuse to forgive.

Forgiveness becomes a mandatory requirement for every believer. If our primary goal is to look like our Savior, we must forgive, I mean, genuinely, from the bottom of our heart. It is of great benefit for a believer to extend that type of forgiveness to every person who has broken their heart, wounded their feelings, or flat out offended them, including betrayal of any kind.

God has another prime objective. The end-time harvest is approaching. Our Lord needs laborers willing to go the extra mile-for the sake of His Harvest. In fact, He makes His intent crystal clear. In Matthew 9: 37-38, we find Jesus instructing His disciples. He draws a word picture of the following analogy so they can understand what Jesus wants them to do: "The harvest is so great, but the workers are so few. So pray to the Lord who is in charge of the harvest; ask Him to send out more workers for His fields."

Now, back to the topic of forgiveness. Our God is ever so patient with His Kids, as He chips away at the bitterness, resentment, hostility, unforgiveness, which we have just addressed... yes, even the hatred that has somehow managed to find its way into the deepest recesses of our heart. Can Christians who truly love the Lord actually harbor resentment, bitterness, envy...? We can, and, unfortunately, some of us still do. These character traits have become so stubbornly embedded that they might have been there for, well, for who knows how long? Only God knows. Once again, the reminder that Jesus gives us, "Remain in My Love," includes genuine forgiveness... His kind of forgiveness...

The Spirit of God reminds us that we need His daily cleansing. The good news is that when we allow the work of the Holy Spirit to reshape us into His image, we can begin to confess our sin, ask God for His Forgiveness and His Grace, and the courage we will need in order to become workers fit for End-Time Harvest work-laborers for Jesus, ready to witness for Him and bring Him Glory.

Oh, Princess of the Living God, we know the only cure for our sin, and that is confession of that sin coupled with sincere repentance. It is simply a matter of telling God how sorry we are for our sins, asking Him to cleanse us from all unrighteousness, and making us whole again. Next, we must turn away from any sin so we can follow His Will for our life. Once we have done these things, we can thank Jesus for shedding His Precious Blood that washes away the stain of that sin. We can thank Him for a forgiveness that only He can give.

We may have sung the words in church many times before. We might even sing it out loud when no one is listening. The lyrics and the music to the song entitled, *Nothing but the Blood,* were written by Robert Lowry. The words reverberate the NIV phrasing of Hebrews 9:22. This verse makes the point unmistakably clear, "Without the shedding of blood there is no forgiveness..." So, "What can wash away my sin? Nothing but the blood of Jesus...What can make me whole again? Nothing but the blood of Jesus... Oh! precious is the flow That makes me white as snow; No other fount I know... Nothing but the Blood of Jesus..."

Heart Whispers...

Dear God, Every drop of Your Blood is Precious, and is the only Atonement for our sins,

Thank You for shedding Your precious Blood, the Blood that washes us clean and cleanses us from all unrighteousness. Thank You, Jesus, that You, and You alone, are our Perfect Atonement... Thank You, God, that even when forgiveness is the last thing, in our human nature, that we want to extend... even when it feels like one of the most difficult things we have to do, You have set the ultimate example of forgiveness for us. Thank You, Lord, that You are there to help us extend the genuine forgiveness You require of us, in order to become obedient to Your Will.

Please give Your Princess a heart filled with thanksgiving for every blessing You extravagantly bestow on her. Thank You, God, for the blessing of beautiful friendships with spiritual sisters, moms, nanas... who adore You, their Maker. May they lift her up should she become discouraged, and lean over the balcony of her life to cheer her on, as she becomes a victorious warrior for You! In the name of the God of our Salvation... Amen.

Bouquets of Grace-Filled Blessings...

"Unparalled joy and victory come from allowing Christ to do "the hard thing" with us. Perhaps, nothing is harder than forgiveness."

-Beth Moore
Praying God's Word
Broadman & Holman Publishers

Gems of Wisdom...

Ephesians 1:7
John 20:23
Colossians 3:13-14

Refreshing Hugs...

Using a small dry-erase board, jot down the name of someone you know you really need to forgive. If the offense, or hurt, is too painful to write down, then just write out a short forgiveness note. When you feel you have completely forgiven that person, take the eraser and thoroughly wipe the slate clean.

Can you hear God whispering the words, "Well done, My Beloved Princess. I am very proud of you!" It is my prayer that you can!

PART TWO: FEELING A MILD CASE OF BURN-OUT COMING ON? BECOME A "CREATIVE IDEA" PRINCESS

"Inherent in the understanding about overload is the need to prioritize. If we have more to do than we can possibly do, then we must choose. And we must choose wisely according to God-honoring criteria."

-Richard A. Swenson, M.D.
The Overload Syndrome
Navpress

JUST SAY NO!

"Praise the Lord, God of our ancestors, who made the king
want to beautiful the Temple of the Lord in Jerusalem."
Ezra 7:27

Ezra was a priest and a teacher of the law. In a decree issued by King Artaxerxes, Ezra was entrusted with articles of worship to be placed in the temple which belonged to the Lord. By the same decree, Ezra was also elected to appoint judges and magistrates to administer justice to the people residing in the Trans-Euphrates area.

To add further responsibility to Ezra's already full plate, the king commanded Ezra to teach the people the law of his God. To anyone who did not adhere to God's law, the king's judgment was punishment by death or banishment from the land.

The use of the word "awesome" to describe Ezra's responsibilities, does not have the same connotation that we use in our contemporary venacular. For Ezra, it probably meant something closer to the description we are familiar with-something that is totally overwhelming, perhaps. Does Ezra become frazzled over the vast amount he had on his plate? No he doesn't. Does he fret and worry over over his likely inability to meet the king's demands? No he doesn't. Rather, we witness this man of God turn directly to the Lord to praise Him. Here's what Ezra does in verse 28, as he exclaims, "praise Him for demonstrating such unfailing love to me by honoring me before the king, his council..."

Ezra's eyes were focused solely on the Lord, and what He could supernaturally accomplish. If our focus is centered upon the circumstances, or the heavy weight of responsibilities we may be faced with on any given day, then our focus needs to be re-directed. If the pasta on our plate, so to speak, is falling to the floor, we are rapidly approaching overload.

What's the solution for what I like to refer to as mega stress? Well, I can only tell you what works for me. If I practice saying the words, "No, I'm sorry that I just can't do that right now", the pressure becomes far less burdensome. The strategy I find that works best for me is to hand over my To-Do list to my administrative assistant Jesus. The next step I take is to ask the Lord a question,

"Lord, is this something You want me to do, or not do?" If I feel that God is leading me to refuse a request for now, but could be a possibility in the future, my response might sound something like this, "I'm not able to do that right now, but early fall might be possible. Could you check back with me around the middle of summer, say around the second week of July? That would be great."

I have a funny story to share with you about empowering my friend Mindy. I had been coaching her regarding how to clarify her boundaries with others in a kind, but assertive way. Mindy was my stylist, at the time, and also a very dear friend. One day, I walked into the salon. I could already tell, by the look in her eyes, that she was having a really tough day. In fact, I had seen that look in her countenance, many times. Now, Mindy is one of the kindest, most loving and service-oriented people I know. However, that particular day she had been stepped on, one too many times, by demanding clients.

When we are in what I refer to as a boundary crisis, we tend to become temporarily needy. I knew what I was suppose to do. I proceeded to give her a big hug, reach into my purse, grab the nearest tube of lipstick, and... I think you may know where I'm going with this. I wrote on her mirror, in huge letters, the little, bitty "no" word, in a few different spots. Mindy and I burst into laughter. With tears streaming down our faces, we both began practicing the "no" word, in different tones of voice. Come on, join me now, let's practice this great boundary setter together. Ready? "No, no, no, no, no..."

At one point, I had needed a little practice in the "healthy boundary" area. With some help from my very special friend, Lenora, I soon caught on. In fact, that was one reason, among many others, that I was drawn to life coaching. The following five-word phrase is what I now refer to as: Healthy boundaries for people pleasers. I have discovered that healthy boundaries are not difficult to practice.

If we keep our focus on Jesus, we soon learn that He is the ultimate authority on maintaining composure while we are in the process of learning healthy boundary setting. It becomes easier to concentrate on gently, but firmly, what healthy boundaries should look like, for each of us.

Now, about that Superwoman cape that I previously mentioned, just a quick reminder to shed, better yet, shread that pesty little thing. And finally, an encouraging word for recovering people pleasers: Keep an arsenal of those healthy boundary phrases ready to use, because, you just never know when they might come in handy...

Heart Whispers...

Dear God, You are the God of Healthy Boundary Setting,

Thank You, Lord, that while our responsibilities may seem overwhelming, at times, the Bible says that Your burdens are light, and that we should shift the weight of responsibilities from our shoulders to Yours. May we worry much less, if at all, and trust You more, in fact, totally! May we quietly listen when You are directing us toward a "yes or no" response. In the name of the God who is our model for setting healthy boundaries for Princess People Pleasers... Amen.

Bouquets of Grace-Filled Blessings...

"Every pleaser must become increasingly skilled at using the word no... It's best to start your answer to the request with the word no... Be firm... Be brief..."

-Jean Baer
How To Be An Assertive (Not Aggressive) Woman in Life, in Love, and on the Job
Signet Books

Gems of Wisdom...

Mattew 5:37
Ephesians 4:15

Refreshing Hugs...

I think this would be an excellent time for a trip to your Ice Cream Palace of choice. Oh, by the way, the Pink Carriage will be arriving momentarily. All boundaries for the day have been cancelled. Just enjoy!

DIVINE DISCIPLINE

"My child, never forget the things I have taught you. Store My commands in your heart, for they will give you a long and satisfying life. Never let loyalty and kindness get away from you! Wear them like a necklace; write them deep within your heart. Then you will find favor with both God and people... My child, don't ignore it when the Lord disciplines you, and don't be discouraged when He corrects you. For the Lord corrects those He loves, just as a father corrects a child in whom he delights.
Proverbs 3:1-4, 11-12

The Christian Psychologist, Dr. James Dobson, in his excellent book entitled, *Love Must Be Tough*, gives keen insight regarding child rearing. Dr. Dobson also draws a parallel between a spouse who has strayed and a Christian who has strayed from the God who has an incredible love for His Kids. The analogy is striking: "...love is not synonymous with permissiveness, passivity, and weakness," says Dr. Dobson. "Sometimes it requires toughness and discipline and accountability." Those words ring as true today, as they did when Dr. Dobson wrote them many years ago.

If God didn't love us, with an unending perfect love, He wouldn't bother to try to bring us into accountability. Nor would He discipline us when we failed to adhere to the rules. An example of this truth is reflected in His words from Isaiah 30:21, as it is phrased in the NIV, "Whether you turn to the right or to the left, your ears will hear a voice behind you, saying, "This is the way; walk in it." Steve Schultz, in his delightfully enlightening book, *Can't You Talk Louder, God?*, cites this same scripture. He says this, "...telling others what God has told you, is about building up, encouraging, edifying the Church-God's people." He goes on to make this astute observation, in reference to the same verse, "If knowing which way to turn isn't encouraging, it'll do until encouragement comes along."

No matter how long we've been a believer, God will continue to tenderly discipline us until we get it right. Why? Well, the best explanation I have, off the top of my head, is that the Lord needs for us to be able to see the path that He has set before us by using our spiritual sight. He is just waiting for us to ask for His imput-His guidance. It's really about the "Wisdom" thing...

It's God's Wisdom that beckons us to place our total, absolute, complete trust in Him, just as Proverbs 3:5-6 reminds us to do, "Trust in the Lord with all your heart; do not depend on your own understanding. Seek His will in all you do, and He will direct your paths."

While we can only see a finite distance away, our Papa God knows every detail of our lives that is sandwiched in between. It's His chastening that stirs within us, a godly sorrow, as 2 Corinthians 7:10-11 puts it, "For God can use sorrow in our lives to help us turn away from sin and seek salvation... Just see what this godly sorrow produces in you! Such earnestness, such concern to clear yourselves... You showed that you have done everything you could to make things right." It's the kind of "godly sorrow" that can seem almost unbearable to endure; it's that "godly sorrow" that drives us to His Mercy Seat seeking His Grace... "I can't believe I did that", we might utter, as our words are laden with sobs of pain. It's that kind of crushing anguish that lurks behind a flood of tears... We stammer, "Oh, how could I hurt the Lord like that... the One I love with all my heart?" It's that godly sorrow that compels us to seek God's Grace. As His Beloved, we can't get through another day without it! Sometimes it's scary to even think that we could.

Princess, you are a precious example of His stunning Grace. It reminds me of the contemporary song "Our God is an Awesome God." And, while that type of grace is totally undeserved by any of us, it is, and always will be, more than sufficient...

Heart Whispers...

Dear God, You are the God of Pure Grace,

Sometimes it is sort of scary to trust You 100% for 100% of the time. But trust You, we must! Thank You, Lord, that Your Mercy Seat is literally lined with Grace; and Your Loving Princess can trust that Your Grace, Your Unmerited Favor over her, unlike an old ragged garment, will never wear out! Thank You that Your Wisdom is always exactly what she will need for the destiny journey that lies ahead of her. Thank You, Jesus, that Your chastening is always coupled with Your Perfect Love... In the name of the God who throws a sheet of Pure Grace over His Treasured Princess, during the stormy times, so that His Perfect Will can be accomplished in her life. Amen.

Bouquets of Grace-Filled Blessings...

"...if He sends storms, or winds, or rains, or sunshine, all must be accepted at His hands, with the most unwavering confidence that...He knows the best way of accomplishing His end..."

-Hannah Whitall Smith
The Christian's Secret of a Happy Life
Fleming H. Revell Publishing

Gems of Wisdom...

Job 5:17-19
Proverbs 3:11-12
Hebrews 12:5

Refreshing Hugs...

Journaling a time when we've experienced God's discipline in our lives, and what that discipline taught us, is refreshing. It increases our trust in the One who holds our hand as we take one more step down our odyssey road.

THE SWEETNESS OF SERVING OTHERS

"So He got up from the table, took off His robe, wrapped a towel around
His waist, and poured water into a basin. Then he began to wash the
disciples' feet and to wipe them with the towel He had around Him."
John 13:4-5

The sweetness of serving others is yet another gift the Holy Spirit lavishes
on the believer. To serve our brothers and sisters in the Lord is truly the epitome
of "Servanthood" Jesus exhibits. The Holy Spirit is our Creative Director.
As He strategically places people in our lives, it is He who gives us creative
resources. There is a direct correlation between "loving" and "serving." As we
serve, under the Spirit's direction, we are given an opportunity to witness to
others about Christ's love.

Indulge me, if you will, to travel back to a time when I was just a "babe"
in Jesus. As a new believer, I had the chance to attend a women's retreat
sponsored by our church. The retreat was held at a beautiful sprawling ranch.
It had been donated to our church family. We awoke, in the morning, to the
tantilizing aroma of freshly baked cinnamon rolls and honey biscuits. We had
awesome times of fellowship, sweet worship, sharing, and lots of laughs. In
the afternoon, finding our outdoor space, we separated from one another for
a quiet, personal time of communion with Jesus; a time of reflective prayer,
and spiritual journaling, if we chose to do so.

The first evening, we split up into small groups. As the Spirit led, we
prayed for each other. We knelt, washing the feet of one another, just as our
Lord Jesus had done with His disciples, in the upper room. That evening,
I learned the true meaning of serving God's people with love. It was a truly
beautiful experience; one that also taught me the importance of intercessory
prayer.

I was struggling with several issues in my life that were draining me of
the energy I needed, as a single mom, to minister to my two children, Adam
and Danielle, who were still quite young. These issues were standing in the
way of my spiritual growth.

Back to the retreat weekend... It was my turn to have my feet washed.
What a truly remarkable experience. I understood, maybe for the first time,

the act of servanthood. The Holy Spirit gave a few women discernment regarding the circumstances that were causing me difficulty. Through these women, God poured out His balm of compassion and love, combined with truth and grace, so they could effectively empower me with the tools I would need to minister more effectively to my family.

When we love, we desire to serve; service becomes a special blessing to the one served, and the one doing the serving. Oh, serving others may seem like such an easy thing to do, yet some of us still struggle with it. If you are facing issues that may be prohibiting you from effectively serving those that God places in your sphere of influence, begin with prayer. Ask the Lord to give you the wisdom necessary to minister to those who may be in need of the blessing of being served.

Lenora, my forever friend, and one of my lifelong "balcony coaches," met me for lunch one day. That same day, Lenora spoke this word to me at the precise time I needed to hear it: "Those who refresh others will themselves be refreshed." She was quoting from God's Word, but did not realize what a great impact it had on me. I was totally blessed and refreshed that day! And, because of Lenora's words, spoken many years ago, I became truly inspired. God's words, coming from my friend's lips, added a new dimension to my newly renamed coaching practice, Princess of Great Destiny...

I began to see another dimension of my niche as having a special emphasis on these four disciplines: *Servanthood & Selflessness & Stewardship & Sharing...* I use these disciplines with young Princesses, ages seven through seventeen. As moms, nanas, aunts, sisters... these disciplines are ones I feel are important in raising up His Daughters, for the next generation.

Heart Whispers...

Dear God, Thank You that You are pleased with every effort we make to serve others,

The privilege of serving is such a blessing; it refreshes the one serving, as well as the one being served. Please help each of us to think less about ourselves and more about those You place in our lives. As we serve, in Your Name, Lord Jesus, may we express our love to You, and give You all the honor, all the glory, and all the praise. In the name of the God who came to serve... not to be served... Amen.

Bouquets of Grace-Filled Blessings...

"Lord...free me to be...the happy foot-washer of anyone today who needs his feet washed...his work commended...his failure forgiven..."

-Elisabeth Elliot
A Lamp For My Feet
Servant Publications

Gems of Wisdom...

Matthew 20:26-28
Galatians 5:13
Romans 12:10-13

Refreshing Hugs...

Just a thought to ponder... Choose a spiritual sister this week. Serve her by doing something special. Make a beautiful memory for her to cherish. Blessings, as you serve in His name.

TEARS SEASONED WITH A CUP OF HOPE

"How painful it was to write that letter! Heartbroken, I cried over it. I didn't want to hurt you, but I wanted you to know how very much I love you."
2 Corinthians 2:4

Passion! 2 Corinthinans 2:4, describes the heartfelt depth of Paul's love for his brothers and sisters in the Lord. Intertwined throughout all of Paul's letters to the churches, we find his zealous love for them, coupled with his rebuke, in love, if necessary. Wouldn't it be marvelous to feel, and be able to express that degree of love and genuine concern? Well, we can! And the best place to begin is in our close friendships.

During our quiet time with Jesus, we can get on our knees, or bow in our heart, asking Him to flood our soul with a river of compassion for believers throughout the world. Because we have a direct line to the Lord, distance is never an issue. We have been given the gift of intercessory prayer for Christians on the other side of the globe, as well as those who reside in our own neighborhood.

Now, I can't read your mind, or your mail, as our contemporary vernacular so aptly puts it, but some of you may be thinking something along these lines: "Gee, Jan, it's not easy for me to express the kind of compassion or concern or love, that Paul expresses, for someone I've never even met. And besides, if you had been emotionally bruised like I have, you would understand." Once again, you are correct. I can't possibly know the extent of the painful circumstances that have reeked havoc on your soul. I don't know the heartaches you have endured. But I have had a few friendships where I have allowed another person to drain my energy tank dry. I have also felt the sting of betrayal.

What I am suggesting is that it may be time for you to move on. And the best news is that God already has a plan to help you step out of your past, out of your pain, and into the joy-filled future He has designed expressly for you.

Here's one option: How about a great big bottle of Elixir of Encouragement? You can do this, Girlfriend, I know you can. Just remember to take a teaspoon of that Elixir, and swallow... And you'll be good to go.

Okay, the last paragraph was all in fun. So, now it's transparency time, once again. If you are anything like me, your heart is simply made of mush. There are signs, you know: You want every romantic movie to end happily ever after; every stray cat or dog to be adopted by an ardent pet lover; every child's tears, boo boo, or runny nose to be wiped away with tender loving care. Well, couldn't we just go on and on?

I cited Apostle Paul's example of "tough love" because we need to learn to love others like God loves us. He isn't looking for perfection; if that were true, none of us would qualify. He simply wants us to make ourselves available to be used by Him. We would never want to intentionally hurt our brother's and sister's in Christ. God loves us with a fervent love, and because He does, there are going to be times that He will need to correct us. There will be times we will find it necessary to correct someone, as well. May we always make a concerted effort to correct, in the spirit of love, because that's exactly what Jesus would do.

Heart Whispers...

Dear God, You are the God of both "Tough Love and Tender Love",

Please help us guard our hearts. Give us the wisdom to know the difference between enabling and empowering, between sharp rebukes and the need to correct. And, when we do need to correct, may that correction be spoken in the spirit of love. In the name of the God who is just plum crazy about His Princesses, despite our weaknesses and frailties. Amen.

Bouquets of Grace-Filled Blessings...

"Sincerity, truth, faithfulness, come into the very essence of friendship."

-William Ellery Channing
Adapted from: *Hugs and Kisses*
A Perpetual Calender
Published by Garborg's Inc.

Gems of Wisdom...

Proverbs 15:23
Colossians 2:2-3
I Thessalonians 3:12

Refreshing Hugs...

Decorate a box with some fabric or pretty wrapping paper. Fill it full of photos, quotations, cards, or prayers you think might encourage someone. Meet them for coffee, if possible, and deliver the box to them, personally.

I was given a beautiful hand painted box that my friend, Sher, gave me when my daddy passed. She called it a memory box and thought that I would like using it as reminders of times that would bring comfort to me, as I went through the grieving process. What a blessing and a truly special gift that memory box has been to me.

Memories are the ultimate gift God gives us as we go from one season of our lives, to the next. Should you need a gift, for any occasion, the idea of a memory box might just be the gift you have been thinking about making, to bless the life of a special friend.

A VALENTINE MADE OUT OF HUGS

"There are three things that will endure-faith, hope,
and love-and the greatest of these is love."
I Corinthians 13:3

Leland Foster Wood wrote a beautiful piece about the family. His words are powerfully expressed, and they exemplify the essence of family love; a sacred love to our Father God. Wood wrote, "...a home is a shelter for love and a setting for joy and growth, rather than a place to be kept up. It is a hallowed place, to which its members shall turn with a lifting up of the heart."

When we turn our focus on love of family, love of community, love of neighbors... the Lord will not hesitate to respond. This kind of love serves to pass on a legacy filled with a strong foundation that embraces God's love, and hands it down to the next generation. And that, in turn, brings glory and honor to the Father.

When Valentine's Day rolls around this year, may we be quick to demomstrate our love to a spouse, a grandparent, a sibling, a friend... May we be quick to forgive, if forgiveness is an issue. May we be quick to show our support for the big dreams one of our loved ones, friends, co-workers...have been working toward reaching. And, may we be quick to generously give to the elderly, the poor, the widow, and the orphan; give not only our financial support, but our time, our resources, our prayers...

When Valentine's Day becomes an every day occurrence to us, that equates to 365 days a year for an opportunity to become a walking, breathing example of God's kind of love, in action.

Heart Whispers...

Dear God, Your Sweet Presence surrounds us every day of the year...

Please bless Your Princess with Your Presence. May she serve others by following Your example, Lord Jesus. May she creatively minister to those You place in her life, with love and joy and gratitude. In the name of the God who blesses us with an abundance of His Love, Joy, Hope, and Grace. Amen.

Bouquets of Grace-Filled Blessings...

"You are blessed by your Father, your Abba, who loves you with the overflowing love of Heaven. It's a legacy of joy you can pass on."

-Mary Hollingsworth
Hugs For Women
Howard Publishing Company

Gems of Wisdom...

Ecclesiastes 3:12
I Timothy 6:18
I John 4:7

Refreshing Hugs...

A Valentine's Day "Hug" suggestion: Ask God for a creative way to "wash the feet" of someone who needs the love of God demonstrated to them this week. Send a loving note to someone who may be lonely or need encouragement. Just a friendly reminder: You can celebrate Valentine's Day, every day of the year, so, use your imagination. Have fun!

HOW DO YOU SPELL P-E-R-F-E-C-T

"...then God our Savior showed us His kindness and love. He saved us, not because of the good things we did, but because of His mercy. He washed away our sins and gave us a new life through the Holy Spirit. He generously poured out the Spirit upon us because of what Jesus Christ our Savior did. He declared us not guilty because of His great kindness. And now we know that we will inherit eternal life." Titus 3:4-7

God does not save us because of the good things we have done. No, none of us are even close to being perfect. Titus 3:4-7 reminds us that our salvation is based purely on His mercy, not on the good deeds that we have done. Romans 3:10, in the NLT, tells us this, "No one is good-not even one."

"What? I love the Lord with all of my heart..." "No one is good-not even one."

"But, I serve at church every Sunday by greeting and helping with the offering!" "No one is good-not even one." "Hey, what about the love offering for our missionaries? I never miss giving to our Missions program!" "No one is good-not even one." "Why, just last Saturday, I gave up going to a basketball tournament just so I could help raise funds for our upcoming Youth Rally." "No one is good-not even one." "Once a month I help bake pies for the Senior Care Center in our neighborhood. And, I stay to help the ladies serve dessert. I know it ministers to the seniors who don't have frequent visitors. They are always so happy to see us! And our pies are always appreciated."

"No one is good-not even one."

In writing the ficticious scenario above, my intent was never to undermine good deeds or charitable acts. As believers, we are to follow in the footsteps of Jesus, who, by His beautiful example, taught us to become generous givers of our gifts and resources. The scenario is intended to explain that as believers, we sometimes fall into the Performance-Based Thinking Trap. I fell into this trap shortly after my conversion to Christianity.

Performance-Based Thinking Syndrome. Sound like an appropriate title? It's the type of thinking that characterizes Christians, who have a tendency to want to rely on their own efforts, works, or good deeds. We call this type of thinking sin. Why? Because it's in direct oppostion to God's truth, as we are told in Philippians 4:13, "For I can do everything with the help of Christ who gives me the strength."

My mother-in-law, Marie, clung to that powerful verse in Philippians. When we moved her from her home state of Ohio, to our city, several thousand miles away, we found a house for her to rent, just a few houses down from ours. She stayed with us until we could move her into her new home. The moving van had finally arrived. As my husband and I helped her unpack a few boxes, we stumbled upon an array of sticky notes that had the verse from Philippians 4:13, written on them. She shared with us that this verse had been instrumental during times of adversity, and had given her comfort and strength during difficult and uncertain times.

A personal example of Performance-Based Thinking: My husband and I moved Daddy to our city, so we can become his primary caregivers. This season of my life became somewhat energy-depleting, and restful night's sleep became few and far between. I was introduced to an excellent natural treatment plan by my internist, Dr. Danka Michaels, who knew exactly what to suggest. Dr. Danka added some exercises for a minor injury I had sustained, coupled with a recommendation for getting a restful night's sleep. I have added to that regimen a little "me" time, on a regular basis. The support of several close friends was also very helpful. I am truly grateful for everyone's helpful imput.

One more example... The Lord brought my friend and hair stylist Kathy, into my life. The way God grew the friendship was by using Kathy as an example of the empowering effect we can have on one another. For the last two and a half years, I have watched Kathy work on getting hair styles as perfect as possible. She goes the extra mile, and beyond, to insure that her clients are as pleased as they can be when they are ready to leave the Salon.

One day, I asked Kathy if she had trouble sleeping at night when she wasn't personally pleased with her work that day. Her response was great. She basically said that her value, as a person, is not predicated [my emphasis], on her performance as a stylist, and I might add, as a color expert, because Kathy is truly gifted in both areas.

I am paraphrasing, but the point is that Kathy's value is not based on her ability to be "perfect" at what she does. Her value is based on the effort she makes while performing her job. There's a vast amount of difference between the two. Our value, as His Child, is based on the One whose love is unconditional. God does not expect us to be perfect at our profession. Neither does He expect perfect performance in our daily tasks. What He does expect is that, like Kathy, we give it our very best. What really matters to God is the effort we put into doing our best, while still maintaining a healthy balance in our relationships with others.

God's faithfulness, in helping us acheive our dreams, is truly an awesome one. He leans over the balcony of our lives, cheering us on for every step we take along our journey. His name is Jesus. And He is our personal Balcony Coach!

Heart Whispers...

Dear God, our Perfect Life Coach,

Sometimes we think that we need to work for what You have offered as a free gift. Thank You, Messiah Jesus, for Your free gift of salvation, the most priceless gift we could ever receive. I ask that You touch the very core of our hearts with Your Word, which is Truth. For each Princess, who may be approaching an unhealthy level of exhaustion, I ask that You pour Your Healing Balm of Gilead, mixed with an extra dose of Your Divine Strength, over her life. Re-Energize her, Lord. Renew and restore her, God. Please sweetly fragrance her life with Your Love.

Remind her that You place the highest value on her, because she is Your Beloved Bride. May she remember that it is not because of her performance, or, her lack of performance, that You place so much value on her life. In fact, if she never did another thing for You, God, Your love for her would never change. Rather, it's because of Your Perfect Love for her, Your Princess. You desire a healthy balance for her, in every area and aspect of her life. In the name of the God who is the Greatest Health Coach ever! Amen.

Bouquets of Grace-Filled Blessings...

"...A part of allowing Christ to heal our thoughts involves admitting our mistakes... and a new willingness to change emerges when we decide that only Christ is perfect."

-Julie Mask
The Woman Within
Thomas Nelson Publishers

Gems of Wisdom...

Colossians 1:28-29

Refreshing Hugs...

If you struggle with perfectionistic tendencies, try this remedy: Purposely leave a few dirty dishes in the sink tomorrow... I'm talking "caked-on food" from last Tuesday's dinner. Don't touch yesterday's trash. But, please, don't tell your family who suggested this crazy idea. They may not like your unconventional boundaries; then again, they might not notice for days... weeks maybe...

WHITER THAN SNOW?

"Come now, let us argue this out," says the Lord. "No matter
how deep the stain of your sins, I can remove it. I can make
you as clean as freshly fallen snow. Even if you are stained
as red as crimson, I can make you as white as wool."
Isaiah 1:18

Whiter than snow? Yes, whiter than snow. The promise, in Isaiah 1:18, was a promise the Lord made to the Israelites. They had allowed their hearts to grow cold toward the very One who loved them with a fervent love; an all-encompassing love; a love that's never-ending... The Israelites had become rebellious and stiff-necked; they refused to listen to their God, much less to obey Him. This was an "If-Then" promise. It still is. If we confess and repent of our sin, then God will do this: Even though our sins are deeply stained, like crimson, God will erase them, as though they never existed.

Hebrews 4:12 reminds us that God's Word is alive and it is powerful. Scripture likens His Word to a knife, "For the word of God is full of living power. It is sharper than the sharpest knife, cutting deep into our innermost thoughts and desires. It exposes us for what we really are." God can discern our thoughts. Now that's rather scary, huh? He knows the intentions we harbor in our hearts-intentions to participate in good deeds or evil ones. So, that means that even before we intend to act upon our thoughts, God is already there. Taking it one step further, when we have a certain thought, God is able to interpret that thought and where it will eventually lead us.

This verse in Hebrews becomes invaluable to the believer. It helps us to focus on God's intentions for our life. It serves as a directional map, or GPS Navigator, powered by the Holy Spirit. He keeps us on a straight path so we won't stray far away from the directional signal He mapped out for us, before we were ever born. Hebrews 4:12 helps to keep us on track. Because of God's promise, we know that we can run straight into the arms of our Papa God, ask for His forgiveness, and ask Him to cleanse us from our unrighteousness. He puts us back on track so we can continue along the path He so lovingly designed for you, and for me. Isn't God just awesome!

Heart Whispers...

Dear God, our Perfect Navigator,

There are times in our walk with You, Messiah Jesus, that we hold back part of our heart. We're ashamed of our weaknesses, thinking You might ask something of us that we don't feel capable of doing. The truth is that without You, Lord, we have no ability to become victorious. Without You, Jesus, we are powerless to change. While others may not forgive us, You take our sins and erase them from Your memory, forever!

Please whisper in the ear of Your Princess, the words she so desperately needs to hear. No matter how stained she feels her sins have been, once she has asked for Your forgiveness, and once she repents, You will make those sins "...as clean as freshly fallen snow." In fact, You will make those sins vanish, forever... In the name of the God who pours His astounding grace over us and washes us as white as snow... Amen.

Bouquets of Grace-Filled Blessings...

"The flagship word of the gospel is grace. No wonder, for grace is shorthand for God wishing us well..."

-Lewis B. Smeads
The Art Of Forgiving
Moorings-A Division of Ballantine Publishing

Gems of Wisdom...

Psalm 51:7-10
Psalm 103:12
2 Corinthians 8:9
Ezekiel 36:25-27

Refreshing Hugs...

Now might be a perfect opportunity to just plop right down on the lap of your Redeemer, knowing that He has been waiting, oh, so patiently waiting, to love on you. Isn't that just the best news you have heard in ever?

GRACE-FILLED GIFTS

"But when the Holy Spirit controls our lives, He will produce
this kind of fruit in us: love, joy, peace, patience, kindness,
goodness, faithfulness, gentleness, and self-control..."
Galatians 5:22-23

"...love, joy, peace, patience, kindness..." There are nine character traits that comprise the fruit of the Spirit; when we yield to the control of the Spirit of God, His fruit becomes more evident in our thoughts, actions, words, and heart motives. Now, I will be the first one to admit that my attitude has not been 100% godly, twenty-four hours a day, for the past thirty plus years... Here's what I do know: The Holy Spirit desires His fruit to dominate and control our emotions throughout all of the "hard stuff." The NIV of Matthew 7:20, states it this way, "...by their fruit you will recognize them." What Jesus didn't say was, "By the type of car they're driving, you will know them." He never said, "By what kind of designer clothing they are wearing-you will know them." Nor did Jesus say, "By the success they have attained, or the amount of power they can wield, you will know them." No, what Jesus did say, emphatically, was that the world would recognize them by the fruit of the Spirit that was evident in their lives.

Jesus set a perfect example for the world to see. Our goal is to emulate the fruit of the Spirit in our lives. And here's why: God is a perfect personification of these nine character traits. When the world looks at the way we conduct ourselves in our relationships, our occupations, socially... what they will see is predicated not on what we say, but how we choose to live our lives. What they will see is our genuine actions and our sincere faith. Our goal, to look more and more like Jesus, becomes evident. Our heart's desire is to display His fruit... And, as His Bride, we want the lost souls of our world to come to Him and learn His ways so that they too, can experience the love, joy, and peace that His Saving Grace brings.

I love Galatians 5:22-23. I committed this verse to memory many years ago. It is a reminder to live, walk, and breathe in the sweetness of the Holy Spirit each day. Am I suggesting we put on a mask so that the world cannot detect the fact that we are embroiled in the middle of a crisis? No. What I am suggesting is a bottom line transparency; to say it another way, no masks! What I am also suggesting is that we kneel, at His Mercy Seat, asking for His Grace...

Beloved Princess, we will need God's Grace to carry us while we are in the rennovation stage. We will need His Grace to come beside us as we walk toward the restoration phase that He has planned for us. And, we will need God's Grace as He works on producing "this kind of fruit in us: love, joy, peace, patience..."

Oh, the Grace of God is so amazingly healing...

Heart Whispers...

Dear God, Thank You, Holy Spirit, that You are the only One who can infuse each Princess with Your fruit,

When we turn the control of our lives over to You, Holy Spirit, You fill us with the fruit of love, joy, peace, patience, kindness, goodness, faithfulness, gentleness, and self-control. Please help each Princess to exude the fruit of the Spirit, in everything she does, so that the world will know that You are God; You are the Holy One of Israel; You are Messiah... You are the Savior of the inhabitants of the universe...

There are those of us who find it really difficult to become transparent. But, as Your ambassadors to the world, we do need to be transparent and sincere. When we are personally dealing with issues, regardless of the turmoil these issues can cause in our daily lives, we can still be used, by You, Holy Spirit, to minister to a world where so many are hurting. This is actually what a balcony coach does; they turn their focus toward another person in order to support and encourage them to become the best they can be; and to do the best they can do, for Your Glory. When we hand over the reigns of our lives to You, Spirit of God, You help us walk in the spirit of love, joy, peace...

As Your ambassadors, God, we are being observed, with scrutiny, to see how we will respond during the tough times life can sometimes bring. May Your fruit, Holy Spirit, be so obvious in our lives, that it can even be seen at a distance. In the name of the God who is the Standard by which we can extend a hand of fellowship to those who need a trusted friend. Amen.

Bouquets of Grace-Filled Blessings...

"Blessed are they who have the gift of making friends... It involves many things, but above all, the power of going out of one's self, and appreciating whatever is noble and loving in another."

-Thomas Hughes
Leaves of Gold
Reflections for Each Day Calendar
Brownlow Publishing Company, Inc.

Gems of Wisdom...

Matthew 7:15-20
Colossians 3:12
Luke 8:15
Ephesians 2:8

Refreshing Hugs...

Perhaps a caring gesture would be to make a recording of some of the Psalms that minister to you, personally, in your own voice. Make arrangements to meet someone you know who needs encouragement, and hand deliver the recording. What a blessing that gift would be.

WHAT? A TIME TO PAMPER ME? SERIOUSLY?

"There is a time for everything, a season for every activity under heaven."
Ecclesiastes 3:1

Our timing is not necessarily God's timing. In fact, He makes it clear that our ways are not His ways; our thoughts are not His thoughts, as He states this fact in Isaiah 55:8 NKJV. Since we cannot completely understand the precision of His timing, we inevitably fall short. So, it's in our best interest to wait on the Lord, just like the song says, "I will wait upon the Lord, I will wait upon the Lord, I will wait upon the Lord..." Rather than jumping head first into our own agenda, as I am still prone, on occassion, to do, it would be to our very best advantage, to wait on Him. There are so many decisions and choices we are called upon to make, each day; how can we know which decision will align with His choice for us?

God tells us that there is a time and a season for everything we plan to do. He has sealed each of His children with the Holy Spirit, and He becomes our Grand Tour Guide. The more we adhere to His guidance, the more closely we come to adjusting our timing with His. Once again, this can only be accomplished when we are submissive in waiting on God to reveal His "Now Time" for us. There have been times, in my own life, when I have really believed I was waiting on the Lord, only to be disappointed when things didn't turn out as I had thought they would. And there's the key... How Jan thought they would turn out, not how He planned for them to turn out.

Eventually, I began following God's agenda, instead of my own. However, there were still times when I would become frustrated because I wasn't able to accomplish the many things I believed I needed to do each day. After seeking His Wisdom, the last thing I asked was for Him to place top priority on His agenda, and place mine wherever He wanted.

It was only about a month after daddy had passed. Honey and I were still grieving the passing of a man who not only was a great dad and father-in-law, but was also a wonderful grandpa and great grandpa. We had been my dad's primary care givers for six plus years, and were really feeling a great loss. In my devotional reading, a few weeks later, I came across a passage of scripture that I hadn't paid too much attention to, until I read the words of Isaiah 58:13-14.

I finally realized the importance of giving our bodies a rest that is imperative to our well-being, spiritually, emotionally, mentally, and physically. I like how the New Living Translation gives the command clarity:

> "Keep the Sabbath day holy. Don't pursue your own interests
> on that day, but enjoy the Sabbath and speak of it with delight
> as the Lord's holy day. Honor the Lord in everything
> and don't follow your own desires... If you do this, the Lord will
> be your delight. I will give you great honor and give you
> your full share of the inheritance I promised...
> I, the Lord, have spoken!"

We made a decision to keep the Sabbath one day a week. It was not an easy decision for us to make, in the respect that my husband's work week consists of a Monday through Saturday schedule. It became necessary for us to choose a different twenty-four hour time frame from sundown to sundown. It is different in the respect that the traditional Friday night to Saturday night Sabbath, that people of the Jewish faith keep, would pose a work conflict for my husband's company. We felt comfortable with this decision because we believe the Lord honors a twenty-four hour respite from work, even if it falls on a different day than the Sabbath, by biblical tradition, is kept.

It has been four plus years now, since we began our Sabbath rest. It has become a blessing for us, and has provided quality time to spend together, re-connecting, after a long work week. It also affords each of us time to spend separately, with the Lord.

I almost feel like a pampered Princess, on the Sabbath. It's a day where I can allow myself time to read, or just relax with Messiah Jesus. I have been suggesting a Sabbath Rest for His Princesses, for several years now. The feedback has been quite positive. What a joy a twenty-four hour respite from work can be! It's almost like taking a twenty-four hour sabbatical, once a week.

Our Messiah tells us many things about a Sabbath Rest. He created the Sabbath for man, not the other way around. We need to rest one full day a week. It provides us with time to sit at the feet of our Messiah, and, it helps us to focus on His direction for our journey. It is, in fact, sacred time spent in His Presence.

So, come on now, hand over those decisions you may be facing-ones that may be causing you stress. That's right, hand them over to your Counselor, the Holy Spirit. He knows your desire to make right choices. In fact, He will stand by your side, ready to help you make healthy decisions.

Should you decide to take a Sabbath Rest, here is what I'd like to suggest: Clear your calendar of work or any decision-making. Once those decisions go from your hand to His, ideally before you begin your Sabbath, I believe you'll feel the stress begin to dissipate. It's such a great thing to know we have a Loving Counselor who, one day a week, wants us to refrain from pursuing our own agenda. We also have a Counselor who will always help us through the hard decisions that life sometimes presents...

Heart Whispers...

Dear God, You are Lord of the Sabbath,

Father God, Thank You for creating the Sabbath Rest for man, and not the other way around. There may be several Princesses, even at this moment, who are struggling to make healthy choices. While I may never have the opportunity to meet them in person, my prayer is that You will help me touch their lives, throughout the pages of this book. Thank you, Holy Spirit, for being both our Counselor and Lord of the Sabbath.

Please bless Your Cherished Princess, as she turns to You for help in making healthy lifestyle choices. And may one of those healthy decisions be to take full advantage of the Sabbath Rest You created for every believer. In the name of the God who desires to counsel us regarding every decision we will be called to make along our destiny path. Amen.

Bouquets of Grace-Filled Blessings...

"...If I could teach you only three things, they would be: first, receive Jesus Christ as your Lord and Savior; second, love Israel, not just the land, but also the people; and third, learn about the miracle God has for you when you remember the Sabbath."

-Larry Huch
The Torah Blessing
Whitaker House

Gems of Wisdom...

Psalm 90:12
Exodus 20:8-11
Isaiah 58:13-14
Mark 2:27

Refreshing Hugs...

Should you decide to take a Sabbath Rest, for a twenty-four hour period, once a week, be sure not to schedule any appointments, or have any phone calls you must make for business purposes. Arrange a blank time slot with nothing you are required to get done. As I have mentioned, in a previous segment, what a difference a Sabbath day of rest can make in our lives spiritually, emotionally, physically...

ABUNDANT GENEROSITY

"Jesus felt genuine love for this man as He looked at him. "You lack only one thing," He told him. "Go and sell all you have and give the money to the poor, and you will have treasure in heaven. Then come, follow Me."

Mark 10:21

Jesus was traveling in the region of Judea when He met up with a rich young ruler... Every time I read this passage, I am struck by the gentility and tenderness of our Lord; all Jesus had to do was to look at the man, and already, He loved him. The Son of God, knowing what was in this man's heart, gave the young ruler an instruction-sell all your possessions and give the money to the poor. We are told that the ruler walked away from Jesus; the obedience He asked from this young ruler was ignored. How very sad. The Spirit of God speaks to our hearts all the time, but then we have to make a decision. If we are intentional and obedient to the voice of the Spirit of God, as He whispers in our ear, we will understand His will for our lives, and we will purpose to walk in His footprints, step by step by step...

It's not like Jesus is asking His children to take a vow of poverty. No. What the Lord is asking is for our complete obedience to Him. Jesus already knew what was in this ruler's heart; He knows what is in the heart of every believer.

There's a song by Marsha Skidmore and David Hook, produced by Maranatha! Music. It is entitled: *Lord Of My Salvation*. The message resounds to it's hearer through the lyrics that form the chorus. The words remind us to pray: "Create in me the purest heart, Restore Your joy to ev'ry part. Deliver me from sin and self, O Lord of my salvation." The Lord gives us every opportunity to change our ways and follow Him wherever He may lead us. He gave the young ruler one instruction: "Go and sell all you have and give the money to the poor..." Because the young ruler was sinful and focused on himself, sadly, when the Lord asked for his obedience, he walked away without heeding Jesus' instruction.

We are without excuse. The bible tells us to heed God's instructions, an example of which can be found in Hebrews 3:7-8, "That is why the Holy Spirit says, 'Today you must listen to His voice. Don't harden your hearts against

Him as Israel did when they rebelled..."' The rich young ruler could not give up his riches; he had allowed them to become the idols he chose to erect in his heart, namely position and power. The ruler had built a citadel; he built this citadel to protect his heart; a heart filled with insecurity about losing his wealth, namely his possessions and his financial status. This young ruler had hardened his heart.

I need to clarify something regarding the whole dialog that occured between Jesus and the rich ruler. The request, from the Son of God, does not always equate to money or possessions, as it does in this passage of scripture. There are many references to the poor in the bible. However, there is a scripture passage, in the Book of Mark, that offers one such account; an example that is a reversal of the example Jesus gives, in regard to the young ruler's hardened heart. The following example does have to do with the issue of money, or, in this case, the lack of it...

> "Jesus went over to the collection box in the Temple and sat and watched as the crowds dropped in their money. Many rich people put in large amounts. Then a poor widow came and dropped in two pennies." Here is what Jesus told His disciples that day, as it reads in Mark 12:41-44, "...this poor widow has given more than all the others... For they gave a tiny part of their surplus, but she, poor as she is, has given everything she has."

The powerful message of this widow is one I hope you will take away with you. The gifts of our time, resources, skills, such as baking or cooking for a shut-in, someone who has recently experienced a loss of a friend or a loved one, or a mom who needs a little "pamper me" time; all these gifts are priceless. The monetary value of the gift is never at the heart of God's message. It's about what is in the heart of the giver; the intention of their motives; these things are the things that make all the difference!

There is another scripture passage found in 2 Corinthians 2:10-15 that speaks volumes about generosity. The NLT phrases it this way, "For God is the one who gives seed to the farmer and then bread to eat. In the same way, He will give you many opportunities to do good, and He will produce a great harvest of generosity in you. Yes, you will be enriched so that you can give even more generously. And when we take your gifts to those who need them, they will break out in thanksgiving to God."

I have this fondness for quotes and cute sayings on plaques, jewelry, bumper stickers, etc. I have one in my kitchen window by Erma Bombeck. It appears in the *Bouquets of Grace* section below. To me, it speaks directly to the focus of God's message and should exemplify the attitude we are to maintain in our heart...

Heart Whispers...

Dear God, our Heart Tenderizer,

Please tenderize the heart of every Princess. Help us to look at the world through Your eyes of compassion. Help us to give of our time generously, to spend with someone who is in need of a blessing. May we give away the bountiful gifts and resources You have given to us; and may we always give them away, in the spirit of love...

Lord, I ask that You bless the hand and heart of Your Princess. Bless her, God, so she can be freed up to share with those who may not even realize how hungry and thirsty they truly are, for the manna only You can provide. Thank You, Messiah Jesus, for Your Mercy, Compassion, Grace, and Provisions... In the name of the God who can change a heart from stone to flesh... in less time than it takes to blink. Amen.

Bouquets of Grace-Filled Blessings...

"When I stand before God at the end of my life I would hope that I would have not a single bit of talent left and could say, "I used everything You gave me."

-Erma Bombeck
Kitchen Plaque

Gems of Wisdom...

2 Corinthians 9:9-13
Exodus 35:22
Hebrews 13:16

Refreshing Hugs...

Suggestion: Set aside some containers that you can put loose change in. As the jars become full, convert the change into bills, and deposit the money in a checking account.

As a family, decide on a ministry for your love offering. If there are children in your home, it's a great way to teach them to share with others who are in need.

BE FILLED WITH THE FULLNESS OF
HIS LIFE & LOVE & POWER

"And I pray that Christ will be more and more at home in your hearts
as you trust in Him. May your roots go down deep into the soil of
God's marvelous love. And may you have the power to understand,
as all God's people should, how wide, how long, how high, and how
deep His love really is. May you experience the love of Christ, though
it is so great you will never fully understand it. Then you will be
filled with the fullness of life and power that comes from God."
Ephesians 3:17-19

Eloquent! To me, the scripture passage found in the third chapter of
the Book of Ephesians reads like a sigh-breathed melody that captures the
longings of the human soul... None of us can begin to fathom the Eternal
Love our Lord has for His Beloved Princess. If we were to catch even the
faintest glimmer of the depth of that love, we would never be the same again.
And that, Princess of the most High God, is precisely the purpose.

Once we come to know the Lord as our Heavenly Bridegroom, everything
else pales in comparison. We cannot help but be deeply moved, to our very
core, by the magnitude of His Love and the power of His Grace... His kind of
Grace has the power to deliver from devastating addictions, the power to heal
the body of a lifetime of disease, to create a new heart-a clean heart-a heart
determined to know Him... His kind of Grace yields the incomprehensible
power to renew a spirit that has been repeatedly crushed for literally years. Yes,
God's Grace is a Transformative Grace, a Restorative Grace, a Saving Grace...

Passion: it's what makes God's heart beat for the salvation of His people.
Passion: it followed Christ to Gethsemene, but would not leave Him there.
Passion: it took Him to Calvary, but held on to Him as they nailed Him
to an old splintered cross, where He shed drops of His Blood, one precious
drop after another. Passion: it stayed with Him as He drew His last breath.
Passion: it defeated death and the grave. Passion: it is why He is our Risen
Lord. Passion: it was the only driving force that would cause Him to do it all
over again, for you, for me, for every child He holds dear. But, Praise God,
He will never have to, because He Lives...

Our Messiah Lives! And it's because of His Passion that we can walk out the Eternal Future He has created for us. Passion: Our Messiah waits patiently until He hears our heartbeat begin to move to the rhythm of His Heartbeat. And my prayer is that each of your odyssey footprints will follow the pattern of that rhythm. May you follow the heartbeat of His Passion, one beat after the next...

Heart Whispers...

Dear God, our Risen Savior,

What a loving, patient, and grace-giving God You are. It is because of Your Passion that You shower Your blessings, Your tenderness, and Your never-ending love on Your Princess. Give her hope for those dreams that match the dreams You paint, exclusively for her. Give her an extra measure of perseverance, as she devotedly works at the task of completing her goals...

When she becomes anxious, give her serenity like a flowing country brook. And if she is concerned about something, give her the assurance of Your Faithfulness so she can trust in Your Love. Give her Your sweet peace, as You lull her to sleep with the lullaby You wrote, just for her... In the name of the God who writes our names in His Book of Life and seals them with His never-ending love and faithfulness. Amen.

Bouquets of Grace-Filled Blessings...

"Great is the Lord, He is holy and just; By his power we trust in his love. Great is the Lord, He is faithful and true; By his mercy he proves he is love..."

-Michael J. Smith
A Song Of Praise To God
Meadowgreen Music Co. by
Tree Publishing Co., Inc.

Gems of Wisdom...

Psalm 103:11
Romans 5:17
2 Corinthians 13:13
Deuteronomy 7:9

Refreshing Hugs...

In your own special style, sing a love song to Jesus. Let your words reflect all those things you can think of that make Him the Great God that He is. Tell Him just how wonderful He is to you. If you decide to take me up on this suggestion, make it fun...go ahead and laugh, giggle, chuckle... Have oodles of fun... Just you and God...

FRESH GRACE

"The unfailing love of the Lord never ends!... Great is His
faithfulness; His mercies began afresh each day."
Lamentations 3:22-23

Smith Wigglesworth, a plumber by trade, became a zealous man of
God. By circa 1900, Wigglesworth began to preach and write devotionals.
Unschooled though he was, God used this simple man to reach thousands upon
thousands for Christ. Before a friend shared a copy of one of Wigglesworth's
books with me, I had never heard of this preacher. But, oh, what a treasure
that book became. I was fascinated by the way God chose to use Wigglesworth
for His glory. Smith was a man who, like Jesus, was filled with compassion
These three words became the hallmark that compelled Smith to share Christ
with the world.

The NKJV of Matthew 9:36, describes Jesus, as He gazed out over
the multitudes of people, as being "...moved with compassion." Our Good
Shepherd looks at us, and He is equally as compassionate today, as He was
over two thousand years ago. Lamentations 3:23 serves as a reminder that
God's Compassion begins again, at the dawn of each new day. This is how
the NKJV describes the depth of compassion Jesus felt for the crowd who "...
were weary and scattered, like sheep having no shepherd."

Despite our weaknesses, our failures, our sin; all the ways we fall short of
the expectations we have of ourselves, and the ones we think others have of us,
God's Great Mercy never fails! He begins each new morning by erasing the
litany of faults we seem to have accumulated since the last time we repented
of them...yesterday. The really good news is that we can choose to greet each
new day by viewing it the same way Jesus does, with a clean slate!

Look up! See Jesus in all of His glory! And may we, as believers, purpose
in our hearts to share His great love, grace, and compassion, with those who
are still seeking...

Heart Whispers...

Dear God, You are the God of Great Compassion,

Thank You for Your compassion and Your faithfulness; they are truly fresh every morning. It is so comforting to wake up with the expectancy, that, one of the ways You choose to show Your mercy is to forgive and totally erase our sin... When we repent, ask for Your forgiveness, and follow Your instruction for our lives, Your forgiveness is instantaneous... With the dawn of each new morning, You take it to the next level, Lord. You provide us with a huge easel and a brand new blank page, ready to be filled with endless possibilities of ways we can bring glory to You.

It truly is quite amazing that even when we fail, or our weaknesses are many, we are still precious to You, Lord. Help us, Holy Spirit, to keep our focus on You and Your directions for our odyssey path. In the name of the God whose mercy, compassion, and faithfulness is fresh every morning, and whose unfailing love has no end... Amen.

Bouquets of Grace-Filled Blessings...

"Great is Thy Faithfulness! Great is Thy Faithfulness! Morning by morning new mercies I see; all I have needed Thy hand hath provided; great is Thy Faithfulness, Lord, unto me!"

-Thomas O. Chisholm
Song: *Great Is Thy Faithfulness*
Hope Publishing

Gems of Wisdom...

Psalm 86:15
Psalm 145:9
Lamentations 3:22-23

Refreshing Hugs...

Take time today to reflect on God's unending faithfulness. Meditate on His compassion and grace. His mercies are like a calming salve poured over our wounded soul. May each Princess remember to thank God for His matchless grace.

PART THREE: FEELING KIND OF INSECURE?
BECOME GOD'S "ANCHOR THROWING" PRINCESS

"...when the winds are blowing and the storms are raging,
there is plenty of fear, but... no danger. ...we are quite safe,
for we have an anchor of the soul that is...sure and steadfast
and will not move... Hope is the anchor of my soul."

-Charles Spurgeon
Finding Peace In Life's Storms
Whitaker House

START YOUR DAY WITH GIGGLES OF JOY!

"Be joyful in hope, patient in affliction, faithful in prayer. Share
with God's people who are in need. Practice hospitality."
Romans 12:12-13 NKJV

I find it so interesting that three of the nine fruit of the Spirit, Galatians
5:22-23, are mentioned in Romans 12:12-13; joy, patience, and faithfulness.
The challenge lies in applying joy to our hope, patience to our times of
adversity, and faithfulness to our prayer life, when several other problems may
need quick resolution. It seems that, with all those possible variables, it can
become easy to lose our focus. I Thessalonians 5:17 addresses this very issue.
The KJV states it this way, "pray without ceasing..."

In my coaching practice, the following are three methods I use to help my
clients live in an attitude of joy, even when things appear to be bleak. Method
#1: To maintain a sense of genuine calmness, when life is anything but calm.
Method #2: To cultivate an attitude of serene patience and perseverence.
Method #3: To establish a strong commitment to bible study; to develop a
consistency in her prayer life; and avoidance of distractions or interruptions
during her quiet time...

The first method is to get quiet so you can have a heart to heart session
with God. Be honest. Our Abba Daddy knows us better than we could ever
know ourselves. Tell Him about your feelings, no matter how negative they
may seem to you. He knows everything about you. Nothing will take Him
by surprise, make Him angry, or cause Him to grow impatient with you. He
wrote the Book about longsuffering. He can handle it-no matter what "it"
might be. Even if you are struggling to exercise a patient attitude, talk to
Jesus. Despite the feelings of hopelessness you may be experiencing, talk to
Jesus. Finally, even if there doesn't appear to be an end in sight... talk to Jesus.

You know, Girlfriend, sometimes a vague sense of hopelessness appears
to creep into our thought life, especially when we are preoccupied with other
things. Martha, for example, became preoccupied with worrying and stressing
over dinner, and making sure that her Messiah would feel as if He were dining
at a Five Star restaurant, in the middle of Jerusalem. We can almost sense
Martha's stress. Jesus had to remind Martha that her sister, Mary, made the

choice to focus on other important matters; like sitting at the feet of her Rabbi, absorbing all He wanted to teach her.

Let's go back to Martha's role, for a moment. Romans 12:13, is a reminder to practice hospitality. Hospitality plays a vital role in our society, and has, for several thousand years. To the Jewish people, who lived at the time this scenario takes place, the table meals represented the close relational ties that were formed at mealtime. It is still a sacred time today. Mary chose to be taught by her Master; Martha, on the other hand, was stressing over the main entree of the dinner menu, and how to please the Lord by cooking a fantastic meal. Martha took her role as meal planner and sous chef, as seriously as Mary took her role as a student with a teachable spirit. Both were on Jesus' list of priorities. Both roles were important. The same is true today. However, if one were to take precedence over the other, like this scenario suggests, Jesus states that Mary's stance came in as top priority.

Okay, so how do I know so much about Martha's high anxiety over a gourmet meal she planned on cooking for her Messiah? Well, if you'll recall, in the intro to this book, I alluded to the fact that, when Honey and I combined our family, every event had to be perfect, with all the bells and whistles. I can relate to Martha because I was also a Perfectionistic Princess-a Recovering Perfectionistic Princess, maybe, but still... I can only imagine the butterflies that Martha might have felt in the pit of her stomach, at the thought of putting a perfect meal on the table for her Lord. You know, I am wondering if this perfectionistic tendency thing is genetically inherited, like somehow showing up in our DNA?

A hope basket, as I suggested creating, in a previous segment, would work well. If you have one, pull a promise out to read. If you find one that really tickles your fancy, tape it to a mirror or your frig. Read it several times a day for the next few weeks. Hope messages serve as positive memory builders, and can help produce a joyful outlook to actually make us giggle. I like that alot!

Indulge me while I share a little secret with you. Patience is not one of my strong suits. In fact, it may just be the fruit of the Spirit that I struggle with most often. But, patience is what is required, while we are waiting for God to help us develop that fruit of the Spirit some of us may need to practice. So...what's a Princess to do? Even if this "patience" thing seems to be an ongoing activity; ongoing as in mega days... weeks... months... learning how to incorporate that fruit does, in fact, require a lot of, well, you know, patience.

If I am undergoing a heavy spiritual attack, for example, suddenly, I might just start giggling. Soon, I find myself laughing like I used to do when my children thought it was their duty to come up with some really great stuff to make mom giggle. Now, instead of lapsing into a state of chaos, I declare the name of Jesus, plead His Blood, and giggle at the enemy...

There's something precious about learning the art of faithfulness in prayer. The odyssey we've embarked on is only in the beginning stages. But, there is a common theme; that theme has to do with a consistent contemplative prayer time. A time of reflection, and, an ongoing dialogue with God throughout our day, is so important. To "pray without ceasing" literally means to talk to God throughout our day.

The battle began to heat up. Soon, I would find myself beginning to converse with God, and thinking it was going along quite nicely, only to find my mind wandering off, on several different tangents. After a while, I wouldn't be talking to Jesus any longer. Instead, I would begin to stress over little insignificant problems that, given enough time, would escalate until they began to resemble a mountain of insurmountable proportions. I began to lose my sense of peace, and waste a lot of energy thinking about circumstances that I could neither alter or control.

Sometimes, what we really need is right smack in front of us. What I really needed was a new perspective on things, topped off with, well, with going on a laughing spree. Wait, let me really emphasis that point: I just needed to start giggling... My friend Denise is a master at this particular art. The recording you hear, when you call her on her cell phone, is a delightful giggle that can make anyone who's feeling a little down, have her heart lifted, just by hearing Denise's message.

I love what Jesus teaches us about living in an attitude of prayer and intercession. We can intercede on behalf of our sisters in Jesus, throughout the world; we can now intercede with peace and patience, even though we're aware that they may be facing grave circumstances. Just knowing that, as we join our voice with countless others, God is working in each situation, for their good. And that's a comforting thought! I hope this has helped you to think about ways of serving your King, joyfully, patiently, and faithfully.

If you struggle a little with perfectionism, forget that "Martha mindset." Your house does not have to pass the white glove test, whatever that might happen to look like. Every meal does not have to appear to have been cooked by a sous chef, even if you happen to cook like one, like my friend Sher does. Your heart for others, and a joyful spirit, is all that is required. May God bless you as you serve Him by interceding on behalf of His Cherished Princesses, around the globe.

Heart Whispers...

Dear God, You are the God of Israel, who never needs to slumber or sleep,

Thank You for teaching us how to be "joyful in hope, patient in affliction, and faithful in prayer." I give You my heart, Lord, and ask that You use me in whatever way You choose, to minister to Your Beloved Princess who may have need of a life coach to come alongside her, partner with her, be supportive of her, and celebrate each victory with her.

I want to be a coach who will lean over the balcony of her life, whispering, "Go for those dreams. Don't put them on the back burner of your life any longer. Be encouraged because your goals are so close to being realized. Reach for your aspirations, and keep praying for those who need your prayers..."

Thank You, God, for Your Provisions and Your Great Grace... Please bless Your Princess ten-fold, as she purposes to pray her way through her day, and live out Your Word, one footprint at a time. In the name of the God who is our Patience, Joy, Hope Supplier... Amen.

Bouquets of Grace-Filled Blessings...

"Before you go to bed give your troubles to God. He will be up all night anyway."

-Anonymous

Gems of Wisdom...

2 Corinthians 4:17-18
Psalm 100:1
Romans 12:12-13

Refreshing Hugs...

For the next few days, let's purpose to practice sitting still for thirty minutes each day. On the first day, let's focus on being joyful in hope, as we pray.

On the second day, may our focus turn toward praying for those we know personally, who may be experiencing difficult times.

On the third day, let's continue our practice of being patient, as God works in the lives of those we may not know personally, but may know about them because they are a missionary, or a missionary family supported by our church family, and we have been praying for their needs.

On the fourth day, let's purpose to pray our way through our days, and through each challenge we may be experiencing personally, with patience, of course. Don't forget the giggling part. The dosage: A little giggling several times a day... Don't be shy...Just do it!

OH, THE GRACE, THE GRACE,
THE GRACE OF GOD...

"...O people, the Lord has already told you what is good,
and this is what He requires; to do what is right, to love
mercy, and to walk humbly with your God."
Micah 6:8

Have you ever felt a little insecure? There have been times in my life when I didn't know what I was here to accomplish. Micah 6:8 can be of great help in teaching us how God wants to direct our energies. I believe it holds the key to where believers are suppose to place their focus. Let's break this scripture down. First, Micah tells us that we need to be in a posture of humility before the Lord. Second, we can become inspired to extend His Love, Mercy, and Grace... to everyone we come into contact with. And finally, if we do this, we will become a blessing to others.

Princess, do you love mercy? Great! Because our Lord loves to show us mercy. Matthew 5:7 is part of the Beatitudes, and this verse reassures every believer with its words, "God blesses those who are merciful, for they will be shown mercy." Next, are you walking in submission and obedience to Him? Awesome! This is a true sign of the kind of humility God wants His precious ones to practice. When we can honestly say, "God, I can't do this myself; I need Your help..." we have His full attention. And, when He responds with that help, He should have our full attention!

The characteristic of humility is high on God's list. If we need help and need to summon the immediate attention of the King of kings, He is there, waiting to answer our cries for help. When we are facing issues of insecurity, we need to consult our Lord. When we are unsure of what our next move should be, or we are just plain "stuck," it's time to ask Messiah Jesus for help.

My husband and I were getting ready to move. While looking through lots of bins, I looked down and recognized a book I hadn't read yet. It was a relatively old book entitled: *Better Than Gold*. I opened the cover to find an inscription that simply read: "To Hy, With God's Love... Remember the words of Micah 6:8." It was signed by a man named Shepherd, who was my uncle's sponsor in his support group. It was a book that my uncle, before he became quite ill, had passed on to me. *Better Than Gold* is a devotional book on the 119th Psalm, written by C.H. Chrisman in 1963. I'll close with a quote by the author, in the forward of the book:

> "It's one hundred and seventy-six verses contain
> the essence of David's heart-throbs over much
> of his checkered career...his inner emotions...
> upon the sacred pages... "O, the grace, the grace,
> the grace of God!"

Did God hear David's heart cry for help, when this man of God had sinned, and needed the grace that only his God could supply? Most assuredly, He did. David learned to put his trust in God, and God alone. Psalm 34:15, 17, reassures us that, when the righteous cry out, God hears. "O, the grace, the grace, the grace of God!"

Heart Whispers...

Dear God, You are the God of Tender Mercies that are new every morning,

You have called Your children to walk in humility, to live a life of justice and fairness, and to love mercy. Please help us to pause often, throughout the course of our day, to acknowledge Your Lordship over our lives. Help us to remember what You require of us. It is in humility of heart, Lord Jesus, that we can find refreshment for our soul. And it is in Your Steadfast Love, that we find secuity-all the security we will ever need. In the name of the God who anchors our soul to His... Amen.

Bouquets of Grace-Filled Blessings...

"Many blessings come to the seeking saints for which they never ask... They are humble and recipients of the mercies of God. It is forever true that God hears...the desires of the humble (Psalm 10:17)."

-C.H. Chrisman
Better Than Gold
Bethany Fellowship, Inc.

Gems of Wisdom...

Micah 6:8
Psalm 25:9-10
Hosea 12:6
James 4:6

Refreshing Hugs...

If you like doing word searches and have access to a Synonym Finder, look up the words: justice, mercy, and humility. What do these terms suggest to you? Write your answers down and look at them from time to time. Write the words of Micah 6:8 on a 3x5 card and commit to memorizing it.

Chrisman says it beautifully: "It is forever true that God hears... the desires of the humble."

HEART CRIES

"Praise the Lord! For He has heard my cry for mercy. The
Lord is my strength, my shield... I trust in Him with all my
heart. He helps me, and my heart is filled with joy..."
Psalm 28:6-7

The Psalmist David confidently relied and trusted on the Lord for his strength. Even when He brought David face-to-face with many enemies, attacking him from all sides, David was fully equipped to meet and defeat his opposition-not because David was mighty, but because he served a mighty God who infused David with His supernatural power.

David's life was anything but exemplary. There was that incident with Bathsheba and what David did to kill off her husband Uriah, so that he could have Bathsheba all to himself. King David was not exactly an angel. Then again, neither are any of God's people. Putting all of that aside, there is still much to be learned from David.

Listen to the hope fulfilled promise nestled among the words of Isaiah 65:24, "I will answer them before they even call to Me. While they are still talking to Me about their needs, I will go ahead and answer their prayers." We have God's promise that, before our heart cries out to Him, He is already there. Kind of mind boggling, huh? To think that before we utter a sound, God hears. Yet another affirmation of God's promise can be found in Psalm 34:15, "The eyes of the Lord watch over those who do right; His ears are open to their cries for help." What comfort, encouragement, and reassurance! What an amazing God!

Heart Whispers...

Dear God, You hear every heart cry of self-doubt, before a sound is ever uttered from our lips,

When fear tries to creep in, because of a litany of doubts like, "I'll never be good enough... I'll never be able to measure up to those high standards... No matter what I attempt to do, I will probably not succeed..." remind us, as Your Beloved Daughters, of Your promises of protection, not perfection. Sometimes, our feelings of low self-esteem may get in the way of staying on the destiny road You have so lovingly created as a blueprint for our odyssey. Thank You, God, that all we have to do is produce a silent heart cry, and You are already responding by answering our prayer.

As You guide Your Princess along the journey you have set before her, fill her with an all consuming assurance that You have heard her heart cries before she can even verbalize them. Before she can express her needs, You "...will go ahead and answer [her] prayers." As You guide us in our faith, Lord Jesus, help us to stabilize our lives, keeping all things in balance, and maintaining the right perspective. Thank You for being our Balcony Coach, Holy Spirit. We cherish Your Grace, Father God. In the name of the God who hears and responds to every doubt that seems to get lodged in the midst of our heart cries, before we utter an audible sound... Amen.

Bouquets of Grace-Filled Blessings...

"To be available, to be imperfect, and give what I had to give, this would be enough. Why? Because God is looking for teachable hearts, not perfect performances."

-Brenda Waggoner
The Velveteen Woman
Chariot Victor Publishing

Gems of Wisdom...

Psalm 34:17
Jeremiah 33:3
Job 1:10

Refreshing Hugs...

The following is my recipe for a Hope Journal:

Prayer Requests: Be Specific

Answered Prayer

Jot down the date

Grace Report

How God chose to answer your prayer

A Hope Journal will encourage you to become a "Hope Spreader" by sharing God's Grace, in a grocery line, at a fast-food drive-in, the DMV... In our contemporary vernacular, it's called, "paying it forward."

ME DISCIPLINED? I'M WORKING ON IT!

"Keep on asking, and you will be given what you ask for. Keep
on looking, and you will find. Keep on knocking, and the door
will be opened. For every one who asks, receives. Everyone who
seeks, finds. And the door is opened to everyone who knocks."
Matthew 7:7-8

Ask, Look, Knock? Keep on asking? Keep on looking? Keep on knocking?
Ahhh! Precious Daughter of the King of kings, God so longs to provide for
you and pour His lavish blessings over your life. Does that mean that God will
give His Princess everything she asks for, and more? No. Here's why: Not all
of what we ask for is necessarily beneficial for us. When we ask our Lord for
something, and what we ask for lines up with His Word and His Will for our
life, then He is more than willing to grant us what we ask for, be it ministry-
related, relational, educational, job oriented, or material things.

On a personal note, God needed to do quite a bit of rennovation work,
in my heart, in respect to making purchases for sheer pleasure. But, I have
noticed that I still suffer from the "buy me" voices that seem to crop up, every
now and then. Oh, you know, the ones that call to us, whenever we approach
a shopping mall, for example. Two items seem to be frequent little culprits
for me. I've already shared that my "candy addiction" looks remarkably like
things you might find in a bookstore-like recently released books, for example.
The second one is clothing and shoe related. Ouch! I pondered over this
dilemma for years. About fifteen years ago, I was just sure I could hear God's
still small voice whispering in my ear, "Ask yourself this question: Do you
really need these things, or would you rather save that money and use it for
your next love offering?" It really is all about that self-talk, Girlfriend. It's all
about what we say, silently, when we are thinking about making that purchase.
Hmmm... Interesting...

When I began to ask God how I could please Him, I knew that I already
had His answer. God wants His Princesses to practice good stewardship.
I needed to hand over my check book to God. Next, I needed to ask Him
where He wanted funds, that were not already allocated for daily expenses, to
be used for His Kingdom Purposes. As a result of this consultation with the

Lord, before I make a purchase, I now consult my Financial Analyst, Jesus. What follows next is to ask myself this question: "Do I really need this thing-whatever this 'thing' is that I think I want, have to have, or simply cannot live without?" Well, I can honestly say, after some self-talk on the subject of extraneous purchases, that very question will cause me to pause and think about how to allocate that extra money wisely. There are literally hundreds of organizations that can use our financial support. For Honey and I, this plan includes a boost in our love offerings to ministries that are near and dear to our hearts, ones that we have been supporting, along with a few new ones we have recently added.

It's been many years now, and what really cinched the decision concerning my personal spending, has been this simple plan. I seek God's Wisdom about any purchase over a determined amount. If the purchase exceeds that amount, I ask the Spirit of God to impress that on my heart. If there is still uncertainty, I ask God to realign my petition so that it matches His will. The last step is to ask Him to completely remove the desire to purchase that "thing" from my heart.

Okay, before you start whining because you think this plan would take away all the really fun stuff, like, spur of the moment shopping trips, especially those that include daughters, daughters-in-love, or our female grandbabies, (no age limit applies), please hear me out. One of the best parts of having children and grandchildren is that we can plan a special occasion spoiling thing for them.

I believe that God is just "tickled pink" (now, Princess, it's just an expression), when we have a Girl's Day Out, and decide to indulge our girls with a new outfit, or manicure or pedicure. Just a few months ago, one of our GrandSugars, Leesi Grace, along with the rest of her family, had moved back to our city. I quickly planned a salon date with her. Leesi told Heather my friend and nail technician, exactly what she wanted in the way of polish and nail art. Heather pulled out all the stops. Leesi was so excited about her electric blue fingernail polish, not to mention the hearts Heather painted on all of her nails. Okay, back to the "spoiling" thing. Once in a while, if we can afford to do so, God is all for lavish gift-giving... We know this because, James 1:17, in the Word, as phrased in the NKJV, tells us that, "Every good gift and every perfect gift..." comes from Him.

Last week, another one of our GrandSugars, Char-Char, came to visit. It was back to the salon with Leesi Grace, and Char-Char. It was also back to

Heather's vast array of glitter polish, for manicures and pedicures. This was Char-Char's first time to the salon and she decided she wanted a different color of glitter polish for each of her toes. Their birthdays are less than three weeks apart. Leesi turned seven last week, and Char-Char will be six, in a few weeks. It was lots of glitz... glitter...giggling... and just plain crazy fun!

One more example of God's principles for good stewardship, once again, using myself as the example. In the past, I would try to justify my need for books. Here's what I use to plead: "Lord, I really need these books. After all, I am a student, working on my coaching certification, and those books would really help me to set up my coaching practice." If I could not justify my book purchase that way, I would back up and try another approach: "God, I write for You. All non-fiction writers who rely on quotes from other sources, as I do, require a large number of reference books." This final justification is like the creme de la creme in the art of negotiating, wouldn't you agree?

I finally had to resort to having a little chat with myself. The dialogue, or rather, the monologue, sounded like this: "Enough Is Enough," Princess Coach, (don't ask... the title just sounded kind of cute). You do not need one more book. You already have one hundred and seventy-seven books that you do not have the time to read. But hey, whose counting? Here's the deal... I might not have time to read them for, well, for who knows how long? They're just sitting there collecting dust bunnies, which, for a recovering perfectionist, is not a good thing!

At the rate I was stocking my library, Honey and I were getting dangerously close to sleeping in a tent, pitched in our backyard, with our little kitty, Cutie Pie. Cutie is the one that gets serenaded by her daddy, (a.k.a. Honey), every night-like clockwork. Yes, my books were beginning to need space of epic proportion. The only place to go next, for book storage, that is, would be the master bedroom-more specifically, the closets, the floor, the bed, under the bed, Cutie Pie's Diva bed...

Now, while this shocking revelation happened quite a number of years ago, it is sill quite painful to recall. The good news, however, is that I learned a big life lesson from a very simple prayer of gratitude, "Thank You, Lord, for giving me the courage to say 'no' to what I really don't need, so that I can say 'yes' to giving more generously, for Your Kingdom Purposes. We could spoil the GrandSugars more often, which is actually part of the job description of nanas and papas. We could treat a single mom to lunch, put together book bags filled with school supplies for children in need; the list of needs, in our country alone, is staggering. And besides, Lord, it can get really chilly... sleeping out on the patio...in the middle of winter...especially when Cutie Pie keeps grabbing all the blankets away with her teeth, so she can burrow underneath them to keep warm..."

Heart Whispers...

Dear God, You delight in teaching Your Daughters principles of great stewardship, as well as generous gift giving to those in need,

To those of us who are frequently tempted to "splurge" when it comes to buying things we really don't need, please help us use restraint when it comes to making frivolous purchases. Instead, those funds can be used to make more of a difference in the lives of so many in our world today, who are in need. Thank You, Lord, that when You extend Your hand to grasp the hand of Your Beloved Princess, Your empowerment will help us to say 'no' to purchasing things that we do not need, so that we can say 'yes' to making a difference in life of someone who is precious to You, and who needs a blessing.

Help us, Father God, to use the provisions You have blessed us with, wisely, for the benefit of others. In the name of the God who entrusts His children with provisions meant to be generously shared, and, when possible, gifts that are meant to be lavishly given... Amen.

Bouquets of Grace-Filled Blessings...

"...when ...the things God has given me to use become idols... I must decide what my heart really wants... She who dies with the most toys still dies. But she who sets her heart on possessing Christ lives."

-Nancy Kennedy
Move Over Victoria-I Know The Real Secret
Waterbrook Press

Gems of Wisdom...

Luke 12:21 NLT

Refreshing Hugs...

You, Favored Princess, have been awesome! Thank you for indulging me while I added a bit of humor to a struggle we sometimes have to deal with, especially when our "wants" get in the way. So, if we must shop, because it just happens to be part of our DNA, (as a Princess, of course), may we remember to use the wisdom and discernment God has endowed us with.

Let's give thanks often, to the generous God we serve. Why, God is so generous, He even hands out a Book of free samples!

THE DAY SPA AT SUSA

"...Let the king appoint agents in each province to bring these beautiful
young women into the royal harem at Susa. Hegai...will see that
they are all given beauty treatments. After that, the young woman
who pleases you most will be made queen... This advice was very
appealing to the king, so he put the plan into effect immediately."
Esther 2:2-4

Mordecai was the leader of the Jewish people at the time of the Persian
Empire. He becomes prime minister. But, more importantly, God uses
Mordecai to reveal His call upon Esther's life. The words of Esther 4:14
warn Queen Esther not to miss a golden opportunity-an opportunity to be
a catalyst for the deliverance of the Jewish people-her people. Mordecai told
Esther that if she remained silent, the relief and deliverance of her people
would be forced to come from another source. Mordecai provokes Esther to
action by posing this profound question: "...What's more, who can say but that
you have been elevated to the palace for just such a time as this?"

I say to you, highly valued Princess of the King of kings, who knows
whether you have come to this point in your faith-the point at which God is
wanting to use your testimony to begin a restoration, a renewal... in the life of
your daughter, or your daughter-in-love, or your Grand Sugar, or your mom,
or your nana, "...for just such a time as this?" Your story may ultimately lead
to someone's eternal salvation. Please do not allow any feelings of insecurity, to
affect your witness for Messiah. Just know that you do not have to be perfect
in order for God to use you for His Glory. God can take your testimony, and
transform it into a harvest of souls for His Kingdom.

Maybe I got a little carried away by entitling this segment, *THE DAY
SPA AT SUSA*. It is true that Esther was given beauty treatments for an entire
year. But, our God looks at the heart, not at external beauty. And besides,
Princess of Great Destiny, who wants to sit around for a whole year having
green yuck stuff applied to her face every day? Who wants to have mud
plastered over every square inch of her body, every week? Okay, this is all in
fun... Let's try not to take the spa thing quite so seriously; although, now that

I'm thinking about a luxurious spa retreat, it just might prove to be a rather relaxing experience, yuk green stuff, and all!

I can just hear my Cajun-French friend, Diane, who can also boast about being a mixture of, well, I don't know how many other countries her heritage represents... I can just hear her voice, calling my name, at an annoyingly high pitch, in the middle of a lovely antique mall, as we were tyring to de-stress that day: "Janiceeeeeeeee..." Maybe I need to clarify. Diane is my "laugh till the tears flow down your blouse that you just had dry cleaned" heart lifter! Oh, how we need such a friend; the type of friend who will speak honestly, when we need to make some necessary adjustments in our perspective. And, we all need a friend like Diane, when we just need to lighten up a bit, or alot, maybe...

Mordecai was a tried and true friend, in addition to being Esther's relative. It was Mordecai that God used to remind Esther that if she remained silent, the Lord would need to pass the mantle for the deliverance of the Jewish people, on to someone else.

Okay, back to the point. When we hand our carefully arranged agendas over to our King, and tell Him how much we desire to be used by Him, for His Kingdom Purposes, circumstances begin to change. At the end of the day, as my son Adam likes to put it, that desire could become a blessing for many. In Esther's case, the blessing came in the form of deliverance for the Jewish people-her people-in the nation of Israel.

Greg, a dear friend of ours, always ends a great time of fellowship with these words, "Walk with the King...and be a Blessing." Greg's beautiful bride, Linda Sue, has been another great encourager in my life. She was chosen by God to lift up my arms at a time when I was growing very weary.

My prayer, Precious Princess, is that God will surround you with friends who will be there for you, no matter what obstacles you may face along your destiny path. Thank you so much, Linda, for sticking by me, during circumstances that called for a loyal friend-like the kind of friend that you have been to me. Thank you for being willing to speak into my life, the words I needed to hear. Thank you for not giving up on me, and for being the iron God wanted to use to sharpen me! You accomplished all of that, so graciously.

Heart Whispers...

Dear God, You are the King who summons us with Your Love, Your Touch, and Your Majestic Grace,

There is such fullness of joy when we spend quality time in Your Presence. I pray, Lord, that Your Princess will experience Your powerful touch upon her life, each time she sets aside quiet moments to spend with You. Bless her worship time, quiet time, bible study time, personal prayer time, intercessory prayer time, family time, fellowship time, leisure time... Lord Jesus, please wrap Your blanket of renewal around Your Precious Daughter, and restore her, as she seeks Your Face and Your Grace. In the name of the God who leans over the balcony of our lives to whisper words of inspiration, encouragement, renewal, restoration, and rejuvenation... to our soul. Amen.

Bouquets of Grace-Filled Blessings...

"Young Esther was an orphan... she had suffered the trauma of exile... Obviously, Esther was too dysfunctional for God to use for anything important... Wrong... Esther... broke the mold to answer the King's summons..."

-Cindy Jacobs
Women of Destiny
Regal Books-A Division of Gospel Light

Gems of Wisdom...

Read the Book of Esther from your favorite Bible version.

Refreshing Hugs...

While it is not feasible for us to take time off from life to attend a year long beauty treatment at The Day Spa At Susa, we do need to incorporate some R&R, (Rest and Relaxation), into our busy...busy...busy... lives.

Remember that bottle of Calgon bubble bath stuff I had mentioned earlier? I thought now would be a fabulous time to try a visualization exercise, just in case the real stuff is not available. So, close your eyes and visualize a life-sized bottle of bubbles. Now, on the count of three, repeat after me, "Calgon, take me away..."

If that Rx doesn't work for you, try this remedy: Set aside an afternoon in the country, taking in God's beautiful creation. And, if anyone wants to know where you disappeared to, just tell them, "It was Jan's idea." I'll promise to come to your defense every single time!

MAKE CREATING YOUR "TO DO" LISTS A FUN PROJECT!

"Teach us to make the most of our time, so that we may grow in wisdom."
Psalm 90:12

Tips On Time Management and Organization Skills are entertwined throughout this book. These tools have become invaluable to me, when working with those of my coaching clients who have expressed a desire to maximize their personal God-Time. I will be sharing a few tips on optimally organizing your home, and involving your family in helping to manage work schedules, activities, etc. For now, however, I'd like to share one example of a time management challenge that I personally experienced on a day I was to speak in front of an audience filled with moms.

Lucy Days... In the past, these insidious days seemed to materialize, out-of-the-blue, once every two or three weeks. Lately, however, they began to escalate at an alarmingly frequent rate. Let me explain. *Lucy Days* are what I call days when I've come quite close to losing it. I love how my friend Diane would phrase the expression, "Losin' it Y'all." Well, at least the "Y'all" part. Now, if you are anything like me, well, Lord help you! Should you have experienced even just an occasional *Lucy Day* yourself, I'll need to move you to the very top of my prayer list.

Without further adieu, here's an example of one such day. The day had arrived when I was due to address an audience of Mops Moms. Oh, thank You, God, for those precious Mothers Of Preschoolers, who just seem to naturally overflow with grace.

I was downstairs finishing breakfast. I heard a very strange noise emanating from our two cats, Muffin and Cupcake, (you'll never guess what was on my mind when I named our two kitties). I looked under the dining room table and gasped. Muffie was pawing at what appeared to be a rather hairy spider. She was playing with the thing like it was a toy. I was terrified, as I watched my kitty torment this little creature. I grabbed a large mixing bowl, turned around, and saw Cupcake pounce on it. It was apparent that I had never taken that course titled: Spider Killing 101. Needless to say, I had to improvise. I finally got the baby tarantula contained, when I realized fifteen minutes had passed. I raced up the stairs, well, actually, it was more like a quick trot. I was running behind schedule.

Next, I jumped, well, maybe not that dramatically. I stepped into the shower and... faster than a speeding bullet-well, maybe more like a quick hop, I reached for the portable shower head. In the blink of an eye, (and that's not an exaggeration), I lost control of that little puppy and doused what remained of my meticulously styled hair. Now's your chance, should you decide to take advantage of it, for a "Oh, poor baby" response.

Suffice it to say, I giggled the entire way to the church, as I got this mental picture of two little kitties using a tarantula as their cat toy of choice. By the sheer grace of God, I managed to regain my composure, and had so much fun speaking to the group. In fact, I was actually the one who received a blessing on yet, another *Lucy Day*.

So, what in the world do these rather chaotic type days have to do with our time management challenges? Basically, everything. The real issue is about how we handle those constant interruptions and annoyingly frequent distractions. Once again, it's about our self-talk; those things we say to ourself when no one else is within hearing distance. Negative self-talk tends to lead us in the opposite direction of where our Heavenly Papa desires that we go. God wants His Princesses to think positive thoughts; thoughts reflecting how we see ourselves, and others.

You see, Princess, you are His Treasure-His Gorgeous Jewel. So, when you think positive thoughts about beautiful you, then He is pleased! Despite an occasional *Lucy Day* challenge, you can be assured that it pleases God, when you use His Wisdom to make the most of your time, and throw in lots of holy laughter, while you're at it.

Heart Whispers...

Dear God, You are the God of our Hopes, Plans, Dreams, Goals...

Thank You that Your Mercy Seat is available for Your Kids to run to, 24/7, when things seem to spiral out of control. I consider praying each *Heart Whisper* in this book, expressly for Your Princess, an honor and a privilege. Thank You, God, that all we need to do is ask, and You are pleased to saturate the lives of Your Daughters, with Your Love and Your Wisdom.

Please grace the intentions, aspirations, hopes, dreams, and goals of Your Princess. May never-ending love surround every moment of her odyssey. May Your Presence never cease to bless her with an abundance of joy, filling her mouth with highest praise for the awesome God You are! May Your Provisions always be filled with favor over every effort she makes to be pleasing to You. Please bless her as she comes in and as she goes out, according to Your Word in Deuteronomy 28:6. Surround her with Your angels and place a hedge of protection around her, and her loved ones. In the name of the God who takes our challenges and turns them into His amazing blueprints for our life... Amen.

Bouquets of Grace-Filled Blessings...

"...In the happy moments praise God ...In the difficult moments seek God ...In the quiet moments trust God... In every moment thank God."

-Anonymous

Gems of Wisdom...

Psalm 90:12
Psalm 95:1-3
Psalm 150:6
Psalm 100:4-5

Refreshing Hugs...

Seek a quiet place. Write down seven things you thank God for. If you are so inclined, write Him a thank you note. Spend the rest of your quiet time reflecting on His Mercy, His Goodness, His Provisions, His Grace, and His Protection over your life...

BLESSED! BLESSED! BLESSED!

"God blesses those who realize their need for Him, for the Kingdom
of Heaven is given to them. God blesses those who mourn, for they
will be comforted. God blesses those who are gentle and lowly, for the
whole earth will belong to them. God blesses those who are hungry
and thirsty for justice, for they will receive it in full. God blesses
those who are merciful, for they will be shown mercy. God blesses
those whose hearts are pure, for they will see God. God blesses those
who work for peace, for they will be called the children of God..."
Matthew 5:3-10

"Blessed!" That simple word which Jesus chose as the beginning of each
scripture in the Beautitudes, found in Matthew 5, contains several different
characteristics, all of which we, as His children, should strive to emulate. When
used in God's Word, "blessed" defines a state of well-being. For example, the
NIV phrases it like this: "Blessed are the poor in spirit." It denotes a contrast
between one who thinks himself to be spiritually superior to the next person,
requiring little of God, versus one who realizes that Christ is his sufficiency,
and, consequently, is continually seeking the Lord's guidance.

Blessed are those who recognize that their total being is dependent upon
the Lord. Blessed are those who continually seek after the things of God-His
righteousness and His Kingdom Principles. And I would say to you, Princess
of the God who is the Strength of your life, you will be blessed when you ask
to become less, so that Christ can become more in you. Blessed are you, His
Beloved Princess, when you kneel to pray, petitioning Him on behalf of the
cares and concerns of others, asking for God to bless them and help them in
every aspect of their lives and their relationships.

Blessed are you, Princess of the King of kings, as you grow to love the
Lord with every fiber of your being; blessed are you when you strive to serve
and obey Him in all you do. Blessed are you, as you hunger for more of God,
and earnestly seek His will for your life.

Blessed are you when you allow His agenda to become yours; when you
offer Him all that you are, so He can help you to become all you were meant
to be. And, most blessed are you, Esteemed Princess, when you sit at the feet

102

of your Messiah, spending valued time with the One who longs to be a part of your goals, your hopes, your dreams, your aspirations...

Heart Whispers...

Dear God, You are the Breath Of Life... the Breath of Heaven,

Thank You for every blessing You so lavishly give Your Princess! Please fill her with Your Sweet Presence; fill her to overflowing. Flood her heart with a steady stream of Your Love, Your Grace, and Your Empowerment... In the name of the God who is the Breath of Life for His Beloved Princess. Amen.

Bouquets of Grace-Filled Blessings...

"...let the thankful heart sweep through the day and, as the magnet finds the iron, so it will find, in every hour, some heavenly blessings!"

-Henry Ward Beecher
Source Unknown

Gems of Wisdom...

Ezekiel 34:26
Psalm 118:26
Ephesians 1:3

Refreshing Hugs...

Read the Beautitudes each day this coming week. At the end of the week, make your own list of heavenly blessings. Post the list where you will see it each day. And, at those times when sleep eludes you, talk to your Shepherd, and count your blessings... instead of counting sheep!

NEED SOME ELIXIR OF HOPE?

"Then the seventh angel blew his trumpet, and there were loud voices
shouting in heaven: "The whole world has now become the kingdom
of our Lord and of His Christ, and He will reign forever and ever."
Revelation 11:15

The Book of Revelation embodies the fulfillment of our hope in our
Messiah Jesus. The NKJV of Revelation 1:3 says this, "Blessed is he who
reads and those who hear the words of this prophecy, and keep those things
which are written in it, for the time is near." The phrase "the time is near,"
is a reference to Jesus coming soon to claim His Bride, His Church; our
Bridegroom is coming to capture His Bride to rule and reign with Him
forever and ever!

Let's take a look at some terminology we find in the above scripture
passage. The seventh angel sounds the seventh trumpet which symbolizes
the consummation of God's reign. When Jesus comes to claim His Bride,
which will be composed of all living believers, and those who have already
died, the reference is to the Rapture of the Church. This will set the stage for
what believers refer to as the Millenium, or, the one thousand year period of
Christ's reign on the earth.

If you were to study the Book of Revelation, you might be somewhat
baffled by the imagery; there also might be much that you would not
understand, or, so it was with me. Should this be the case, please don't be
alarmed. There are numerous excellent resources to peruse through that cover
all sixty-six books of God's Word. For the sake of time and space, I will not
go into detail regarding some of the common viewpoints which relate to the
Great Tribulation. However, I recommend you do a search on the net, if
you have access to a computer, and look up the many time-line graphs and
charts available, by credible theologians. It would truly be worth your time
to explore those sites.

You may, at this point, be questioning the validity of what an end-time
study has to do with our odyssey toward balance, and the destiny God has
mapped out for each Princess, no matter her age or stage of life. Let me clarify.
One of the most difficult emotions we, as females, may encounter along our

journey, is that of hopelessness. Ahhh, there's the key. If our hope is in God, regardless of the state of world affairs, the financial state of our government, global warming trends, earthquakes, famine, violence, child abuse, human trafficking, homelessness, and a multitude of other crisis' that our world is facing today, we know that hope is our only answer. It is hope in our God, who can provide the only Rx, that can help us, and our neighbors around the globe, to be overcomers. To say it another way, hope is God's elixir for every imaginable crisis we could face in our world today.

Where there is hope, precious child of God, there is more hope... Jesus is standing by to offer the remedy. That source of hope stems from the very throne of the King of kings and Lord of lords. When we begin to regain our hope, not in our own strength, for we have none, but our hope in Messiah Jesus, we can be assured that God can not only handle the state of the world, but that He is the solution, and the resolution, for our emotional well-being, as well. Stress begins to melt away, when our hope rests on our Rock, for the healing needs of our world, and, for each of us, personally.

Heart Whispers...

Dear God, You are the God of All Hope,

My prayer is for those who do not yet know You as their Messiah, their Savior, their Papa God... Please open up the eyes of their spirit to receive You into their hearts, and make Yourself real to them. Speak to each one, Holy Spirit, that they may know of Your unfailing, everlasting Love... that they may know that Your Banner over every one of them is Love! Teach them Your ways and Your Word, which is Truth.

Thank You for the hope You give us in you, God. In the midst of a world steeped in an atmosphere of hopelessness, and surrounded by a cloud of helplessness, because they do not yet know that Your lovingkindness is better than life... may Your promise for the kind of peace that only You can provide, be implanted in their souls by You, Holy Spirit, because Your Princess shared her testimony... May they know, in the very depths of their heart, that they are so very special to You. In the name of the God who whispers our blessed hope with these words, "Yes, I am coming soon!" Amen.

Bouquets of Grace-Filled Blessings...

"The word which God has written on the brow of every man is hope."

-Victor Hugo

Gems of Wisdom...

Psalm 146:5
Hebrews 6:19
Psalm 39:7
Colossians 1:27

Refreshing Hugs...

If you have put together a "Hope Basket," now would be a good time to pull out a "hope booster." Once you have read it, pass it on to someone in need of the only Elixir of Lasting Hope...Messiah Jesus... The Elixir is God's Eternal Promises for you, His Beloved Princess...

THE BALM OF RESTORATION

"O Lord, You have examined my heart and know everything about me.
You know when I sit down or stand up. You know my every thought
when far away. You chart the path ahead of me and tell me where
to stop and rest. Every moment you know where I am. You know
what I am going to say even before I say it, Lord. You both precede
and follow me. You place Your hand of blessing on my head. Such
knowledge is too wonderful for me, too great for me to know."
Psalm 139:1-6

When it is just God and you... when you have removed the distractions and
clutter that have been standing in the way of your focus on Him... you'll be
able to hear His whispers of loving affirmation. Listen to the description of
the treasures you will discover when you become still, before your loving
Heavenly Father. They come from the pen of David, as he so eloquently
expresses them in Psalm 16:11,

"You will show me the way of life,
granting me the joy of Your Presence
and the pleasures of living with You forever."

Are you feeling a little down in the dumps? Don't despair. The Psalmist
David, in the NKJV of Psalm 16:11, phrases the verse this way, "You will show
me the way of life, granting me the joy of Your presence and the pleasures of
living with You forever." Have you grown disheartened at unkept promises?
Take heart, Jesus is your Promise Keeper. Has discouragement kept you from
reaching your goals? Look up! Jesus is your Balcony Coach, encouraging
you to stay on track... God wants you to use His directions for your odyssey
travels, as your compass...

Remember, Jesus is our First Responder. John 1:14 tells us that, "Jesus
was full of unfailing love and faithfulness." He was on the scene when others
rejected you; called your idea foolish; criticized the very dream that God
Himself had planted in your heart... He was also there when you, His Princess,
felt abandoned, with no where to turn, or so you thought. Oh, Princess of

the Eternal Reigning King, every tear you shed... every sigh you whisper... strikes a tender chord in His heart. And, He cries in unison with you when the hurt sears your very soul. Every time your heart gets broken, seemingly beyond repair, so does His. Then comes His response as He whispers, "Give your brokenness to Me and I will restore and renew your heart."

Soon, things are beginning to look different. God is beginning to surround you with people who have godly compassion, and yet are able to challenge you to change your perspective, or to give up your negative self-talk. He has placed them along your odyssey road to inspire you to look up-look up to the One who holds your heart in His hands. They inspire you to look up, instead of hanging your head down in shame, at yet another failed aspiration. You are His Precious Daughter. He takes such delight in showering you with His Unending Love. Look up!

Are you beginning to sense a longing in your soul to hear the whispers, to hear His words of further direction for your journey? You can, you know. Just listen for His soft voice; listen for His encouraging words; listen for His Grace-Filled whispers of affirmation; listen, as He speaks proudly into your ear, "You are My Beloved Bride; I formed you, I fashioned you; I walked ahead of you so that you could follow in My Footprints... You are the apple of My eye. You are My Cherished Princess. I adore you! You are so special to Me. This is the next part of the blueprint I have formulated for your life... "...this is the way, walk in it..."

Heart Whispers...

Dear God, our First Responder,

Speak Your sweet words that will drift quietly into the heart of Your Princess, Lord. She wants to please You. She needs Your affirmation. She needs to know that the pleasure You take in her has nothing to do with her performance, but has everything to do with who she is in You, God.

Help Your Princess to know just how much You value her, and how precious she is to You. Please whisper words, God, that are filled with all the promises You have stored up for her... Whisper, Lord. Whisper... In the name of Jehovah Shammah, the Lord who is there... and... the God whose signature of Grace is present on each page of our lives. Amen.

Bouquets of Grace-Filled Blessings...

"...don't wait for catastrophe before you un-wrap grace. Embrace it today... There is only one minute in which you are alive. This minute!..."

-Barbara Johnson
Extravagant Grace,
Devotional entitled *Present Moment Grace*
Zondervan Publishing

Gems of Wisdom...

Joel 2:25
Psalm 84:11
Psalm 139:17

Refreshing Hugs...

A good way to envision closure on the past is to try this: Fill a teapot with boiling water until it is half full. Allow the vapors of steaming water to escape. Turn off the stove. Now, put the teapot somewhere out of sight for a week. The next time you check it, the water will have all but evaporated.

Try imagining your disappointments and your discouragement, that have been lodged in your memories from the past, and have caused you pain, in the same way as the teapot example. Allow them to evaporate from your memory. Remember to give God praise, honor, and glory.

IT'S TIME TO THROW AWAY THOSE
ROSE COLORED GLASSES

"Look! A messenger is coming over the mountains with
good news! He is bringing a message of peace...
Nahum 1:15

Ahhh! Upon closer examination of Nahum 1:15, we find that it points directly to deliverance-deliverance of the people of Judah from the hands of their enemies of Ninevah. The messenger, Nahum, was bringing news that never again would they be invaded by their adversary. The name "Nahum" means "comforter" or "full of comfort." God selected Nahum to bring comfort to Judah's people. Unfortunately, they chose not to adhere to the message Nahum brought. That message contained, first of all, condemnation for Judah's rebellious, disobedient attitude, believing that they could act as they pleased without adhering to God's commands; Assyria's fall was a warning to Judah; it was a warning the people of Judah refused to acknowledge. They openly rebelled against God through their immoral behavior. Judah subsequently fell at the hands of the Babylonians who had risen in power to take Assyria's place.

Let's take this idea of deliverance one step further. If applied to all those who belong to Jesus, then our close relationship with our Lord Jesus, coupled with a knowledge of God's truth, will set us free. Jesus came to earth and went to the cross, aften enduring horrendous persecution, so that we could be set free! Our enemies come in many forms; enemies in the form of unhealthy relationships, enemies in the form of addictions of any nature, enemies in the likeness of anything or any person that would attempt to distract us from the destiny God created exclusively for you, and for me.

If you are addicted to anything that might hinder your closeness to your Maker, begin by quieting your heart. Be totally honest with yourself. You didn't get to this place with a bag full of issues, by over-night travel. No, some of these issues have been a lifetime in surfacing. Give your feelings, your apprehensions, your fears, your anxieties, your insecurities to God. Make sure you have plenty of tissues handy for those tearful moments. But, don't stay in the past too long. Afterall, you did things differently then, remember? You'll only be in this place for a season. The Spirit of God wants to move you ahead to a place called "The Present".

A note to His Beautiful Bride: As we grow in the knowledge and the grace of the Lord, and as our focus begins to shift to Him, God will fling back the curtains of our soul, exposing the deepest part of our heart, and we will begin to see our Savior in everything-the helping hand of a friend, the beautiful melody of a songbird, a tree, as it grows stately and mature, a child, as he or she sheds the selfish nature we all inherited at birth, and begins to grow into a giving, loving, nurturing young adult.

Ever so slowly, after years of circling repeatedly around the same mountain of issues, your perspective will begin to change. It may not be particularly comfortable, as God's imprint begins to move across the place we'll refer to as "stuck." But remember His promise? He will never give His Princess more than she can handle... Never!

You may be in a challenging position right now. However, the good news is that your Abba Daddy, in His infinite wisdom, knows all about your "stuck" places. In fact, He was there when you faced what seemed to be an insurmountable challenge... He stood there when you were "stuck" in the quick sand of indecision, not knowing which way would lead to safe passage and deliverance from your dilemma.

I would say to you, His Beautiful Treasure, you are just steps away from that freedom. Am I saying it will be a cake walk? Absolutely not! It will take much work, on your part. But, despite the obstacles you're facing, look up! Call upon the only One who knows your weaknesses, the One who is totally committed to setting your feet on higher ground.

If you are stuck, ask the Holy Spirit to surround you with those who are willing to walk alongside you, be supportive of you, yet challenge you with truth, as you begin to take control of, and responsibility for your choices. Jesus has given you all the authority you need, in order to be an overcomer. Remind yourself often, if necessary, that you are the victorious Princess He had in mind, when He created awesome you!

I pray that your victory will inspire you to inspire others, by sharing your story. May God bless you richly, as you bring the good news to others, planting seeds for the Lord, for His glory!

Now, Princess, stand back and watch, in amazement, as He waters those seeds, nurtures them, and causes them to grow, for His Kingdom Purposes!

Heart Whispers...

Dear God, You are the God of Life Transforming Changes,

Thank You for Your Word, for it is Truth. Thank You, God, for the power that is in Your Name, available for use by every believer... I pray for that Princess who may be "stuck" and in need of hearing Your Whispers of Grace and Healing for her odyssey; the path that will help set her free! Empower her, God, with the courage to tell her story, and share the transforming changes You have helped her accomplish in her life. May she give You all the glory, honor, and praise. In the name of the God who pardons our sin, sets us free, and presents us with opportunities to share His Grace freely!

Bouquets of Grace-Filled Blessings...

"The power of God is available to help solve our problems, but only if we acknowledge them honestly. Wrong dependencies keep us in bondage, and Jesus waits to set us free..."

-Nancy Groom
From Bondage To Bonding
Navpress

Gems of Wisdom...

John 8:32
Ephesians 1:19

Refreshing Hugs...

Suggestion: Write the words of John 8:32 on a 3X5 card. Post it where it is in plain sight so you will see it often. Repeat its words until they become real to you... "And you will know the truth, and the truth will set you free."

YOUR SPIRITUAL LANTERN

"For God, who said, "Let there be light in the darkness," has
made us understand that this light is the brightness of the
glory of God that is seen in the face of Jesus Christ."
2 Corinthians 4:6

Michaelangelo, after painting the Sistene Chapel, reflected upon his work. In different intensities of light, the artist's painting took on varying hues of color. The magnificent Sistene Chapel became Michaelangelo's gift to mankind. It was based on his interpretation of the creation of the world, and of God's miraculous works. Instead of an easel with a canvas perched on top, the artist decided to display the splendor of God's Glory on the chapel's ceiling. God "...commanded light to shine out of darkness," as the NKJV words it. The NLT continues the remainder of the verse, "...this light is the brightness of the glory of God that is seen in the face of Jesus Christ." God's light, when it shines in our lives, displays His Glory, to a world submerged in darkness.

God will open spiritual eyes that have been blinded, when we allow Him to shine through us. When others see the hope we have in God, and hear about what the Lord has done in our lives, personally, many will be curious and want to know more about the Amazing God, we serve.

I would say to you, Princess of El Shadai, lead by your example. Take your spiritual lantern and shine for His Glory. You are a living example of God's light. You may be the only light a person will take notice of. And, even though you may be in the beginning stages of your odyssey, and may have some difficult challenges, God will make you strong in Him. Please remember this: Despite our slightly out-of-balance emotional state, our physical limitations, our job instability, our feelings of insecurity... God makes us strong in Him, so we can share Him with the world.

Jesus is standing next to you, Princess, ready to shine His Glory through you! May you take comfort in His Word and allow Him to do for you those things which you cannot do on your own. Your job is just to trust Him and allow Him to take care of the rest! So, shine away, Princess, shine away...

Heart Whispers...

Dear God, You are the Brilliantly Shining Light,

Thank You for Your reminder that, no matter where we go, and no matter what we may be contending with, You will shine through each Princess... Your Glory, Lord, will be reflected in our attitudes, as well as our burdens for the spiritually lost. Remind us that it's not about our problems, our issues, or our circumstances. It's about You, God. It's about Your Power to shine Your light through Your people. In the name of the King of Light, Glory, Power, and Majesty! Amen.

Bouquets of Grace-Filled Blessings...

"There is no book like the Bible for casting a light on the dark landing of human life."

-F.B. Meyer
The Secret of Guidance
The Moody Bible Institute of Chicago

Gems of Wisdom...

Psalm 119:105
Matthew 5:14-16
I Peter 2:9

Refreshing Hugs...

In your quiet time with the Lord, instead of turning on the lights, light a candle. Use this experience to remind yourself that you are a light that God longs to use to display His Light brightly for the world to see...

GREAT SHEPHERD OF GRACE

"My sheep hear My voice, and I know them, and they follow Me.
And I give them eternal life, and they shall never perish; neither
shall anyone snatch them out of My hand. My Father, who has
given them to Me, is greater than all; and no one is able to snatch
them out of My Father's hand. I and My Father are one."
John 10:27-30 NKJV

What a mighty God we serve! What incredible provisions He has bestowed upon us, His sheep: "And I give them eternal life, and they shall never perish." What unmatched protection He provides for His flock, "...no one is able to snatch them out of My Father's hand."

"There is more in Jesus, the Good Shepherd, than you can pack away in a shepherd. He is good, the great Chief Shepherd; but He is much more. Creation is too small a frame...to hand His likeness. Human thought...too contracted; human speech too feeble, to set Him forth to the full." C.H. Spurgeon penned these profound words-yet these words cannot do justice to the magnitude of God's greatness.

Precious Princess, there is a glorious place for you and for me, in His flock. No matter where you are at emotionally; no matter what heavy decisions you may be facing; no matter what physical limitations you may be dealing with-our Good Shepherd has prepared a special place in His fold for you.

Are you battling financial strain that has caused you to be short on funds, with mouths to feed, rent to pay, and endless mounds of bills piling up, that are staring you in the face? There's hope. Tilt your head upward, and gaze upon the Good Shepherd. Jesus is in the process of sending help.

Perhaps you are worried about your child who has strayed from home. Be at peace. The Lord keeps track of every last one of His sheep. He knows exactly where that child is, and is preparing to bring that lost one home, and to restore that strained relationship.

Let's give thanks to our beautiful Shepherd, for the way Jesus completes every prayer He utters for us with His Promises. Listen to the trustworthy, time-proven words of our Messiah, as they are found in the NKJV of 2 Thessalonians 2:16-17, "Now may our Lord Jesus Christ Himself, and our God and Father, who has loved us and given us everlasting consolation and good hope by grace, comfort your hearts..."

Beloved Princess, feed upon the words of Lamentations 3:21-23, as the verse is phrased in the NIV, "Yet this I call to mind and therefore I have hope: Because of the Lord's great love we are not consumed, for His compassions never fail. They are new every morning; great is Your faithfulness."

God wants us to know, and claim, His promises, like this one found in Deuteronomy 33:27, as it reads in the NIV, "The eternal God is your refuge, and underneath are the everlasting arms..."

One final word of encouragement can be found in Matthew 17:20, as it reads in the NKJV, "...assuredly, I say to you, if you have faith as a mustard seed, you will say to this mountain, 'Move from here to there,' and it will move; and nothing will be impossible for you."

There's hope! There's help! There's healing in Jesus. Be blessed by the vast storehouse of promises your Good Shepherd has provided for every child of God. Wait patiently as the Lord brings each one to pass...

Heart Whispers...

Dear God, even the great author, C.H. Spurgeon, could not find words adequate to describe Your Majesty and Your Glory, for by his own admittance, "...human speech is too feeble."

Remind each Princess to give thanks each day-in fact, many times during the course of each day-for Your Protection, Your Promises, Your Compassion, and Your Grace. In the name of the God who is our Great Shepherd, Beautiful Savior, Promise Maker, Promise Keeper, and Friend. Amen.

Bouquets of Grace-Filled Blessings...

"One of the greatest revelations of the heart of God given to us by Christ is that of Himself as our Shepherd... It discloses the depth of His understanding of undone people to whom He came eagerly and quickly, ready to help, to save, to restore..."

-W. Phillip Keller
A Shepherd Looks At Psalm 23
Zondervan

Gems of Wisdom...

Read Psalm 23 from your favorite Bible version.

Refreshing Hugs...

Read Psalm 23 once a day for the next week. Ruminate, (chew on repeatedly, meditate, ponder), the nuggets of wisdom King David used in this Psalm to express the Lord as our Shepherd.

Make a list of the many ways Jesus has been your Great Shepherd. Write a note of thanks expressing your gratitude to God for His caring, loving concern that is never-ending!

PART FOUR: FEELING A TINGE OF REJECTION?
BECOME A "BALCONY COACH" PRINCESS

"...abiding in the truths of Christ's love and acceptance brings
freedom and joy... we need to affirm God's truth: He (or
she) is deeply loved, completely forgiven, fully pleasing, and
totally accepted by God, and complete in Christ."

-Robert S. McGee
The Search For Significance
Rapha Publishing

WHEN GOD WHISPERS, "GOOD JOB, MY PRINCESS!"

"O Lord, please hear my prayer! Listen to the prayers of those
of us who delight in honoring You. Please grant me success now
as I go to ask the king for a great favor. Put it in his heart to be
kind to me. In those days I was the king's cup-bearer."
Nehemiah 1:11

Nehemiah's prayers touched the very core of God's heart. Why? Because our God loves for His people to honor and fear Him, giving Him the highest respect and regard. Nehemiah 1:11 speaks about Nehemiah's genuine servant's heart. He was appointed the cup-bearer to King Artaxerxes. A cup-bearer to the king was a position that was considered a respected one. Any person holding such a position must be willing to give up his own life to spare the life of his master. It was Nehemiah's responsibility to sample the drink before giving it to the king. In the event the drink was poisoned, the cup-bearer would sacrifice his own life to protect his king.

Throughout the book of Nehemiah, we read the prayers of this faithful servant for his God. As we intercede for others, we can ask God, as Nehemiah did, to listen to those prayers. We can intercede for them while they are in the workplace, or are in any position where they need to find favor in the sight of others. We can pray for those who may be facing distressing circumstances. We can also pray for success, on a personal level, just as Nehemiah did.

Through a long process of overcoming rejection and people pleasing, I learned to gain my acceptance from God, and not from others. I have also learned that while others may reject me, God will never reject me. This one was really difficult for me, but, I no longer feel like I have to please the immediate world so that I can gain their approval. Instead, I have learned to pursue the primary objective, and that is to please God.

Do I stay perfectly on target 24/7? That would be an impossible feat for any of us to acheive, because, the simple fact is that none of us are perfect. However, I believe I am making progress, thanks to the Holy Spirit, my personal Life Coach. Every once in a while, I still catch myself going overboard when it comes to trying to please Honey, our kids, their spouses, our thirteen GrandSugars, my friends, our kitty cat, Cutie Pie... I just threw that one in for free.

If you find yourself needing to seek approval from a certain individual, or group, I'd like to suggest that, as you continue on your destiny path, you keep on asking for God's Wisdom. Should you struggle with feelings of rejection, take the authority Jesus has given you, and pray that those feelings will no longer have any power over you, to keep you caught up in the pleasing cycle. Be persistent in your prayers until you experience a breakthrough.

Should you find yourself wanting to please, in order to gain approval, I have a suggestion. Decide to please out of personal choice to do so, not out of the need to gain someone else's approval. May you be blessed with those "heavenly goosebumps" every time you hear God clapping His hands, rejoicing, and exclaiming, "Good Job, My Princess!"

Heart Whispers...

Dear God, You are the God whose applause we will honor and cherish,

It is a privilege and an honor to serve You through our service to others. At the same time, God, please remind those of us who may still be struggling with the "pleasing" thing, that we don't need to hear the handclap of the world because of our good deeds. What is necessary, however, is our desire to please You, like Your faithful servant Nehemiah succeeded in doing.

May our top priority be, to please You in everything we think, do, and say. I pray for the Princess who may be feeling stuck because of low self-esteem issues. Please whisper the truth to her heart, Holy Spirit. Share with her how much You value and esteem her, and how just plum crazy You are about her. In the name of the God who is so pleased with our decision to be obedient to Him, that He claps His hands, in delight... Amen.

Bouquets of Grace-Filled Blessings...

"The individuals whose lives have glorified the Father share one common trait: they overcame their need for human approval so they could be obedient to God."

-Les Hughes
The Sound of God's Applause
Broadman & Holman Publishers

Gems of Wisdom...

Zephaniah 3:17, 20
Matthew 25:21
Revelation 2:7
Revelation 21:7
1 John 5:4-5

Refreshing Hugs...

Imagine a large blackboard with one word written twenty-five times in capital letters: REJECTED. Now, imagine a large eraser. Take that eraser and wipe out that word twenty-five times. At the top of the blackboard write the words: ACCEPTED by my Lord, my Savior, my Messiah, my King. Each time the thought of being rejected comes to your mind, visualize the word: ACCEPTED.

If the blackboard image doesn't work for you, an alternative would be to take a blank sheet of paper and a pen and write these words:

God loves and accepts me just as I am. I love God. My top priority is to please Him by becoming more like Jesus, every day.

Have a blessed day now!

FEELING A SLIGHT TILT IN YOUR HALO?

"Then Jesus said, "'Come to Me, all of you who are weary and carry
heavy burdens, and I will give you rest... Let Me teach you, because
I am humble and gentle, and you will find rest for your souls...'"
Matthew 11:28-30

Overwhelmed... Overloaded... Overworked... Overcommitted...? Sound
like the aftermath of dealing with the countless responsibilities and challenges
we, as moms, nanas, daughters, care-givers, wives, sisters, friends... need to
deal with on any given day? Unfortunately, the end result is oftentimes sheer
exhaustion. I know I've touched on this subject in a previous segment, but I
think it may be worth a closer look, once again, from Jesus' perspective.

Before we continue, take heart. I don't want you to become discouraged.
Jesus reminds His Princess that she cannot accomplish everything on her
daily "To Do" list in any given twenty-four hour time frame, day after day...
week after week... month after month...without suffering consequences. It is
truly impossible. It is definitely unrealistic. It is absolutely not doable, period.
But, the great news is that we serve a God who wrote the book on taking a
Sabbath Rest for one twenty-four hour period each week. And, the one sure
way to accomplish that is to hand over our overloaded and overwhelmed lives
to Jesus...

The more deeply we enter into a personal relationship with our Savior,
the more we can begin to look at things from His perspective. And the more
we get what Jesus needs for us to get... the quicker we will adopt the habit
of taking a Sabbath Rest. To do so means to abstain from work so that we
can rest our body, mind, and soul. We can give our burdens to Him, and,
in exchange, He gives us the opportunity to rejuvenate, restore, repair... the
constant, non-stop, ceaseless cycle we have functioned under... some of us,
for a long, long time.

Okay, once again I'll use a personal example. There have been
innumerable times in my life when I have come face-to-face with three or more
circumstances that appeared to be impossible to resolve, and to compound
matters, they were all going on simultaneously. God used my friend Lois to
speak truth into my life, and she did it in such a sweet way by talking, followed

by praying, and concluding by asking for the Lord's help. Lois helped me to regain my perspective, and to focus solely on Jesus. When I began to shift my focus from the circumstances to the Lord, what looked impossible to resolve, began to get worked out. I prayed through each problem until, before long, I witnessed God turning the "impossible" into awesome solutions; three of them, to be exact.

Here are a few of the steps of the *Princess Personal Action Plan* I use with those clients who need to clear away all distractions, for a little while; distractions that may be impeding their ability to develop a system analysis for their job, complete a work project, come up with a creative schedule to increase productivity in the work flow of their employees... If you work out of your home, find that quiet space; a space with no distractions or interruptions. This takes some creativity, but is so worth the little extra time it takes to create a sanctuary, versus the wasted time, anxiety, and frustration caused by constant distractions.

Step #1:   Clear every distraction; electronics seem to be at the top of the list these days. Bring a pen and note pad to jot down some ideas or instructions you believe God is wanting you to concentrate on. Find a place where it's just you and God; a quiet place, perfect for spending good quality time with Him, without any interruptions; wherever that space can be created. Silence... No sound, except God whispering His dreams and plans for your future, and your own breathing...

Step #2:   Take your eyes off of the things that would appear to take "Superwoman" in the flesh, to accomplish. Remind yourself, once again, that Superwoman is a myth. She does not exist. She is a figment of the imagination. You, on the other hand, are His Princess. Just know that God has no unrealistic expectations of you. None. He created you for His good pleasure. He wants to spend quality time with you; time that's not divided with those things that tend to interfere with your God-time. Your total focus is on Him, for the duration of your quiet time.

Step #3:   Practice getting so comfortable with God, and this special time you have allocated to spend alone with Him, that you are already counting the number of days before your next date with Jesus...

There have been times when some of my clients were approaching overload status, and just needed some guidance on how to creatively de-stress. The feedback indicated that these initial three steps proved helpful. Once again, this method may or may not work for you. Or, you may see some benefit in adapting a portion of these first steps. Regardless, the Lord is so cool! He waits, ever so patiently, as we figure out how to approach life at a slower pace, taking full advantage of the enjoyment we can derive, for example, from becoming still and just enjoying the sights and sounds of nature.

Watching a butterfly that God has painted with magnificent colors, preparing to take flight, ever so gracefully, is so incredibly calming. Observing the fluttering wings of a hummingbird provides a great object lesson on focus. We look, with fascination, at the fluttering of their wings, as they suspend themselves in mid-air, preparing to gather nectar from one flower to the next. It's awesome to watch them approach the portals of a nectar feeder, equipped to handle five or six hummingbirds simultaneously.

We live around the block from a manmade lake with three tributaries. We have so much fun when we take our GrandSugars for a walk around the main lake. Leesi giggles, with sheer delight, the minute she spots a mama duck coaching her babies on how to dive and catch fish for their dinner... Isaiah's attention might rest, for a moment, on the waves gently shifting back and forth, but his gaze quickly shifts to people walking their dogs. He is so good with pets... almost as good as he is at soccer. Leesi Grace is also an ardent pet lover. Whenever they visit, Leesi has running conversations with our kitty, Cutie Pie, that only she can understand! In another month, they'll be moving back from out-of-state. The whole family will be staying with us, while the house they purchased is being renovated. We are hoping for some clement weather so we can take full advantage of the lakes, and the serene background they provide.

Char Char, on her recent visit, loved watching the swans as they gracefully swam around the first lake. She is amazing to listen to, as she captures the sight, then quickly repeats what she has seen, in detail-facial expressions, hand movements, and all, as she relays the experience days later. You know, there is so much to be learned by watching the fascination, in the eyes of our young children or grandchildren, as they take in the sights and sounds of nature. We can also learn so much from them, when it comes to slowing down life's hectic tempo, to leisurely take it all in!

God waits, ever so patiently, as we begin to relax enough to take in the beauty of nature that can be found in a field filled with wildflowers... a natural habitat where the wildlife God created, find refuge. A babbling brook... a multi-tiered waterfall... a sunset so elegant that it can "wow" us with an array of breathtaking hues, and, no two are ever alike...

Ecclesiastes 3:11, as phrased in the NKJV, reminds us of God's Grace, which is so powerful that it can take sinners, like us, and transform us... "He has made everything beautiful in its time." And that includes a tranquil, relaxed, transformed, de-stressed... you!

Heart Whispers...

Dear God, You are Creator of every tranquil moment, every inspiring testimony, and every outpouring of Your Marvelous Grace,

You are the God who creates a wonderful masterpiece on the canvas of our souls, and not one of them is the same. While it's not always an easy thing to give You the canvas of our lives, especially when we tend to see that background as bleak, with little to offer. The hope comes in knowing that this is where You can create stunning results. Regardless of our shortcomings, God, You fill in that blank canvas with something exquisite. You create an atmosphere that can help lift the hearts of those who are feeling overloaded and overwhelmed.

So, thank You, Lord Jesus, for turning the "impossibilities" of our lives into awe-inspiring testimonies, to share with the world; testimonies that speak of the ways in which You miraculously empower each Princess to touch the lives of countless souls who are searching for Your Love.

Help us, Spirit of the Living God, to slow down the pace of our lives. Should Your Princess be anxious, please help her to relax so she can enjoy spending quiet time with You, in Your Presence, at Your feet, just listening...

Thank You, Father God, for the canvas of nature You have so lovingly placed in clear view, for our enjoyment. May each Princess give You the canvas of her soul so You can create a painting that reflects Your Glory and Your

Splendor... In the name of the God who is our Master Painter, and the Artist of our souls. Amen.

Bouquets of Grace-Filled Blessings...

"...when we acknowledge that we are paupers at the door of God's mercy... God can make something beautiful out of us. This poverty of the spirit is the second major characteristic of saved sinners with tilted halos living by grace."

-Brennan Manning
The Ragamuffin Gospel
Multnomah Press

Gems of Wisdom...

Titus 3:7
Ephesians 2:7
2 Thessalonians 2:16-17
Titus 2:11

Refreshing Hugs...

During your next quiet time, practice genuine humility before your Savior. Ask the Spirit of God to remind you of any attitudes that you need to work on, such as unforgiveness, a judgmental spirit, impatience... Princess, you're now ready to take the next step on your odyssey to that street called "Precious Grace Road."

A MIRACLE RX FOR OUR YEARNING HEARTS

"There is salvation in no one else! There is no other name
in all of heaven for people to call on to save them."
Acts 4:12

The stage is set. Peter and John are standing before the Sadducees, a Jewish sect whose members were of the priestly line and who were in control of the functions of the temple. Greatly agitated at Peter and John for teaching the people about Jesus, and His resurrection from the dead, they seized the two apostles and put them in jail. When brought before the rulers and asked by what authority they were teaching, Peter, "...filled with the Holy Spirit," proceeded to explain their position.

Our salvation is found in none other than the Lord Jesus Christ. We are called by God to give a defense to everyone who asks our reason for the hope that is in us... It is God's desire that we are certain of our salvation. We know that we are saved only by placing our trust and faith in Jesus and confessing Him as our Lord, our Savior, our God. We must also repent of our sins and ask the Lord for forgiveness... And, according to God's Word, we, as His disciples, are to help those who are seeking and searching for Him...

These actions are fundamental to every Christian. Taken a step further, God wants to use the healing some of us have experienced personally, for countless people who are struggling with what I call, "issues of the heart." And, the greatest healing and miracle of all is the salvation of the human soul. It is the healing of the soul's yearning to know the God of Glory as Savior...

Now might be a good time to wander slowly through the Book of Psalms. Or, at your own pace, read through the Gospels... Invite the Holy Spirit to travel back in time with you; back to a time, so very long ago, when Messiah Jesus walked along the Sea of Galilee, instructing His disciples to follow Him... asking them to trust Him, wherever He would take them... no matter what He might ask of them... just to trust Him...

Here's a soothing thought: God's angels are on stand-by 24/7. Every time someone makes the most crucial decision they will ever make in their lifetime, by becoming a believer, we are told that the angels in heaven rejoice with resounding joy. Have you ever imagined that heavenly scene taking place when you became a believer, or someone you loved became a believer? Do you think Jesus' disciples ever imagined the angels rejoicing when they gave their life to their Messiah?

Let's pause, for a moment, and thank the Lord for our salvation. Let's thank Him because He is in the process of using the gifts He has carefully deposited into each one of our lives-gifts He has given us to use, for the benefit of those He will strategically place along our odyssey path. He may bring those who are struggling, or sad, or lonely...

Let's thank Him for teaching us the fruit of the Spirit so we can grow to be more like Him. Let's express our gratitude to the Lord for using our prayers, our hands, our resources, and our spiritual gifts to minister to those who do not yet know Christ as Lord.

May God richly bless you, His Princess, by opening doors of opportunity for you to witness and to minister to others, for Him... for His Glory... for His Kingdom!

Heart Whispers...

Dear God, Your Touch is Life-Changing...

I pray that the eyes of the unbelievers; the eyes of their spirit, may be opened to receiving You into their hearts and their lives. Help Your Princess to become a powerful witness to those You direct her to, Holy Spirit. Mighty God, fill the mouth of Your Princess, so she may proclaim the awesome things You have done to captivate her soul; answering her yearning for more of You, God. Thank You for Your Touch, a Touch of Your Grace, a Touch of Your Healing, that You give, without measure... In the name of the God who is the only Rx for healing for our yearning hearts... Amen.

Bouquets of Grace-Filled Blessings...

"There is no touch in the universe like the touch of His nail-scarred hand. All who touch Him are made whole... salvation, healing, deliverance, and power are in His touch. The Master's touch makes all things new."

-Kathyrn Kuhlman
Healing Words
Creation House

Gems of Wisdom...

Matthew 9:20-22
Revelation 21:3-5

Refreshing Hugs...

May you experience a fresh touch from your Master's hand, for all your tomorrows...

PRAYERS WHISPERED FROM A MAMA'S HEART

"My heart rejoices in the Lord! Oh, how the Lord has blessed me! Now,
I have an answer for my enemies, as I delight in Your deliverance.
No one is holy like the Lord! There is no Rock like our God."

1 Samuel 2:1-2

"Now, I have an answer for my enemies, as I delight in Your deliverance.
No one is holy like the Lord!..." Oh, Princess of the Rock of your salvation,
wouldn't it just totally delight your heart to be able to "...have an answer for
[your] enemies?" Wouldn't it just make your day to be able to "...smile at your
enemies..." as the NKJV phrases it. Wow! There is such amazing power that
our Lord bequeaths to His Beloved Princesses. All we need to do is have faith
in our Rock; all we need to do is "smile" when the enemy of our soul begins
to taunt us. All we need to do is use the authority God gives us, the authority
of His Name, His Word, His Blood... Hannah had an abiding faith in the
God she knew would hear her whenever she cried out to Him!

Hannah, mama of Samuel, touched the very heart of the Father, on
behalf of her child. When Hannah prayed, it came from the very depths of
her heart. Mama, as she prayed for her son, knew the secret of dedicating her
child, Samuel, to the Lord.

Let's take a step back to I Samuel 1:10. In the tabernacle, we find Hannah,
who has been unable to conceive a child, petitioning God to give her a son.
"Hannah was in deep anguish, crying bitterly as she prayed to the Lord. And
she made this vow: "O Lord Almighty, if You will look down upon my sorrow
and answer my prayer and give me a son, then I will give him back to You. He
will be Yours for his entire lifetime, and as a sign that he has been dedicated
to the Lord, his hair will never be cut."

Eli, the priest, had watched Hannah as she prayed, "Seeing her lips
moving but hearing no sound, he thought she had been drinking..." Finally,
Hannah explained to Eli that she was "not drunk! But...very sad, and...
pouring out [her] heart to the Lord." Eli told her to "cheer up!" And, he added,
"May the God of Israel grant the request you have asked of Him."

Hannah's lips were moving, but no verbal utterance was heard by the
priest. Why? Because Hannah was praying from the deepest recesses of her

heart; praying to the God she would eventually entrust with the well-being of her son, Samuel. What Hannah did, when she relinquished the son she had pleaded for God to give her, was inspiring. She dedicated her son Samuel, to the Lord.

This is what transpired, in I Samuel 2:21-22, "The next year Elkanah... went on their annual trip to offer a sacrifice to the Lord. But Hannah did not go. She told her husband, Elkanah, "Wait until the baby is weaned. Then I will take him to the Tabernacle and leave him there with the Lord permanently." What a role model Hannah became to future generations. Her exclaimation, "No one is holy like the Lord! There is no Rock like our God," said it all. Like Hannah, we can also choose to proclaim words of exaltation, as they truly bring glory, honor, and praise to the Mighty God we serve!

Heart Whispers...

Dear God, You are the God of Extraordinary Love,

Please bless the prayers of each mom, nana, aunt, friend... as their prayers come from their hearts. As You unfold Your plans for their family, or the future of other loved ones, may every God's Girl, no matter her age or stage of life, help plant seeds for Your Great Harvest! Thank You, Lord, for Your extraordinary Love! In the name of our Covenant Making, Covenant Keeping God. Amen.

Bouquets of Grace-Filled Blessings...

"As Christian parents, we have a solemn obligation to constantly...on a day-by-day basis, lift up our son [daughter] in prayer. We are responsible before God for his [her] spiritual, emotional, and physical well being..."

-Lee Roberts
Praying God's Will For My Son
and
Praying God's Will For My Daughter
Thomas Nelson Publishers

Gems of Wisdom...

Psalm 127:3
Psalm 128
Matthew 19:13-15
Isaiah 11:6
Proverbs 22:6

Refreshing Hugs...

Perhaps you might like to create a scripture basket. As you discover articles, quotes, or God's promises pertaining to His Kids, store these in the basket. Each day, as you pray for your child(ren), or a friend's child[ren], a neice or nephew, or grandchild ... pray God's promises for them. And give God thanks, because, children are a gift... a reward from our Heavenly Father!

LEARNING TO READ THE BLUEPRINTS

"As he was nearing Damascus on this mission, a brilliant light
from heaven suddenly beamed down upon him! He fell to the
ground and heard a voice saying to him, "Saul! Saul! Why are you
persecuting Me?" "Who are you, sir?" Saul asked. And the voice
replied, "I am Jesus, the One you are persecuting! Now get up
and go into the city, and you will be told what you are to do."
Acts 9:3-6

What a dialogue that takes place between the Lord Jesus and Saul of
Tarsus, a Jew and a man of high position among men, but one who was guilty
of oppressing God's people. The Lord reached down into the very soul of this
man, and exposed the wickedness embedded there. On that very road, ravaged
with dust, the same type of dust God used to form and fashion Adam, Saul
had a dramatic, life-changing conversion experience. And Saul, whom the
Lord renamed Paul, would never be the same again!

It is an astounding realization when we become aware that our
disobedience greives the Spirit of God. When we are saved, washed in the
precious blood of the Lamb, and sealed by the Holy Spirit, we, like the Apostle
Paul, will never be the same again.

We must learn, very early in our Christian walk, that obedience to God
comes by reading His Word and consequently doing what He instructs us to
do. Like the Apostle Paul, and every believer throughout this vast world, the
Holy Spirit begins to tug at our hearts regarding our rebellious attitudes that
have somehow managed to wriggle their way into our hearts...

There are so many things, "I am still learning," as Michaelangelo put it.
But here's what we do know: As we submit to God, He so graciously unfolds
His plans for us. And I would say to you, precious one, learn to follow in
His footprints, the same footprints our Savior leaves for every believer. Copy
His precepts, carefully patterning your core values, your ideals, the spiritual
disciplines, your heart attitudes... after His.

The Word of God is the pathway to our spiritual, emotional, physical, and
relational well-being. When we, as believers, learn to focus on Messiah Jesus,
our Master Character Builder, He takes the unholy attitudes that earmark our

rebellion, along with the emotional junk that we have dragged around with us like a piece of heavy baggage, and pour His healing balm over our souls. The Word tells us that when we come to Jesus and make Him Lord over every aspect of our being, "Our old sinful selves were crucified with Christ so that sin might lose its power in our lives..." Romans 6:6.

The blueprints are engraved in His Word. So, let's continue to walk down our individual path, the odyssey road of your life, and of mine. Let's purpose to develop an eagerness to study His Precepts, Commandments, Counsel, and Covenant Promises, written in His Word. He has designed an individualized path for every believer, which includes places God may want to send us, people He wants to introduce into our lives, and the type of discipleship He has custom designed for each of us to do. Dusty and challenging as the road can sometimes become, the prize, eternal life with our Messiah, is so worth it all!

Heart Whispers...

Dear God, our Blueprint Engraver,

You are a most incredible God. You have laid out the blueprints necessary for living a godly life, engraved with Your signature, and etched ever so carefully into our souls. Thank You, Lord, that we no longer have to guess, when we are called upon to make a decision. We can now make healthy choices for our life because You have empowered each Princess to follow Your lead. Thank You, Lord God, for modeling a healthy lifestyle for Your people. In the name of the God who is our Savior, our Healer, our Mentor, our Renewal Life Coach... our Messiah... Amen.

Bouquets of Grace-Filled Blessings...

"The Bible is alive, it speaks to me; it has feet, it runs after me; it has hands, it lays hold on me."

-Martin Luther

Gems of Wisdom...

Hebrews 4:12
Colossians 3:16

Refreshing Hugs...

If you have begun a *My Princess Goals Reached And Dreams Realized Daybook*, jot down a few short and long term goals. Submit them to God's scrunity, giving Him permission to amend or delete any goals that don't coincide with what you believe to be an outline of His personal blueprints for your odyssey.

Make these goals open-ended so God can add others He may want included, to the list. I will be cheering from the bleachers with every successful adventure-packed step you take, to reach each goal and realize each dream.

THINK LOVELY THOUGHTS

"...whatever things are true, whatever things are noble, whatever
things are just, whatever things are pure, whatever things are
lovely, whatever things are of good report, if there is any virtue
and if there is anything praiseworthy-meditate on these things.
The things which you learned and received and heard and saw
in Me, these do, and the God of peace will be with you."
Philippians 4:8-9 NKJV

"Logos." What an intriguing word! In Greek, "logos" is translated as,
"The self-revealing thought and word of God." In the above scripture passage,
God is saying that we are to think upon certain things, "...whatever things
are true, whatever things are noble, whatever things are just, whatever things
are pure, whatever things are lovely..." Our world was created by the Word,
or "logos" of God. To say it another way, God's Son Jesus is the Word made
flesh. In Philippians 4:8-9, we are instructed to think about all the truth and
loveliness contained in the Word of God.

As human beings, our thought patterns are one of the most intricately
structured patterns imaginable. We have been given the ability, by our
Creator, to control those patterns, changing negative thoughts into positive
ones. The Word teaches us this: "...do not be conformed to this world, but be
transformed by the renewing of your mind..." Romans 12:2 NKJV.

For over twelve years, on Monday evenings, I had the privilege, and the
pleasure of facilitating a variety of different support groups ranging from
issues like grief and loss, co-dependency... Monitoring self-talk, or what we
say to ourselves when no one else is around, is key.

In just a matter of weeks, the work of the Holy Spirit became so evident...
They were able to identify negative thoughts that often led to negative self-
talk. The support of the other members of the group provided much needed
positive feedback. Within another few weeks, they began to see the fruit
of their efforts. The hard work they were doing became readily apparent.
They began to notice changes in their thinking patterns. God's Grace was
exactly what was needed in helping to turn their negative thought patterns
into positive ones, "... whatever things are lovely, whatever things are of

good report..." The exhortation, found in the NKJV of Philippians 4:8-9, encouraged them to focus on, "...whatever things are true... noble... just... pure..."

The last few minutes of group time was spent in pairing up with a partner for the sole pupose of praising and affirming a member of the group who had successfully identified negative talk. The next step was to change those unhealthy thoughts into healthy ones. Once they had begun that process, they also began receiving affirmation for their progress. What was so rewarding was the privilege of hearing group members express their desire to begin working toward changes they wanted to see take place in their relationships, their jobs, their short-term and long-term goals...

Should I be speaking to a Princess who may need some assistance in the area of negative self-talk, I encourage you to call upon the Holy Spirit. Seek God's Wisdom in helping you to change your unhealthy thought patterns into healthy ones. Reflect on all the virtues God mentions in Philippians 4:8-9. Write out these verses and place them in a visible spot. Memorize them, and, as you do, think about the depth of God's incredible love toward you, His Jewel.

Heart Whispers...

Dear God, Author of Pure Thoughts, Lovely Thoughts, Noble Thoughts...,

I crave a fresh word from You, Lord. Make Your Word come alive to me, as well as those who are reading these words... Give Your Princess clear direction, and the steps You highlight for her in Philippians 4:8-9, so she may accomplish her goals. Help her to think beautiful thoughts that reaffirm Your Goodness, Grace, Patience, Faithfulness...

Help her to test the thoughts that come into her mind, and the motives that reside in her heart, as 2 Corinthians 10:5 instructs believers to do. By doing so, she will be able to make sure that they line up with scripture. These instructions will lead her to live a life of obedience to You, Father God. Thank You, Lord, for filling her with Your Spectacular Love... and Your Awesome Grace! In the name of the God who desires to fill our thoughts with Loveliness, Truth, Good Reports... Amen.

Bouquets of Grace-Filled Blessings...

"The main weapon in mental warfare is deliberately to feed your mind on God's truth and power. Think about the greatness of the Lord. Fill your mind with His Word..."

-Stormy Omartian
The Power of a Praying Parent
Harvest House Publishers

Gems of Wisdom...

Philippians 4:8-9
Hebrews 1:3
Ephesians 1:19-20
Ephesians 6:10
John 17:17

Refreshing Hugs...

Suggestion: Meditate on Philippians 4: 8-9, every day for a month. As you monitor your self-talk, work on bringing your thoughts into alignment with, and obedience to the Lord. Practice transforming your negative self-talk into positive affirmations about yourself, based on what God says about you.

Our dear friends, Pastor Bob and Lenora, put a beautiful recording on their answering machine. The caller hears Lenora, reminding that caller that they are the most important person Pastor Bob or Lenora would speak with that day! What a precious way to greet those who call. What a great way to affirm a person's value!

COMMITTED TO A LIFE OF
PURPOSE AND MEANING

"Then He called His disciples and the crowds to come over and listen. "If any of you wants to be My follower, He told them, "You must put aside your selfish ambition, shoulder your cross, and follow Me. If you try to keep your life for yourself, you will lose it. But if you give up your life for My sake and for the sake of the Good News, you will find true life."
Mark 8:34-35

While Mark 8:34-35, seems to run contrary to our human nature, Jesus spent a great part of His ministry teaching His disciples that the precepts in His Word are perfectly aligned to His Truth. Left to our own devices, we might tend to choose our own course of action, not His. That decision could ultimately lead to unhealthy consequences. The Lord knew this before we were ever formed. That is the very reason Jesus tells us to "...put aside your selfish ambition, shoulder your cross, and follow Me."

Jesus called His disciples to a point of total commitment. His call has not changed. The commitment He is calling us to make today, is the same commitment He called His disciples to make over two thousand years ago. Commitment is a big word, but simply defined it means, "Submitting and yielding yourself to someone without conditions."

The cross that Jesus refers to is the daily cross we are called to bear. This cross may include all of our challenges... obstacles to accomplishing goals... frustrations... grief... loss... financial hardship... physical or emotional infirmities... The "cross" also encompasses our willingness to put Him first, before our life, our comfort, our agenda, and, our own stubborn will...

Ahhh... Now, let's examine the upside of this commitment. God promises that we will gain Eternal Life, which can never be taken from us, not ever! What an amazing insurance policy! The benefits are incomparable... And there is no expiration date. Hallelujah!

Obedience is what God asks of His Kids. Difficult as it may appear to be, the reward will far exceed the commitment to obey, that He asks of us. And the commitment we are asked to make is, "...for the sake of Jesus, and for the sake of the Good News..." When we decide to surrender to His ways, God promises that we "... will find true life."

In order to fulfill this commitment, we will need to release all that binds us, or holds us back. We will need to live intentionally and purposefully. We will need to resist every temptation to go our own way...to do our own thing. We will need to count the cost, then weigh that cost against the ultimate reward... Eternal Salvation... Eternity spent with God...

If you know of someone who has not fully committed to follow Messiah Jesus, just yet, lift her up to the Father. Cover her in prayer, and ask another "sister" to do the same. Perhaps you could offer to take her with you to your home church. Share your testimony... Continue lifting this precious one up to the Lord, and listen to the Holy Spirit's leading. May God bless you as you share your faith, and what God has done in your life. Now, get ready to take the next step along your destiny journey...

Heart Whispers...

Dear God, our Perfect Reward,

You are our Perfect Reward, God! If there is a Princess who has not yet given all of her heart to You, Messiah Jesus; if she has not completely surrendered her will to Yours, God, then I pray that, as she makes the most important decision of her life, she will choose to give her "all" to You!

May she make You the Lord of her life, her Savior, her Messiah... Holy Spirit, I thank You that You are standing next to her right now, ready to breathe Your breath of life into hers... I pray that Your anointing and Your call on her life, God, will bless her, and cause her to be a blessing, wherever You lead her...

Thank You, Messiah Jesus, that You were willing to die, so that we might live... You rose from the grave so that Your Beloved Princesses could experience that abundant life You speak of in Your Word. As your Daughters, we look forward, with great anticipation, to spending eternity with You... In the name of the God who restores that which was lost, sets our feet on higher ground, and, as the NKJV of Isaiah 40:31, phrases it, "...those who wait on the Lord... renew their strength; They shall mount up with wings like eagles..." Amen!

Bouquets of Grace-Filled Blessings...

"There are no crown-wearers in heaven who were not cross-bearers here below."

-Charles H. Spurgeon
Morning and Evening
Thomas Nelson Publishers

Gems of Wisdom...

Psalm 3:8
2 Thessalonians 1:3-4
Psalm 27:5
Luke 14:27

Refreshing Hugs...

"...God hath not promised Sun without rain, Joy without sorrow, Peace without pain. But God hath promised Strength for the day, Rest for the labor, Light for the way, Grace for the trials, Help from above, Unfailing sympathy, Undying love."

-Annie Johnson Flint
Poem: "What God Hath Promised"

After reading the above portion of Annie's poem, please close this book. Take some time to reflect upon the words of truth and grace in the poem, and on the powerful promises God makes to you, His Special Jewel. God is, indeed, our Perfect Reward!

SHOW ME HOW TO GET THERE, LORD!

"God blesses those whose hearts are pure, for they will see God."
Matthew 5:8

Prior to a road trip, people have their cars checked by a mechanic. Tires, oil, water, engines, brakes, accelerators, windshield wiper fluid, compressor, turn signals, sideview mirrors, front mirror, fuel pump... the list for safe freeway travel, as well as driving on city streets, is seemingly endless. We can spend a great deal of time and possibly money, checking our vehicles to insure the safety of our trip. But, I was thinking about how long it had been since I had done a "heart motive" check. Ouch! Way too long, was the ultimate conclusion I had drawn.

Jesus teaches us that, "God blesses those whose hearts are pure, for they will see God." It is the Lord who know our hearts. He knows what motivates us, and why we say the things we say and do the things we do. "The eyes of the Lord search the whole earth in order to strengthen those whose hearts are fully committed to Him," is the lesson we learn from 2 Chronicles 16:9.

God knows our weaknesses, as well as our strong character traits. He wants us to know them, as well. Before saying a word, before acting upon any decision that might affect not only our own well-being, but that of others, as well, it would be in our best interest to do a heart check-up...

Dr. Tim Clinton, President of AACC, and founder of ICCA, International Christian Coaching Alliance, makes a powerful point in his life coaching training, to those who aspire to be great coaches. In his teaching on leadership coaching, Tim drives the point home, "People who separate themselves don't make excuses, they make adjustments."

What is the condition of your heart today? If you are desiring to be more like Jesus, are you willing to grant the Lord permission to do some "heart surgery?" Is your goal to seek pure heart motives? Do you strive to put the needs of others before your own? Tough questions, I know, but important ones! Just a word of caution that was of help to me, and hopefully will benefit you, as well. Do not attempt to scrutinize the intentions of your thoughts, words, or motives, without help from the Holy Spirit. It is only by God's guidance in His Word, that purity of heart can be cultivated. It is a process. It will take time. But, the end result will be a heart of genuine love and compassion toward those He brings into your sphere of influence.

I don't begin to have all the answers, but what I do know is that by giving God glory, often, for bringing me through some burning embers, He continues to purify my heart. What I do know is that when I give the Spirit of God permission to do all the "heart surgery" He needs to, as often as He needs to, He continues to purify me.

Please join me in giving God all the glory, honor, and praise, for what He has done, and, for what He will do to conform us into His image, one day at a time. I applaud you, as you become even more intentional about your longing to commit your will and your ways to Him...

Heart Whispers...

Dear God, our Heart Strengthener,

Your intentions, for Your Princesses, are that we live with a heart full of pure motives that will dictate our actions as "other centered." Please show us how to get there, Lord! We commit to following Your lead...

I ask that You bless Your Princess, as she gives You her words, her attitudes, her heart motives... so that, at the end of the day, she will glow with Your Love and Your Grace, as she becomes "other centered" like You, God. In the name of the God who is our Chief Heart Surgeon. Amen.

Bouquets of Grace-Filled Blessings...

"...It takes time to learn about motives and how to determine whether ours are pure."

-Joyce Meyer
Me and My Big Mouth
Harrison House

Gems of Wisdom...

Psalm 16:7
Psalm 19:14
Proverbs 27:19
Proverbs 4:23

Refreshing Hugs...

Psalm 49:3 says this: "For my words are wise, and my thoughts are filled with insight." Before criticizing anyone, yourself included, meditate on the wise words of this Psalm, instead.

There is an old adage that is a reminder to:"Think before you speak." But, if you are still struggling in this area, Designer's Duck Tape is now available. The only catch is that I get first grabs!

FEASTING AT HIS TABLE

"He brings me to the banquet hall, so everyone
can see how much He loves me."
Song of Songs 2:4

The love-inspiring words of Song of Songs 2:4, so poignantly remind me of the Valentine's Day cards my daddy gave me on that special day, every year. He passed four plus years ago, just short of his ninety-fifth birthday. He was blessed to have lived a beautiful life, which he continually poured out, unselfishly, on the dreams and hopes of those he loved. Daddy was my first example of what it looked like to be a balcony coach. He believed in me, even when I, at times, wasn't certain that I still believed in myself. He would lean over the balcony of my life, cheering me on, as I set a small goal and reached it. With each goal I set, he would encourage me to set a little larger goal the next time...

My husband has been my life coach for the last two and a half decades. Honey and I sometimes disagree, having a little different take on how something should be handled, for instance. But while our ideas differ, at times, I know that he always has my best interests at heart, as he does with each of our children and GrandSugars. It's what we do when we love someone-we put their needs above our own.

God reminds each Princess, in Song of Songs 2:4, as it is worded in the NKJV, that, "His banner over [her] is love." In fact, one of God's Hebrew names is Jehovah Nissi, which refers to His covering or protection over each of us. This covering represents His Love, which is Awe-Inspiring. If you were to imagine the deepest love you have ever experienced for another human being, it would not begin to touch the depths of God's love for His Kids. However, none of us can ever begin to love God as deeply, completely, and perfectly as He loves us.

Let's take a glimpse into God's future design for every believer, and what that blueprint will look like for the Bride of Christ, in the New Jerusalem... Let's look at the way the NLT phrases Isaiah 25:6-10:

"The Lord has spoken! In that day the people will proclaim,
"This is our God. We trusted in Him, and He saved us. This is
the Lord, in whom we trusted. Let us rejoice in the salvation He
brings! For the Lord's good hand will rest on Jerusalem."

Now let's look at Revelation 21:1-7, as it is phrased in the NLT,

"And the one sitting on the throne said, "Look I am making all
things new! And then He said to me, "Write this down, for what I
tell you is trustworthy and true." And He also said, "It is finished!
I am the Alpha and the Omega-the Beginning and the End.
To all those who are thirsty I will give the springs of the water of
life without charge! All who are victorious will inherit all these
blessings, and I will be their God, and they will be My children."

It is my prayer, my sister in the Lord, that when you meet with Jesus in
your quiet time each day, you will fall head-over-heels in love with Him, all
over again. Claim God's Promises as you read His Word. Meditate on His
Goodness, His Grace, His Faithfulness...

May your meeting times blossom into a purpose-filled way to spend
precious moments; time expressly carved out for you and your King. May
these priceless times become beautiful memories, embedded deeply in your
heart, forever...

Heart Whispers...

Dear God, You are Yahweh Roi, our Shepherd,

Your Love, Lord, for Your flock, is simply breathtaking. Just how much
You love us is impossible to comprehend. Thank You for the covering You
provide... May the love Your Princess has for You, be expressed in fresh new
ways. May that love, Messiah Jesus, grow and grow and grow...

Please fill her with an abundance of Your Presence that brings peace and
tranquility to her soul. In the name of the God who loves us so much that

He invites us into His Presence, so that we can glorify Him and enjoy Him now, and throughout eternity, in the New Jerusalem... Amen.

Bouquets of Grace-Filled Blessings...

"In commending us to glorify Him, God is inviting us to enjoy Him."

-C.S. Lewis
C.S. Lewis - The Inspirational Writings
Inspirational Press, A Division of
BBS Publishing Corporation

Gems of Wisdom...

Psalm 34:8
Psalm 16:11
Isaiah 25:6-10
Psalm 111:1

Refreshing Hugs...

Enjoy each tender moment, as you meet with God today. Get quiet. Listen... with rapt attention, and anticipation, because, God can hardly wait to whisper His Love Sonnets in your ear...

THE NEED SUPPLIER

"And this same God who takes care of me will supply all your needs
from His glorious riches, which have been given to us in Christ
Jesus. Now glory be to God our Father forever and ever. Amen.
Phillipians 4:19-20

"When you come to the place where I am all that you have, you'll find
that I am all you need." Etched on a bookmark, this sentiment seems like a
revolutionary new way of expressing our need for our God. But, simply put,
it serves as a reminder to put our needs in their proper perspective. All of our
heart's deepest needs can be found in Jesus... "...God...will supply all your
needs from His glorious riches...given to us in Christ Jesus."

Need Peace?	*He is your peace.*
Need Hope?	*He is your hope.*
Need Reassurance?	*He is your reassurance.*
Need Rest?	*He is your rest.*
Need a Safe Haven?	*He is your safe haven.*

I remember reading about a young missionary in Japan who became
discouraged and began to question her reason for living. After having given
so much of herself to the Japanese people, as well as to her own family, she
found herself depleted emotionally, mentally, physically, and spiritually.
These feelings grew stronger and continued for many months. She felt
overwhelmed by her own unmet needs. As the Lord began to touch and
heal her, Philippians 4:19 became the hope she clung to. God really is the
only One who could meet every need she would ever have, and bless her life
richly in Him.

God wants us to consider Him as the Source for every need we have. How
precious and timely is God's Word for us as we continue on our odyssey. How
great are His Covenant Promises; they are His way of assuring us, His Bride,
that He will never leave us, but will be there for us whenever we need the
kind of stability that only He can provide. This young woman met God at a

time when she needed Him most. We can be assured the Lord stands equally ready to meet every need we have, and more...

The following scripture verse, found in Ephesians 3:20, encourages our hearts, when we need that reassurance: "Now glory be to God! By His mighty power at work within us, He is able to accomplish infinitely more than we would ever dare to ask or hope." What an Amazing Promise from an Amazing God!

Heart Whispers...

Dear God, You are Jehovah Jireh, our Provider, and the only One who can ever be the supplier of our deepest needs,

You are not only our Promise Maker, You are our Promise Keeper! You're our Provider for every need that we could ever imagine having. We thank You for the astounding works You are able to do in us, and through us, when we are yielded to Your Plan for our odyssey destiny. Thank You, Lord, for the remarkable, as well as the incredible, for You truly are the God of both!

Whisper in our ear, Lord God, a reminder for us to look at the supernatural in the everyday circumstances we encounter. You are Lord over "...infinitely more than we would ever dare to ask or hope."

Bless the life of Your Princess so that she can embrace a life of continual blessing, and can give inspiration to others who are in need of hope. Through this prayer, Lord, I place this Princess in Your loving care. Should she be experiencing discouragement, I ask that You summon her to the foot of Your throne, Father God, and cover her with Your blanket of encouragement...

Surround her with those who will encourage her to work toward successfully fulfilling both her goals and her dreams! Plant her feet upon Your unshakeable ground. Remind her of Your Covenant Promises, Lord. In the name of the God who is the Solid Rock on which we stand! Amen.

Bouquets of Grace-Filled Blessings...

"... It is in the soul and spirit of man that needs are more frequently undefined, unaddressed, and unmet... Only God... can meet your deepest needs."

-Charles Stanley
Our Unmet Needs
Thomas Nelson Publishers

Gems of Wisdom...

I Peter 1:3-5
Matthew 6:8
Hebrews 4:16

Refreshing Hugs...

When you go to the Father for help with your needs, be brief, but specific. If you are journaling, write from the depths of your heart. Chart the progress you are making.

A suggestion: Write God a note, thanking Him for every step of progress He has helped you take, and for every bountiful provision He has given you. Have a blessed, stress-free day!

THE FRAGRANCE OF GRACE

"...Now wherever we go He uses us to tell others about the
Lord and to spread the Good News like a sweet perfume.
Our lives are a fragrance presented by Christ to God... To
those who are being saved we are a life-giving perfume."
2 Corinthians 2:14-16

My daughter Danielle and I were out walking on a beautiful summner evening. It was many years ago, but I remember it like it was yesterday. The moon was full, hanging like a large orange sphere, suspended in the sky. Danielle and I were sharing about our day when suddenly, some gorgeous flowers growing in our neighbor's garden caught her eye. I talked about how beautiful they were, and how I would love to walk up and smell them. That's all I needed to say. Knowing my love for flowers, Danielle and her friend Saundra knocked boldly on the neighbors' door, a few days later. My daughter asked if she could have some of the flowers. What a lovely bouquet Danielle brought me. This time, I not only admired their beauty, but I could enjoy the sweet fragrance of their perfume throughout our home.

God calls us, as Christians, to be the aroma of Christ. The NKJV states it this way "...the sweet savoring fragrance of Christ "...among those who are being saved and among those who are perishing." The NKJV of Philippians 4:18, talks about our lives as reflecting "...a sweet-smelling aroma, an acceptable sacrifice, well pleasing to God." Princess of the Everlasting Father, you are a continual "sweet-smelling perfume" to a world that is rapidly perishing for lack of hearing the Good News of salvation, and eternal life spent in God's Presence. So, I'd like to challenge you to be creative! There are many ways you can be an influence on those that God has placed around you. All it takes is a little time and thought.

Step outside your problems or difficulties for the time being... Send a card to a shut-in to let them know someone cares about them... Make up a basket filled with scripture inspirations, some fresh-baked cookies, some tea bags, and a note of encouragement... Grocery shop for a friend or take someone to a doctor's appointment, like my friend Kathy does on her day off. Kathy has a heart for people who are unable to do for themselves. She gives of her time and support, and does it out of a heart of compassion. She also serves as a volunteer for a house, set up by the church, to distribute food, clothing, household items...as an outreach for those in the church community who are in need.

Perhaps you could donate your time, like our home bible study co-leader, Susan, does. Once a week, Susan takes their dog, Rambo, to the hospital, to love on people who are ill. She also takes books that have been read by either herself or bought at garage sale or donated by others for her to give away. What a beautiful way to bless, and minister, to those who need both!

The list of opportunities to serve are truly endless, but oh, the sweet blessings you will impart to a precious soul. Your ministry to others will provide a wonderful aroma of "essence of healing balm," when you serve others in His Name. Thank you for being a blessing... a sweet aroma, to someone who may not have experienced the Love, and the Gift of Salvation, that only our Savior, Messiah Jesus, can give...

Heart Whispers...

Dear God, You are the God who blesses our lives with Your Sweet Perfume-the Gift of Salvation,

Fill Your Precious Princess with Your "Sweet Fragrance" as she begins her day. Help her to walk, throughout the day, basking in Your Love, and filled to overflowing with Your Peace, Your Joy, and Your Grace. May she always glorify You with her words and her actions. Please give Your Princess a portion of Your Tenderness, so that she might be a continual blessing to those around her. In the name of the God who blesses us with creative ways to minister, both to the lost, and to our "sisters" in Him... Amen.

Bouquets of Grace-Filled Blessings...

"She comes with perfume. Expensive perfume. As she anoints him, the aroma of extravagant love fills the room. So pure. So lovely. Flowing from the veined alabaster jar of her heart..."

-Ken Gire
Intimate Moments With The Savior
Zondervan Publishing House

Gems of Wisdom...

John 12:3
Luke 7:37-38

Refreshing Hugs...

A grace-filled thought would be to buy a bouquet of fresh flowers, or, if you have a garden, to make up a bouquet. Tie them with a bow and include a lightly scented note, graced with words of affirmation, perhaps from the Book of Psalms. Present them to someone who may be in need of a fresh whiff of God's Grace. And be blessed for being a blessing, wrapped in human kindness...

TRUE SERVANTHOOD

"Jesus, knowing that the Father had given all things into His hands, and that He had come from God and was going to God, rose from supper and laid aside His garments, took a towel and girded Himself... and began to wash the disciples' feet..."
John 13:3-5

Oswald Chambers, in the combined volumes of *The Devotional Writings of Oswald Chambers: My Utmost for His Highest* and *Daily Thoughts For His Disciples,* clarifies the meaning of true servanthood. It can be found in his devotion entitled: *The Destitution of Service,* "...Christ's... idea is that we serve Him by being the servants of other men... The real test of the saint," Oswald continues, "is not preaching the gospel, but washing disciples' feet...doing the things that...count everything in the estimate of God."

By virtue of the fact that we are Christians, we are considered "members of one body." Colossians 3:15, admonishes us to act accordingly. Collectively, as one body, God calls us to serve one another. The verse closes with these words, "And always be thankful."

Jesus is our Messiah!	*Be Thankful!*
He died to save us from our sin!	*Be Thankful!*
He rose again to give us abundant life!	*Be Thankful!*
He lives in us so we can be victorious!	*Be Thankful!*
He reigns in our hearts!	*Be Thankful!*
He puts eternity in our hearts!	*Be Thankful!*
He is Love!	*Be Thankful!*

True servanthood means stepping outside of yourself and putting your own challenges and problems aside, momentarily, so you can become a "balcony coach" to others who may be struggling. To forget your problems, for the time being, by serving and becoming a blessing to others, sums up one of the purposes for which this book was written. To put your own challenges aside in order to extend a helping hand to another, is the Rx Jesus taught us by His example. Simply put, we become a servant for the express purpose of seeking God's highest and best for another... And, by serving others, we are serving God.

Thankfulness and peace begin to rule in the heart of His Princess, when she serves others, because she is also serving Him. In the words of Psalm 50:14, "What I want...is your true thanks to God..."

Heart Whispers...

Dear God, You are our perfect example of a Selfless Servant,

Thank You for the ultimate sacrifice You made on the Cross at Calvary. Thank You, Lord, that You live in us and give us new life! Thank You that when we declare You as the Lord and Savior of our lives, having confessed all of our sins and having asked for Your forgiveness, that You not only grant that forgiveness, but You cleanse us from all unrighteousness. Thank You, God, that You grace our hearts with so many blessings...

I ask, Lord God, that You bless Your Faithful Princess for every unselfish act she has put her heart into, on behalf of another. Help her, Spirit of God, to grasp the magnitude an act of kindness can mean for a single mom, an elderly shut-in, a mom who needs surgery, but has no one to help at home, as she recovers, a teen-ager who needs to work, but transportation is either not readily available, or possibly, too expensive, parents who have a sick child in the hospital, with no one to watch their other children while they are ministering to that child. Grocery shop and cook for their family...

Serving is all about a passion; one that is born deep in the heart of a servant of God, to minister to others. May Your Princess cultivate a heart filled with gratitude for the opportunities that You give her, Holy Spirit, to partner with You in serving those in need. May she share Your Kingdom Purposes with those she meets, along the pathway of her odyssey journey. Please bless her, God, with a profound sense of peace and well-being in the depths of her soul. In the name of the God who came to serve His Bride with His Love, Grace, Compassion, and Blessings... Amen.

Bouquets of Grace-Filled Blessings...

"...Draw near to the divine Servant who gave His all for you. Let His fire ignite the flame of humble servanthood in your heart; then find someone else and serve them as Jesus served you."

-David Cape & Tommy Tenney
God's Secret To Greatness
Regal - A Division of Gospel Light

Gems of Wisdom...

John 13:1-9
Luke 22:27
Romans 12:10-13
John 12:26

Refreshing Hugs...

Find a quiet spot outdoors. Give Jesus thanks for modeling true servanthood... If you have begun a Gratitude Journal, make a list of all the times and all the ways you can think of that God has brought someone into your life that you have had the honor of serving.

Regarding a true saint of Christ, Oswald says this,"...not one who proclaims the Gospel merely, but one who becomes the broken bread and poured out wine in the hands of Jesus Christ for other lives." What a beautiful description of a true servant's heart.

PART FIVE: FEELING A SLIGHT BIT UNFORGIVING? BECOME A "GRACE PLANTING" PRINCESS

"It may not be an easy thing to live in sweet fellowship with all those with whom we come into contact, but that is why we are given the grace of God... If I am not willing to forgive those who may have committed some single offense against me, what a mean, contemptible thing it would be for me to ask God to forgive the ten thousand sins of which I have been guilty!"

-D.L. Moody
The Joy Of Answered Prayer
Whitaker House

CREATED TO CONNECT

"But now you belong to Christ Jesus. Though you once
were far away from God, now you have been brought
near to him because of the blood of Christ."
Ephesians 2:13

Many of us have experienced a longing for family or friends who live
far away. Our heart yearns for them and we'd love to see them often, but
sometimes we are not able to do so, because, we are restricted by finances, or
time off of work, or perhaps, weather conditions... My husband and I have had
several experiences that parallel this example. With us it now includes four
of our seven children and their families, who all live in different parts of the
country. It also involves five couples, our dear friends, who have moved to five
different states. Sometimes, it's not an easy thing, when we've prayed together
for many years. Or, when we have shared our hearts, our joys, our sorrows,
our issues, our children's activities, and now, each couple's GrandSugars and
what activities they are involved in...

There are some things that are not easy to share over a phone line.
One day, I suppose I was close to experiencing a mini pity party, because it
seemed as if everyone had moved far away and I wasn't sure when Honey
and I would be able to re-connect with our special friends. I began to
realize, that particular day, just how important it was to pray for each of
our friends and their families, each day, just as we pray for our children
and their families. Prayer is one way to remain connected, even if separated
geographically.

I began to pray the words of Ezekiel 34:26, over our family, and, the
families of our friends. In the beautiful style of a word picture, the Lord,
through His prophet Ezekiel, whispers this promise...

"I will cause My people and their homes...to be a blessing. And I
will send showers of blessings, which will come
just when they are needed."

Suddenly, there it was! There was the realization that when we pray scripture and ask for our friends to receive blessings from the Lord, and favor in the eyes of those they need that favor from, the Lord begins to do just that. When we believe God's Promises of blessings for us, we can be assured that He always keeps His Promises!

We may not be able to see our loved ones or friends in person, very often; we can, however, communicate in a number of different ways... by phone, letter, e-mail... When we continually speak God's blessings and favor over the lives of our family and friends, and, when we continue to ask our Abba, to shower blessings over others, we know that we are "Created To Connect." And that "connection" is a most precious blessing. We were created to "connect" with our God, first and foremost, as Epheisans 2:13 states. And that "connection" is foundational to our relationship with others...

May the Holy Spirit draw you near to Him. May you share sacred moments with the One who loves you. And, may each of your relationships contain "Showers of Blessings" descending down from the heart of your Abba Father, straight to the hearts of those you hold dear!

Heart Whispers...

Dear God, You are the Great Heart Connector,

When we hurt, You hurt... When we weep, You weep... When we are in need of comfort... You, Holy Spirit, are our Comforter. When we need favor, You provide us with that favor. When we need to connect, You are right there to connect with us. And, when we need earthly connections, You provide those with whom we can form godly relationships.

Please bless Your Princess with that special "balcony girl," one who is able to laugh with her... cry with her... pray with her... and love her enough to correct her... that special one who will become her encourager! I ask, Lord, that You bless the odyssey path You have personally mapped out for her, with each step that she takes... In the name of the God who delights in providing us with Showers of His Richest Blessings... Amen.

Bouquets of Grace-Filled Blessings...

"We were designed to connect with others. Connecting is life... In connecting with God, we gain life. In connecting with others, we nourish and experience that life as we freely share it."

-Larry Crabb
Connecting
Word Publishing

Gems of Wisdom...

Galatians 6:2
Philippians 2:1-4
Ephesians 2:19
Colossians 1:3-8
Hebrews 10:25

Refreshing Hugs...

Set aside two or three times a month, for a few hours, to meet with one of your friends. If they live out-of-state, or, perhaps, out of the country, establish a set time via your cell... in order to do some voice-to-voice, or, face-to-face catching up.

Purpose to learn something about that friend that you were never aware of before. Perhaps you might put together a scrapbook, including pictures and some events you attended together. These become invaluable, and serve as some beautiful memory-making moments the two of you shared, when you both lived in the same location.

Laugh, have fun, but also be prepared to offer what they might need in terms of a listening ear, a kind word, or perhaps some constructive input regarding an action plan they might be planning to put together. These ingredients may be just what that special friend is needing, and can be blended together to even further enhance your close, connected relationship.

THE POWER OF FORGIVENESS

"The Lord is righteous in everything He does; He is
filled with kindness. The Lord is close to all who call
on Him, yes, to all who call on Him sincerely.
Psalm 145:17-18

Life in Ravensbruck Concentration Camp, according to Corrie Ten
Boom, was a faith-building experience extending from God's heart to hers.
Sentenced to a life of persecution beyond what most of us would ever be
capable of conceiving, much less able to endure, Corrie survived. Not only
did she survive, but her faith in God continued to increase daily. Corrie's
experiences at Ravensbruck are recorded in the book entitled, *The Hiding
Place*. Corrie expressed her undying passion as she exclaimed, "We must go
everywhere. We must tell people that no pit could be so deep that Jesus was
not deeper still. They will believe us because we were here."

In the midst of a place where people were herded like cattle, and continuously
tortured day after day, Corrie survived. This woman of great faith acheived a
richness of depth in her relationship with her God that many of us long to have.

Much can be gleaned from this woman of God...this courageous woman
of valor. Corrie could have excused feelings of bitterness, anger, hatred...
justifying those feelings on the cell she was forced to occupy, in a prison in
Holland; being separated from her sister, after being arrested at their home
in Holland for hiding the Jewish people. She and her sister Betsie were
emprisioned in Holland, for a little over three months. The sisters were then
transfered to Vught, a German concentration camp in Holland, and were
placed together there. The final transfer, for the sisters, was to the dreaded
Ravensbruck concentration camp in Germany.

The Ten Boom family, motivated by God's love, became instrumental in
hiding many, in Holland, from the German military. Corrie, along with her
family, helped provide food, shelter, and most of all love and human kindness
to countless people who had no place to hide. All of this took place by the
orchestration of the Holy Spirit... And, through it all, our Mighty God gave
strength to Corrie, and the members of her family, who risked their own lives
to hide Jewish men, women, and children...

Corrie miraculously survived the perils of the camp, but sadly, her sister succumbed to the brutal and atrocious treatment at the hand of the soldiers in the Ravensbruck concentration camp, coupled with Betsie's fragile physical condition. Corrie's life, and testimony, has remained a hallmark of courage for every Christian! Years later, Corrie was giving her testimony. At the end of her story, a man came forward to ask her forgiveness for murdering her sister Betsie. Corrie granted the man those forgiving words of grace he so wanted to hear... She did so by extending the same grace she knew her Lord extends to His own.

Heart Whispers...

Dear God, You are the God who gives us Your Supernatural Strength so we can be overcomers,

Corrie Ten Boom's life demonstrates the forgiveness that You desire each Princess to exemplify, toward those who have hurt us deeply. The desire of our hearts should be to reflect that same measure of forgiveness that Corrie extended to her sister's perpetrator.

Thank You, Lord, for Christians, throughout history, who defended their faith, regardless of the cost to their own well being... May we be found faithful, Lord Jesus, as we go out into the world and spread the Good News of Your Gospel of Salvation, Love, Grace, Truth, and Forgiveness. In the name of the God who gives and gives and gives, without measure, to those who will listen and receive... Amen.

Bouquets of Grace-Filled Blessings...

"And so I discovered that it is not on our forgiveness any more than on our goodness that the world's healing hinges, but on His. When He tells us to love our enemies, He gives, along with the command, the love itself."

-Corrie Ten Boom
The Hiding Place
with John & Elizabeth Sherrill
(U.S.A.- A Crossings Classic)

Gems of Wisdom...

Psalm 86:5
John 20:23
2 Corinthians 2:7
Matthew 6:14-15
Matthew 5:23-24

Refreshing Hugs...

If there is someone who has hurt you, or offended, wounded, or hurt someone you love, and you need to extend forgiveness and grace to that individual, ask the Holy Spirit to help you by giving you the grace to forgive. If the individual is no longer alive, or, is not a safe person for you to be in contact with, write a letter stating your forgiveness, then discard it. This gesture may help bring the closure and peace you may be seeking.

WARM FUZZIES AND A LATTE

"...may the God of peace, who brought again from the dead our Lord
Jesus, equip you with all you need for doing His will. May He produce
in you, through the power of Jesus Christ, all that is pleasing to Him..."
Hebrews 13:20-21

What was it like to be a child? For some of us, childhood memories were
of a warm, carefree, fun-filled time, all wrapped up in a secure enviornment.
There was a sense of being protected and nurtured. Basic needs for affection,
shelter, clothing, food... were all met. Of course, not all of us grew up in a
nurturing enviornment. And, even if that were the case, the best of homes is
never perfect. Sadly, there may even have been times that we wrestled with
feelings of anger or rejection...

Whether you are a single parent, married, a single person, or married
with children, and just wanting some viable solutions to help you de-stress
your life, I'd like to give you lots of encouragement! Let me share what
worked for me as a "stressed-out" single mom, and a new believer, challenged
with Type A personality issues... When I finally got sick and tired of being
sick and tired, I began to surrender my daily burders to Jesus. I was tired
of living on the edge of an emotional tightrope, and began to trust that the
Lord's Promises to His Kids were, in fact, written in stone. It was soon after
I had become a believer, that the Lord began transforming my life, one small
change at a time.

The Spirit of God showed me that, as a single parent, there were
times when I had a tendency to operate out of a sense of guilt, attempting
to compensate for the lack of a two-parent home. In order to provide a
more stable home enviornment, I knew things had to change... I knew I
had to change. Why was I such a perfectionist? Did you know that, by
definition, being a perfectionist gives one the ability to make everybody
around them crazy, including themselves? Okay, that might be a slight
exaggeration, but hey, if the "Glass Slipper" fits... And, that certainly was
the case with me.

I don't begin to have all the answers, but I do know this much, the
Lord won't yank that agenda, the one you so painstakingly constructed,

out of your clutches! You must take the first step and offer it to Him to downsize.

Oh, my poor daughter, Danielle. The whole thing started when I bought her that first calendar. She was only seven, but noticed that my commitment "To Do" agenda was very full, color-coded, with little breathing room. That night, she retreated to her room, only to emerge later, with her first calendar, bringing it to mom as if it were a blue ribbon prize. Beginning at 7:00 AM and ending at bed time, she had color coded her schedule... And I thought mine was full? All I could say, under my breath, of course, because I would never hurt her feelings, was, "Oh My Gosh! I've created a miniature me-another Type A Personality, in miniature form...

I know I have said this before, but it's so true that I believe it is worth repeating: None of us can do it all! If you happen to be a Type A, my best advice would be to release that "To Do" list to Him. He can help you prioritize, and bring order to your over-committed, no "me time," life...

There is such a freeing moment that occurs when we surrender our heart, time, goals, and struggles, amidst all the "To Do's" we feel we must get done... yesterday... It is such a liberating feeling to just hand them over to Jesus. God wanted to be included in the smallest details of my day. He was the only One who was able to make sense, and bring order, out of the gazillion thoughts, (please give me a Princess Pass Card on this exaggeration), churning around in my brain. He was the only One who could bring a wonderfully calming state to my rampant emotions, whacked-out feelings, or whatever one might choose to label them.

Can you stand some more good news? Jesus wants to help you reorganize your mind. He wants to deliver His Darlin's from what I like to call, the "Mad Hatter Tea Party Syndrome." This syndrome could more commonly be referred to as "Life." The Lord is beckoning you to slip away with Him to your quiet place. Can you sense His Sweet Presence drawing you to Him? He would like nothing more than to have you fall back into His arms and rest... rest, while He cradles you in His Peace.

Once you have learned the secret of truly resting in the Lord, He wants to teach you how to be filled with outrageous "Tickled Pink" Delight!!! Even if your immediate world appears to be falling apart at the seams... God plans on being there to share in your up and coming debut...

INTRODUCING...

SPARKLING... GLITTERING... SHIMMERING...
PRINCESS MOMENTS...

NOW FEATURING:

WELL RESTED... ENERGIZED... FOCUSED...
CREATIVE... LOVING...

SIMPLY AMAZING...

YOU!

Heart Whispers...

Dear God, our Perfect Event Planner,

Please help Your Princess set aside precious moments, each day, to rest in Your Love. May she invite You, God, to wander into her thoughts, her schedule, her dreams, her goals...any time You desire. Should any of those areas need readjusting, I pray that she will hand them over to You, Lord, to do with as You will...

Since some of us grew up in a less than desireable enviornment, I ask that You fill in the gaps; those areas where emotionally distant family members may have made it difficult to cultivate a healthy lifestyle of our own. Bless Your Beautiful Princess with Your Simply Lavish Love! In the sweet, sweet name of the God who decorates our lives with His Forever Grace... Amen.

Bouquets of Grace-Filled Blessings...

"Surrending to God means allowing Him to do what He wants to do with your life; it puts you smack-dab in the center of God's will..."

-Joni Lamb
Surrender All
Waterbrook Press

Gems of Wisdom...

Romans 12:2
James 4:7

Refreshing Hugs...

Write down a few things you believe the Lord is asking you to relinquish. Then journal your thoughts and feelings regarding giving those things up. Be as honest as possible. Then ask God for the grace to surrender them to Him, one by one.

Now, stand back. Get ready to be amazed by your Amazing God. He is the Great Restorer of your life... For every one thing you surrender to God, you are one step closer to His Perfect Will for your life! Perfect!

GETTIN' RID OF ALL THAT STUFF

"The Son reflects God's own glory, and everything about Him represents
God exactly. He sustains the universe by the mighty power of His
command. After He died to cleanse us from the stain of sin, He sat down
in the place of honor at the right hand of the majestic God of heaven."
Hebrews 1:3

As I was meditating on this scripture verse, I began to fumble around
for the right words to attempt to describe the awe-inspiring, powerful "word
picture" that Hebrews 1:3 paints for the finite mind. I came to the conclusion
that there are really no words in any language to give justice to this scripture.
It is simply incomprehensible to grasp, much less wrap our minds around the
concept that the entire universe is held together by the very Word that spoke
this world into existence...

Jesus does not just personify an image of God-He is God. Revelation
4:11, expresses it so perfectly, as the verse describes the scene this way, "...the
twenty-four elders fall down and worship the One who lives forever and ever.
And they lay their crowns before the throne and say,

"You are worthy, O Lord our God,
to receive glory and honor and power.
For You created everything, and it is for
Your pleasure that they exist and were
created."

When we praise Him, we tend to become acutely aware of our inadequacy
to bring glory to the Lord. We are struck with the reality that we have so many
shortcomings... shortcomings that, when brought to bear in light of God's
holiness, leave us feeling totally unworthy. But, since we were created in the
image of the God, we must emulate the Lord Jesus by observing His response
to life's circumstances. By following His footprints, we then learn how to live
out our Christianity, day by day...

If we are to be like our Messiah, we must act like Him. If we are to act like
Jesus, we must begin to think as He thinks. In the NKJV, Romans 11:34, describes

it this way: "For who has known the mind of the Lord?... For of Him and through Him and to Him are all things, to whom be glory forever. Amen." Another verse, found in I Corinthians 2:16, as it is phrased in the NKJV, is explicit when it comes to our ability to think like Christ, "But we have the mind of Christ."

So, if we purpose in our hearts to saturate ourselves in the Word, He will show us how to really think like He does... The Holy Spirit empowers us, so we can renew our mind, and "get rid of all that stuff" that distracts us and keeps us from staying closely connected to Him.

Renewing your mind simply means, to fill your mind daily with the following four Spiritual Disciplines: Prayer, Praise, Worship, and the Word of God. While there are many more disciplines, these four should give you a good starting point. Allow the Spirit of the Living God to help you renew your mind, as you seek Him daily...

Heart Whispers...

Dear God, our Master Prayer Warrior,

Your Word is filled to overflowing with Your Healing Balm that is perfect for every need. Empower Your Princess with Your Strength and Your Presence. Help her, Holy Spirit, to renew her mind, getting rid of all that "stuff" that could clutter her thoughts, turning her focus on other things that are distracting her from placing her focus on You.

May Your Princess develop a heart filled with desire and determination to glean all she can about You. May she continue to grow closer and closer to You, God, with each passing day... In the name of the God who paints our destiny, one footstep at a time... Amen.

Bouquets of Grace-Filled Blessings...

"Be diligent in your search. Be hungry in your quest, relentless in your pilgrimage... read about Jesus... seek him... seek your king... Can you think of a greater gift than to be like Jesus?"

-Max Lucado
Just Like Jesus
Word Publishing

Gems of Wisdom...

Hebrews 11:6
2 Corinthians 3:18
Psalm 119:2
Acts 17:11
Psalm 42:1-2
Colossians 3:1-4

Refreshing Hugs...

Suggestion: Read Psalm 119 in its entirety. Encourage someone to read a portion of God's Word every day. Keep them accountable by asking them to share regarding what they have read, and how it might have impacted them. Did their reading lead them to praise or prayer or worship? This works great as a reciprocal study where you share, as well.

THE MANY FACETS OF GOD'S LOVE

"Because Your lovingkindness is better than life, my lips shall praise You.
Thus I will bless You while I live; I will lift up my hands in Your name."
Psalm 63:3-4 NKJV

The Lover of our soul, El Shaddai, God Almighty, continues to pour His unending Love into our hearts. We can't help but praise Him and thank Him for His incredible lovingkindness which, in the NKJV of Psalm 63:3, states it this way, "…is better than life."

As a result of His Unfailing Love, our souls are set free to take flight. The Spirit of God can take us into the very throne room of our heavenly Father. It is at the foot of His Throne that we are given the freedom to express our gratitude, not merely with words, but with our obedience.

King David, in Psalm 145:3-7, and 147:1, 5, 7-8, proclaims these truths, in poetic fashion, which serve to guide us in praising God with all the praise that resides in our heart and in our soul, "Great is the Lord! He is most worthy of praise! His greatness is beyond discovery! Let each generation tell its children of Your mighty acts. I will meditate on Your majestic, glorious splendor and Your wonderful miracles. Your awe-inspiring deeds will be on every tongue; I will proclaim Your greatness. Everyone will share the story of Your wonderful goodness; they will sing with joy of Your righteousness."

Praise God every opportunity you get! Prayer and Praise are two out of the three most precious commodities we have been given by our Messiah. So, seize every opportunity you have been given, by your Maker, to use them to bring God Glory!

My prayer for you, Precious Princess of the Living God, is that you will take time to explore the magnitude of the lovingkindness of the King of Glory in His Word. I pray that your mouth be continually filled with praise and adoration, like David's was, for the One who has given you life, and the destiny He longs to bring to pass in you! Praise the God who desires to set your feet dancing with joy, to the rhythm of His Heartbeat!

Heart Whispers...

Dear God, You are so Great and Worthy of all Praise,

We can praise You now, Lord God, in our earthly bodies. But one day, You will transform these fleshly bodies into glorified ones, and we'll be able to praise and glorify You perfectly. May Your Princess await that day with great anticipation... Until then, God, please fill her with Your Glory and Your Grace. May she use her testimony for Your Praise and Honor! In the name of the God of all Truth... the God who is our Rock, our Redeemer, our Refuge, our Shield, our Salvation, our soon and coming King... Amen.

Bouquets of Grace-Filled Blessings...

"God wants us to be passionate about knowing Him... (John 17:3)... Nothing else matters...God wants to wrap His arms around you and fill you with a passion to know Him more."

-Tricia McCarey Rhodes
The Soul At Rest
Bethany House Publishers

Gems of Wisdom...

Exodus 3:14
Isaiah 44:6
John 6:35
John 10:9-16
Revelation 1:17-18

Refreshing Hugs...

Give yourself the gift of Refreshing by looking up all the scriptures that pertain to His desire for you to become passionate about knowing Him more. Read Revelation 1:17-18. Start with the three I AM'S of God that He mentions in these verses. Then look up other "I AM" verses. A bible concordance would be a great starting place. Should you have one in the back of the bible version you use, that would be great. If not, look them up on the internet, or at your local library.

If you are keeping a journal, perhaps you would like to write God a letter asking Him to fill you with a passion to know Him...to really know Him...

Blessings to you, as you study the treasures that are hidden in the depths of His Word. And may you develop an even greater passion in your soul, to know what God says about Himself, His Love, and the Power and Truth contained in His Word...

WELCOME TO THE PRESENT

"And He received honor and glory from God the Father when
God's glorious, majestic voice called down from heaven,
"This is My beloved Son; I am fully pleased with Him."
2 Peter 1:17

The following is the exclaimation that bursts forth from the mouth of John the Baptist, in John 1:29, "Look! There is the Lamb of God who takes away the sin of the world!" John continues, in John 1:30-31, as he makes this proclaimation, "He is the one I was talking about when I said, 'Soon a man is coming who is far greater than I am, for He existed long before I did.' I didn't know He was the One, but I have been baptizing with water in order to point Him out to Israel.'"

When a hunger is birthed inside every child of God-a hunger for more of our Savior, then we will begin to see Jesus in a way we have never seen Him before. Maybe, at this moment in time, you are intentionally seeking more and more of Jesus, determined to make Him the very center of your life. Once again, I want to encourage you; Jesus has all the time you need, in order to help you go deeper into a study of God's Word.

I'd like to suggest, once again, getting alone with God-I mean really alone. When it's just you and Jesus, without all of the distractions modern conveniences can sometimes present, ask the Lord to quiet your heart. Be totally honest about what you are feeling- your apprehensions, your fears, your sadness, your grief, disappointment, anxieties... Give God all of it so He can exchange your emotions, with His peace.

Be patient with yourself. If you are struggling with issues, you probably didn't arrive there with a bag full of those problems, by overnite travel. No, some of the challenges you have found yourself confronting, have been there for awhile. They may just now be surfacing. Make sure you have plenty of tissues handy for those tearful moments. Just a word of advice-don't stay in the past too long. Afterall, you did things differently then. Here's a dash of hope: you'll only be in this place for a short season. Princess, the Spirit of God wants to move you ahead to a place called "The Present".

As you grow deeper in your study of the knowledge and grace of God; as you begin to work on the issues that have troubled you, or caused you pain, they will begin to diminish in intensity. In fact, God wants to fling back the curtains of your soul. Why? So you will know that He is right there, and, in fact, He has never left your side. Be assured, His Precious Princess, that He never will. You see, God is working all things together for your best interests, because you love Him, and because He chose you. He chose you so that He could work His purposes in your life, just as He promises in Romans 8:28.

In the meantime, God is so very patient. He will wait, as you begin to see His healing touch in the helping hand of a friend, the beautiful melody of a songbird, a tree as its branches begin to grow stately and mature. He will wait, as you begin to take note of a child who sheds the selfish nature inherited at birth, and grows into a giving, loving, nurturing adult. The scars of many years of dealing with emotional pain will begin to dissipate. God's imprint will move across those memories, causing them to slowly fade away.

Your Abba Daddy knows all about you. In fact, He was there when you had to deal with that failed relationship. He stood by you when you felt stuck in the quicksand of disillusionment. He was at the scene when others rejected you or called you foolish for reacting the way you did. He was also there when you felt abandoned-left out in the world with no place to turn for comfort-or so it seemed. Every tear that you shed struck a tender chord in His heart. And, He cried in unison with you. Every time your heart was broken, so was His. Every time your dreams were shattered, He felt the anguish, as He held out His arms to hold you tightly.

God desires to whisper His encouragement to your heart, "Dream bigger dreams, My Jewel. Don't Quit. Keep on reaching for your goals. I am right here beside you. You can do this. In fact, My Daughter, let's do this together..." As you listen for God's affirmations, things may be starting to look a little different. I exhort you, my sister in Jesus, to look up. Look up to the One who will give you the strength, the stamina, the courage to go forward. Look up to the One who is able to put new dreams in your heart. Look up to the One who says, "Nothing is too difficult for Me...'"

Are you beginning to sense a longing in your soul to hear the words your Father God wants to whisper to you? Close your eyes and listen with your heart. Listen for His soft voice. Listen for His encouraging words. Listen, as He whispers proudly in your ear, "You are My Beloved Princess. I long to dream your biggest dreams with you. I long to help you reach your highest goals and aspirations..." Listen for His whispers... Listen...

Heart Whispers...

Dear God, El Roee, You are the God who sees into the heart of every precious Daughter of Yours,

Bless Your Princess with Your sweet words, as they drift quietly down into the depths of her heart. Affirm each of her efforts to be pleasing to You. Thank You, Lord, that the pleasure You take in communing with her has nothing to do with her performance, but has everything to do with who she is to You- Your Special Daughter.

May she discover just how much You value her, and how priceless she is to You. In the name of Jehovah Shammah, the God whose signature is present on each page of our lives. Amen.

Bouquets of Grace-Filled Blessings...

"...don't wait for catastrophe before you unwrap grace. Embrace it today. Remember... the past is gone. The future is unknown. There is only one minute in which you are alive. This minute! Right here, right now."

-Barbara Johnson
Present Moment Grace
Devotion from *Extravagant Grace*
Zondervan Publishing House

Gems of Wisdom...

Psalm 84:11
2 Corinthians 13:13
Ephesians 6:24
Ephesians 1:7

Refreshing Hugs...

As I write the end of this segment, I am reminded to give thanks often for you. And while our personal odysseys may never cross paths during our time here on earth, I'd like to reiterate the words of Romans 1:8, "...How I thank God through Jesus Christ for each one of you." Blessings!

NEXT TIME I'LL ASK GOD TO FIX IT!

"This is real love. It is not that we loved God, but that He loved
us and sent His Son as a sacrifice to take away our sins."
I John 4:10

In John 14:6, Jesus says this, when speaking with His disciples, "I am the way, the truth, and the life. No one can come to the Father except through Me." There is no other access to our Father God, except through Jesus. We, as a universe made up of billions of people, have tried a multitude of other ways-ways too numerous to be counted. We have looked to men as idols, we have declared animals to be gods, we have tried alcohol, drugs, possessions... The list is too exhausting to even think about. But, to no avail. Why? The reason is simple, "Jesus is the way, the truth, and the life." There is no other way!

I began my odyssey by traveling, in my mind, back to my past. I definitely didn't want to live there again, but I believed that if I could better understand my past, I might, with a huge dose of God's Grace, be able to gain access to those insights which would bring restoration and wholeness to my life.

Almost immediately after meeting the Lord, I became saddened at the thought of the things I had tried, in order to "fix" my family of origin; in order to fix Jan. I made this astute observation: Superglue can't fix it! It just gets so sticky... you know what I mean? Nothing can fix the past, not one single thing. It is what it is. But, God can fix a myriad of broken promises, painful memories, hurt feelings... You name it-God can fix it. He can redeem those failures, those words that should never have passed through our lips, those judgmental thoughts, those decisions that led to devastating consequences...

It took literally years before I finally came to the conclusion that what I had been told many years ago was true. God is the One who places a void in our hearts for Himself. And, God is the only One who can fill that void. I had been attempting to fill that void through so many other ways. Here's what I discovered: Only when we come into communion with our Lord, only when we surrender, only when we lay down our stubborn will-then, and only then, will He become the only One we will ever need to please. Only God can be all that we need. All the rest of our relationships can be beautiful and sweet, kind and loving, and that is so precious, but, our relationship with our Savior is the ultimate gift!

Please join me, in this moment, in committing to commune with our Papa God, through His Living Word... Commiting to spend time at His feet in Contemplative Prayer... Committing to devote time, each day, praising and worshipping Him. Committing to give God thanks for the love He gives so lavishly-for the sacrifice He made, to wipe the slates of our lives clean. Extraordinary Love from an Extraordinary God...

Heart Whispers...

Dear God, You are an Extraordinary God,

Thank You for Your atoning sacrifice. You redeem our past, give us rich opportunities to fulfill Your Great Commission in our present, and You speak blessing and anointing over all our tomorrows... Thank You, Lord Jesus, for gracing us with the assurance of a future Eternity to spend in Your Presence... Glory!

Bouquets of Grace-Filled Blessings...

"Think of the most beautiful gifts you could ever imagine in your heart and mind. God is saying, Just wait! These are nothing compared to what I have for you to open for all eternity!"

-Sharon Hoffman
Untie the Ribbons
Whitaker House

Gems of Wisdom...

Psalm 107:1-2
Psalm 68:19
John 4:10
Ecclesiastes 4:12-13

Refreshing Hugs...

The following is a memorable quote I found in a perpetual calendar that puts our response to life's day-to-day challenges in the proper perspective:

"It's usually through our hard times, the unexpected and not-according-to-plan times, that we experience God in more intimate ways. We discover an unquenchable longing to know Him more."

Anonymous
365 Stress-free Moments for Women
Calendar compiled by Joanie Garborg Barbour Publishing, Inc.

SPEAKING WORDS OF TRUTH WRAPPED IN A BLANKET OF GRACE

"Then the Lord touched my mouth and said, "See,
I have put My words in your mouth!"
Jeremiah 1:9

Not exactly what some might refer to as a popular guy, the Old Testament prophet, Jeremiah, on the contrary, was sometimes referred to as a prophet of gloom, but much can be learned from this man upon whom the hand of God rested. Jeremiah 1:4-5 tells us that God had a special calling for him, "The Lord gave me a message. He said, I knew you before I formed you in your mother's womb. Before you were born, I set you apart and appointed you as My spokesman to the world." With every child of God, before He forms us in our mothers' womb, He knows all about us. What an amazing realization... God knows each of us personally!

A man, who was quite verbal with His feelings, we know Jeremiah as a man who was often given to criticism; some of that criticism was self-directed. Jeremiah expressed his feelings toward man, and, to his God, as well. Yet a wonderful truth was revealed to Jeremiah when the Lord proclaimed, "...I have put My words in your mouth."

Sometimes we look to our own intelligence, or we depend upon our own feelings or emotions, which are expressed in the way we articulate our thoughts. While we are not all called to be prophets, every Princess is called to be a spokeswoman for the Lord. We may be assured that God has put His hand upon us. While the calling of each Princess takes us down a different pathway, we are always to look to our God, and not to our own abilities or gifts. The reason is that it is God who endows each Princess with unique abilities and gifts, before we are ever born. It is God who sees the entire picture of our life, as it is unfolding.

Our intelligence is limited, but His is unlimited. Our feelings may betray us, but His Grace, upon our lives, never fails. Our words, at times, are inadequate, but His Word is always perfect.

When we look to Jesus, trusting with all our heart in a loving God, we begin to rely upon His words more than our own. When we put ourselves in the hands of our Master, we become yielded vessels, to be used for His Glory. We can ask God to put His words in our mouths and He will do it...

So, I would say to you, let your words become His words, to be used for His Glory! May the words you speak be uplifting, edifying, encouraging, and filled with His Grace, always!

Heart Whispers...

Dear God, You endow us with spiritual gifts, specially customized for Your Girls,

Oh, how I long to be a vessel used by You! Please put Your words in my mouth. Each time I am called to enpower or inspire a client, a Grand Sugar, a mom, one who serves me, a child, a co-worker, a family member, a nana...help me to speak Your Truth. Each time I am called upon to exhort, may I always do so in a spirit of love and grace.

Thank You, Lord God, for the ministry of encouragement You desire each Princess to replicate. Help us to become like the one You called Barnabas, which means, "Son of Encouragement". God, please bless this Princess as she directs her efforts, with intentionality, to be in the direct center of Your will for her life. And, as Your ambassador, may she be a source of encouragement to many. In the name of the God who encourages and inspires His Kids to walk in His ways, and to extend the gift of grace, enveloped in love, just as He does. Amen.

Bouquets of Grace-Filled Blessings...

"We all need encouragement. We can live without it... but unless we receive that warm nurturing, we never reach our full potential, and we seldom bear fruit."

-Florence Littauer
The Gift of Encouragement
Word Publishing

Gems of Wisdom...

Psalm 19:14
Proverbs 25:11
Hebrews 3:13

Refreshing Hugs...

Speak a word of encouragement to at least three people this week. Season each word with grace! Read Hebrews 3:13 each day, for the next five days. As you do, think about some creative ways you can extend the gift of encouragement to the next Princess the Lord places on your heart.

SPRINKLED WITH TEARS...
DRENCHED WITH JOY...

How painful it was to write that letter! Heartbroken, I cried over it. I didn't want to hurt you, but I wanted you to know how very much I love you."
2 Corinthians 2:4

An excellent example of the Lord's love and compassion, the Apostle Paul expounds upon the passion with which he loved his brothers and sisters in the faith. Woven throughout Paul's letters to the churches, we find his zealous love for them expressed in such a poignant fashion.

The Holy Spirit filled Paul up with such an abundance of His Love that it virtually spilled over into every letter Paul wrote. Wouldn't it be marvelous to feel, and to be able to express that degree of love? Here's what we can do; we can get on our knees, or, if that is not possible, we can bow in our heart before our Papa God. We can ask Him to flood us with a river of His compassion for others.

Now, I can't read your mind, or your mail, as we say it in today's vernacular, but you may be thinking something like this: "Gee, Jan, it's not easy to express that kind of compassion if you have been wounded like I have, or, if you've felt the degree of emotional pain that rocks your world..." Well, you are absolutely right. I don't know the extent of the painful ordeals that have reeked havoc upon your soul. I don't know the heartaches, or, the depth of loss you have experienced. However, I have been in relationships which have inhibited me from becoming the victorious woman that God designed me to be. Having said that, I take total responsibility, in the respect that I allowed it to happen. Instead of investing my energy into learning how to establish healthy boundaries, I kept quiet.

Now, for the good news: God has a plan, a plan that just might prove to be of help for your dilemma. Here are some steps you might consider implementing to help you in becoming genuinely compassionate, without creating an atmosphere that may cause co-dependent issues to arise, in any given relationship. The premise is based on a decision to step outside of your own problems, in order to become an encourager, a balcony coach for another person. As she shares her hopes and dreams, you are now focused on ways in which you might inspire her to attain those hopes and dreams. This step can be accomplished through walking alongside her, offering her hope and encouragement.

True selflessness, as Jesus demonstrated it, comes by developing a posture of placing someone else's needs before our own. I have placed the following suggestions in a sequence of steps for you to ponder. My prayer is that these steps will help you, should you struggle with feelings of guilt or shame-feelings that may be inhibiting you from reaching out to help the next person become the victorious Princess God designed her to be:

Step #1   In your quiet time, ask the Spirit of God to help you get beyond your feelings of guilt concerning your sins. Please know that He wants you to leave your past with Him. Visualize the Lord drowning your feelings of guilt over your past by pitching them into the depths of a vast ocean... The NKJV of Jeremiah 31:34 states the promise God makes in a new covenant that He establishes with Israel, "...For I will forgive their iniquity, and their sin I will remember no more".

Step #2   Whatever that wound looks like to you, declare it gone in the name of Jesus, along with the power it might still hold over your life. Declare it broken, forever, because of the shed Blood of Jesus. Repeat this step, as often as necessary, until you get the closure you are seeking.

Step #3   Now, consider stepping outside of yourself in order to begin interceding for someone God has given you a burden for. I took a magnetic board and created a collage by putting pictures of people, along with photos of the foreign countries where they live. I've attached a small paragraph that serves as a reminder for me to pray specifically for needs that they have.

At the back of this book, you will find five blank pages allocated for your personal journal entitled: *My Princess Prayer Odyssey Daybook*. You have my permission to make as many additional copies of the title page as you wish.

This daybook can provide you with a day by day account of where God is taking you in your spiritual walk, the Princesses He places on your heart to minister to, memories of family events, and a way to keep track of people from other lands, who have so many needs that you may be praying about. This daybook can lead to making a financial commitment, as a family, to support a given ministry, or a missionary/missionary family who is sponsored by your church family. Should you want more information regarding how to begin a *Princess Prayer Odyssey Daybook,* please see my contact information at the back of this book.

Step #4   Ephesians 6:18 reminds us to, "Pray at all times and on every occasion in the power of the Holy Spirit. Stay alert and be persistent in your prayers for all Christians everywhere." This step will take time, practice, and patience. Continue to pray, with persistence, until you begin to see the fruit of your prayers, coupled with the prayers of others, bring help to those precious ones being prayed for.

Step #5   Because there are times when we are not equipped, financially, to sponsor a missionary, or an entire family with children in need of nutritious meals, on an ongoing basis, consider the following idea: Every time you go food shopping, have a list of staple food items that are on sale like, cereal, canned goods, etc. As you do your own shopping, pick up one or two items that you can store in a space in your own home. When you have collected a few grocery bags full of food, take them to your local food bank, or a grocery store that has a barrel for food donations.

If your church provides a pantry, that would be great. If you collect these grocery items over a period of several weeks, this becomes a great way to give to those who are truly in need, without putting a strain on your weekly or monthly grocery budget. Your love offering will be greatly appreciated and will be an awesome blessing, for sure!

Step #6   Thank God for the love He is pouring into you so that you can become a seed planter of encouragement and compassion, wherever your *Princess Prayer Odyssey* takes you!

If you are anything like me, your heart is simply made up of mush. Here are some signs...

You want every romantic movie to have
a sign posted at the end that reads:
"Happily Ever After..."

You want every stray animal to be adopted
by ardent pet lovers.

You want every child's boo boo to have a
magic boo boo healer applied immediately!

You want everyone to suceed in reaching
their goals or realizing their dreams...

And, well, couldn't we just go on and on? If you do happen to have a
heart made of mush, don't let that discourage you. Oftentimes, our tears and
prayers can become healing for someone else.

Let's purpose to thank God each day for His Love that He gives so
extravagantly and abundantly. It is His delight to bless you. I am praying that
you receive, with open arms, the blessings of contentment, encouragement,
and never-ending grace-grace that He showers over your relationships, dreams,
goals, ministry...

Heart Whispers...

Dear God, You always correct with Your Truth, Your Love, and Your Grace,

Help each Princess to welcome correction; without it, we will surely miss the
life lessons You are passionate about teaching us. God, give us the wisdom
to know the difference between becoming an enabler, and becoming an
encourager. Bless each Princess, as she becomes passionate about being an
encourager, for Your Glory! In the name of the God whose enthusiasm is
contagious! Amen.

Bouquets of Grace-Filled Blessings...

"Grace always remembers that it's not your job to get people to like you, it's your job to like people. You are only a decision away from pouring out grace..."

-Barbara Johnson
Filled to Overflowing
A devotion from the book:
Extravagant Grace
Zondervan Publishing House

Gems of Wisdom...

Proverbs 15:23
John 1:16
I Thessalonians 1:1-4

Refreshing Hugs...

Just for fun, decorate a shoe box with pretty wrapping paper. Fill it full of quotations, cards, or prayers which have been a source of encouragement for you.

The next time you are facing something that is discouraging to you, pull out a few quotes or prayers. Once you are finished with them, pass them on, every chance you get! Refill the box often.

My prayer for you today is that you'll be blessed by the abundance of His fabulous grace!

MARVELOUS FRIENDSHIPS

"A man who has friends must himself be friendly, but
there is a friend who sticks closer than a brother."
Proverbs 18:24 NKJV

I marvel each time I read about the love between Jonathan and David. These two men shared a friendship that was a personification of Proverbs 18:24. They shared a bond that refused to be severed. Jonathan and David gave to one another out of the abundance of their hearts; and because they did, they experienced a genuine agape love, a godly love.

If you have experienced rejection in a past relationship, and I don't know of one of us who hasn't, you may be wondering if a friendship like Jonathan and David's could even be possible. In my own experience, rejection and betrayal on the part of a few friends, had scarred my heart; it caused me to react to any notion of a close relationship with extreme caution. Risk another person who might betray me? Not this lady! I never wanted to go through that kind of emotional pain again.

Fast forward... Once again, the Holy Spirit came to the rescue. He touched those damaged places, so damaged that I had little hope of ever having the type of close friendships that Jonathan and David experienced. But God, in His Wisdom, knew differently. There were those who remained true and loyal to our relationship, as they continued to pray for me, day after day, month after month. All the while, God was at His Potter's Wheel, re-working the clay, which represented my heart, over and over and over again, (see Ezekiel 11:19-20). Jeremiah 18:6, also likens us to clay in the hand of the potter. Of course, as believers we know that our Lord is our Master Potter. In Jeremiah 18:6, God was referring to the Israelites, and the hardness of their hearts, and the disobedience they displayed against Him. But we know that, even as believers, we are capable of hardening our own hearts. That was the case with me.

A friend is one who is loyal, one who looks at the good she can bring into that relationship. A friend is one on whom you can rely, to be there for you with godly counsel. A friend who will intercede on your behalf; one who will lend a helping hand, when needed. These are the kind of friends that I like to refer to as heaven sent. Friends like this are placed in our lives because they want God's highest and best for us. A friend, like one I have just described, is a special gift from God. We have touched on this topic in a previous segment. Once again, if you have not experienced such a friendship, ask the Lord to bring a special friend, or friends into your life-friends that will stay by your side, no matter what.

I can honestly say that any one of these friends would go the extra mile for me, and I would do the same for them, in a heartbeat. Three of these women and their families moved out-of-state several years ago. But God, in His loving compassion, moved one of the friends back. Over the years, these dear friends have continued to lift me up, in prayer, asking God to help me in my writing, in my relationships with our seven children and their spouses, my studies, my life coaching practice, and with the daily pressures of a plate filled to overflowing with responsibilities. Here we are, many years later, and I know that they continue to ask the Lord to lift my spirit, should I be growing a little weary.

I feel truly blessed to be surrounded with special friends who rejoice with me in my triumphs, mourn with me when I have suffered a loss, and celebrate with me when God has given me yet another dream to dream... It's my desire that you experience friendships such as those I have described...

So, in my intercessory prayer time, each day, you have my commitment to pray for you, should you want to have close relationships. Though we may not have met personally, I will be asking the Lord for bountiful friendships that will fill your life with special spiritual moms, sisters, dear friends... ones hand-picked by Jesus, just for you!

You see, Beloved Princess, you are so loved by your Abba Father. Keep praying; patiently wait for the blessings God wants to bring in the form of friends, into your life. They will become friends who will pray for your needs, encourage you, inspire you to become the best you can be. They will be friends who will be, oh, so much fun to be around. You know, when we give God our best, He delights to bless us without measure. May God bless you with a rich harvest of friendships, and may you strive daily to be a blessing to each one, in return.

Heart Whispers...

Dear God, You are the God who delights in blessing us with a harvest of friendships,

Please bless each Princess with the gift of special friends You bring into her life. Please bless each one of those friendships with "...showers of blessings" and rays of bright sunshine, even on the cloudiest of days. In the name of the God who showers us with His Love, and with special friends that we will delight in treasuring, always. Amen.

Bouquets of Grace-Filled Blessings...

"Soulmates are rare gifts from God, "second selves sent to strengthen us in our sojourn of life... it is possible, through the strength we have in Christ, to show unfailing love. David and Jonathan provide the needed model..."

-Dee Brestin
The Joy of Women's Friendships
Sharing The Gift of Intimacy
Victor Books

Gems of Wisdom...

I Samuel 20
I Samuel 23:15-18

Refreshing Hugs...

If you have photos taken with a friend, frame a few special ones. Enclose a card telling her just how special the friendship is to you, and how much you appreciate her. Tie the package with a beautiful bow. Then call her and plan a lunch date. As you hand her that special gift, give her a big hug! Have fun!

POURED OUT LOVE

"And this expectation will not disappoint us. For we
know how dearly God loves us, because He has given us
the Holy Spirit to fill our hearts with His love."
Romans 5:5

One of the Hebrew names for God is Yahweh Nissi, which means, "The Lord My Banner." The word "Nissi" means standard or banner. The Holy Spirit is our Banner. It is the Spirit of God who establishes a standard by which we are to live. God has poured His love into our hearts through the Holy Spirit to set an example, a standard for His people.

When we become filled with the Spirit, we begin to really walk by faith-faith in a God who loves us more than we can ever conceive. In turn, we become willing to pour out our love for those God places along our destiny road.

So, I say to you, Beloved of God, pour into others; pour your time, your gifts, your resources...pour into others. It will become an awesome investment, and the rewards will be eternal.

As I pen these words, I am praying for you, my "sis" in Jesus. I may never have met you, but God knows your words before you speak them. He knows your decisions before you even realize the need to make them. He knows your hopes, your aspirations, your dreams, some of which you may have been too afraid to utter because you may think they might take a "Parting Of The Red Sea" miracle to attain. Well, I happen to know the One who can make that miracle happen, and so do you.

My prayer for you is that the Spirit of God will give you a fresh outpouring-an infusion of His blessings over your hopes and dreams. This is His desire for you, so that through your prayers, others may realize their dreams, and they, too, will get blessed. May your relationship with your Father God, become deeper, richer, and sweeter than ever...

Heart Whispers...

Dear God, Yahweh Nissi, You are our Banner and Your Banner over us is love,

Fill Your Princess to overflowing, with Your Love, Spirit of God... Bless her spiritually, physically, emotionally, relationally... Thank You, God, for pouring Your richest, most abundant blessings over the lives of Your Kids... Your Love, Lord, is Awe-Inspiring... In the name of the God who persues us relentlessly, loves us unconditionally, and blesses us immeasurably... Amen.

Bouquets of Grace-Filled Blessings...

"People who have received "the blessing" will live lives full of the fruit of the Spirit...commit...to being servants of God...servants to the body of Christ-never demanding, never requiring...always desirous of giving of themselves as a conduit of the Holy Spirit."

-Thomas E. Trask and Wayde I. Goodall
The Blessing
Zondervan Publishing

Gems of Wisdom...

Isaiah 61:6-7
Ephesians 1:3
Proverbs 10:22

Refreshing Hugs...

Ask God to saturate your heart with His love daily, and to empower you to live a life of poured out love, as you become, like Trask and Goodall say it,"...a conduit of the Holy Spirit."

WHAT A LADY!

"Who can find a virtuous and capable wife? She is worth more
than precious rubies... Charm is deceptive, and beauty does not
last; but a woman who fears the Lord will be greatly praised..."
Proverbs 31:10-31

Proverbs 31:10-31, epitomizes the life of a true woman of God. When I
met Linda and Greg, friends of my husband, twenty-five years ago, I knew
that Linda, an awesome woman of God, modeled the essence of a "Proverbs
31:10-31" woman. For the past twenty plus years, I have watched as Linda,
mom of seven children, walks out the characteristics of a godly woman.

Let's take a closer look at the character that defines this type of woman.
For the sake of space, I will paraphrase. In versus 10 through 19 we find her
getting up before dawn to prepare breakfast for her family. She is described
as being energetic, a hard worker, and one who watches for bargins. She stays
up late into the night and is, in all probability, highly organized. We know
she has a charitable heart because, in verse 20, we are told that, "She extends
a helping hand to the poor and opens her arms to the needy."

This woman "...has no fear of winter for her household because..." she has
seen to it that "all of them have warm clothes." Verse 24 speaks volumes about
her character; a character that is further defined in these words, "She is clothed
with strength and dignity, and she laughs..." This Princess doesn't fear what the
future may bring. Why? Because she is a "Just In Case" lady. God has prepared
her for whatever unknown circumstances may arise, that might adversely affect
her or her loved ones... She is, indeed, "...a woman who fears the Lord..."

Verse 26 emphasizes her godly attitude which is reflected in this manner,
"When she speaks, her words are wise, and kindness is the rule when she gives
instructions." Verse 27 points out that "She carefully watches all that goes
on in her household and does not have to bear the consequences of laziness."
In verse 28 we find that, "Her children stand and bless her. Her husband
praises her..."

Take heart! This woman is not "Superwoman." Rather, she models for
today's woman the kind of integirty, tender loving care, and godly attributes
God wants His Faithful Daughters to possess. My friend, Judy, models a

Proverbs 31 woman so beautifully; it just seems to come so naturally to her. Judy has been an inspiration to me for many years. What a prayer warrior! What a mentor! What an encourager! What a lady!

If we set our hearts on following the paradigm God has carefully crafted for us, we can truly say we are "works in process." If we are feeling inadequate, we shouldn't. Jesus is our Balcony Coach, and will be cheering us on, every step of the way! Guaranteed!

While we have many hats that we are called upon to wear each day, the Spirit of God takes delight in helping us fulfill our roles as daughters, sisters, wives, moms, nanas, aunts, chauffeurs, avid sports enthusiasts for our kids, be it football, baseball, soccer, gymnastics, basketball... Or, maybe it's French lessons, bake sale promotions, charity fund raisers, tutors, Sunday school helpers... Whatever the role, our goal is to be godly examples of women who glorify God, in our thoughts, in our actions, and in our words.

My prayer is that the Lord will place godly women in your life, just as He placed Nancy S, Sherry, Lenora, Diane, Linda, Judy... into my life. God's Girls who will model godly qualities, and are "...clothed with strength and dignity." As they speak into your life, may they speak words that are seasoned with wisdom, integrity, encouragement, and good old-fashioned praise, for every one of your accomplishments! What a blessing they will become to you, His Precious Jewel...

Heart Whispers...

Dear God, You are the Master Craftsman who creates a unique call upon the life of each Princess,

It is obvious that we are faced with a choice... We can read about the multitude of attributes exemplfied by the Proverbs 31 woman, and get totally depressed because we see no way to measure up. Or, we can look at this woman and think, "I can really learn so much by the example God gives me, regarding the qualities He wants me to embrace... Creator God, may You find Your Beloved, choosing to practice the latter. May she walk out Your Promise of a life filled with Your Abundance, with intentionality and purpose. May she be determined to follow the example of godly women in Your Word, like the Proverbs 31:10-31 woman, the Titus 2 woman, Deborah, Mary, Ruth...

Thank You, Father God, that You are not nearly as concerned about our "doing" as You are about our "being." You have equipped Your Princess with the beautiful examples in Your Word, with everything she needs; everything that pertains to living a God-Focused life. You have also provided her with an "other-focused" example to follow. When she is called upon to serve others, may she do so without hesitation...joyfully! In the name of the God who leads by example, and reminds us, through His servant Paul, in I Timothy 6:11, to "...Pursue a godly life, along with faith, love, perseverance, and gentleness."

Bouquets of Grace-Filled Blessings...

"Women of strength have a passion for God's call on their lives... Look around. When you find a woman with a passion for God's call on her life, you will find a woman of strength."

-Neva Coyle
A Woman of Strength
Servant Publications

Gems of Wisdom...

Luke 2:36-38
Proverbs 31:10-31
Titus 2:3-5

Refreshing Hugs...

Choose a woman you know; one whom you admire for the strength of character and dignity she models. Think of two or three occasions where she has shown graciousness and kindness to you, or to a mutual friend. What trait stands out for you that you might like to follow as a role model?

Perhaps you can write her a note telling her what you appreciate about her and thank her for modeling grace, strength of character, gentleness, and kindness...

PART SIX: FEELING A SMIDGEN DOWN? BECOME A "HEART LIFTING" PRINCESS

HOPE

Hope means to keep living amid desperation,
...to keep humming in darkness
Hoping is knowing that there is love...
In the eye of another...to see that he understands you.
As long as there is still hope there will also be prayer.
And God will be holding you in His hands.

-Henri J. Nouwen
"Hope"
Excerpt from *With Open Hands*
Ave Maria Press

A TRANSFORMED LIFE

"In the beginning God created the heavens and the earth. The earth was empty, a formless mass cloaked in darkness. And the Spirit of God was hovering over its surface. Then God said, "Let there be light," and there was light. And God saw that it was good..."
Genesis 1:1-4

The word "Genesis" comes form the Greek word "geneseos" which, when translated, means "history of origin," "birth," or "geneology." The first five words in the Book of Genesis, "In the beginning God created..." are words we, as believers, can reflect on, when we consider the works of our incredible Creator. In the Hebrew translation, there's a veritable storehouse which God opens up for His children; a myriad of ideas for a believer to reflect upon, not the least of which is the majesty of our awesome God. And to think that He simply spoke the world into existence! Truly amazing!

The origin, or "birth" of nearly seven billion people who currently live on planet earth, not to mention all those who came before us, is also an amazing phenomenon. All of our abilities to reason, to formulate concepts in our minds, to create with our hands; all these are developed accomplishments because God created us with the gifts necessary to perform them. Having said that, here's more food for thought: We begin as tiny infants with a continuous list of needs. And, so it is with our emotions. If our strong emotional needs for love, acceptance, and a healthy self-esteem go unmet, our existence becomes mundane, stagnant, and void of challenge.

If we want to see change taking place, in the realm of emotional balance, we need to begin by asking God to reveal the not-so-obvious attitudes we have formed, that are not pleasing to the God we so desire to please. We need to allow our Master Creator to place us back on the Potter's Wheel, so He can help us correct the negative thoughts or feelings, or both, that we have embraced, rather than confronted.

Warning: This Process Will Not Be Without Pain.

But, if we are to grow; if we are to be conformed more and more to His likeness, we must be willing to make sacrifices...

Permission... sometimes it is a scary proposition. To allow God to begin a process in us that may result in reshaping those aspects of our character that need refining, is not always easy... The process may not be a simple one, for any of us, but it is imperative. If we want to look more like our Lord, we will need to adopt a heart attitude that is willing to accept His refining methods, including being placed, once again, on His Potter's Wheel. Here's the great news... God delights in reshaping, sculpting, conforming, and fashioning His Princess into His likeness... All He needs, to begin the process, is your consent, and mine.

May God bless you, His Precious Princess, as you allow Him to perform the necessary rennovation so that you will look even more like Jesus... Why, I do believe you are beginning to see the signs of what looks like an awesome transformation, as you yield to every turn of the Potter's Wheel....

Once again, I will be praying for you, as the Master Potter is about the serious business of transforming His Beloved Bride...until... she is pure and spotless...

Heart Whispers...

Dear God, You are the Master Heart Sculptor,

Thank You for so many blessings... more than we could possibly grasp in a lifetime. God, I ask that Your favor rest upon the life of Your Princess, as she gives You permission to reshape and remold her character to be conformed more and more into Your likeness. In the name of the God who is our Master Heart Sculptor and Character Shaper... Amen.

Bouquets of Grace-Filled Blessings...

"...an important truth about the growth process. It cannot be willed. It can only be enhanced by adding grace, truth, and time, and then God produces growth."

-Dr. Henry Cloud
Changes That Heal
Zondervan Publishing

Gems of Wisdom...

Jeremiah 18:6
Isaiah 64:8

Refreshing Hugs...

Take a few moments to give the Master Potter praise and thanks for giving you His Grace. It's His Grace that is necessary to help you make the changes that promote balance. It's His Grace that will enable your focus to rest on Him and the destiny odyssey He has created, exclusively for you.

RECIPES THAT SATISFY

"Blessed are those who hunger and thirst for
righteousness, for they shall be filled."
Matthew 5:6 NKJV

Jesus, in His Sermon on the Mount, nourishes our spirit with His words. He tells us that if we hunger and thrist for His righteousness, He will fill us. He will never reject us. Never! In fact, Jesus promises that we "shall be filled". It's a promise we can cling to each and every day.

Food and water are essential for our survival, but equally essential for our earthly existence is our personal relationship with our God. For Jesus says of Himself, in John 6:48, "I am the living bread that came down out of heaven..." Now we know that food and water can satisfy for a time, and are vital for our sustenance. However, our Messiah, in John 6:51, reminds us that He is "the living bread..." and, as such, He can satisfy totally and completely, here and now, and throughout all eternity. In John 6:51, Jesus ends the verse by proclaiming that, "If anyone eats of this bread, he will live forever; and the bread that I shall give is My flesh, which I shall give for the life of the world." You know, it is just not possible to get any better than that! It is the Messiah that satisfies now, and eternally.

Julian of Norwich makes reference to turning our thoughts to God, and His Goodness, as being truly pleasing to our Lord. Furthermore, it brings much benefit to our soul, as well. He says this, "...For of all the things our minds can think about God, it is thinking upon his goodness that pleases him most and brings the most profit to our soul."

Joel Osteen, in his book, *Break Out!*, talks about the favor of God on our lives. Using Nehemiah as an example, he encourages us to do this, "When the dream looks too big, don't give up. Be like Nehemiah and say, 'Lord, thank You that Your gracious hand is upon me.'" What an awesome promise God makes for us!

If we draw our sustenance from the Lord, and believe, like Nehemiah believed, that "The gracious hand of God is upon [our] life," feelings of discouragement will have to go! It is simply not possible to be discouraged, and, simultaneously, to be focused on God's Goodness and His Favor.

Psalm 16:5, is yet one more scripture verse, out of innumerable others, that are treasures; each one is so worth meditating on. "Lord, You alone are my inheritance, my cup of blessing. You guard all that is mine..." So, feast on His Word, and meditate on His Goodness. Take time to bask in His Presence, daily. Pastor Osteen, in the same book, continues to inspire us with these powerful words, "...remind yourself that because you keep God in first place, because you honor Him with your life, there's something about you that's indefinable. It's Almighty God breathing in your direction..."

Heart Whispers...

Dear God, You nourish each of us with Your Word, Your Presence, Your Graciousness, Your Favor...

Please help Your Princess decide, in her heart of hearts, to crave the life sustaining nutrients You provide for the health of her spirit, that are contained in Your Word... just as we crave nutrients for the health of our bodies. Thank You, Lord, that Your gracious hand is, indeed, upon each Princess. Thank You, God, that when she asks anything that is in accordance with Your will for her life, Your response is affirmative. In the name of the God whose Gracious Hand and Favor rests upon every Princess. Amen.

Bouquets of Grace-Filled Blessings...

"...do as Nehemiah did. Declare: 'The gracious hand of God is upon my life...' The more you brag on God's favor, the more of His favor you will see."

-Joel Osteen
Break Out!
FaithWords

Gems of Wisdom...

Psalm 45:2
Psalm 16:5-6
Nehemiah 9:15

Refreshing Hugs...

Psalm 34:8-9 says this: "Taste and see that the Lord good. Oh, the joys of those who trust in Him!..."

Just for fun, let's entitle our hug: "Food For Thought." Make a favorite family meal this week. Next to each plate, place a copy of this Psalm, along with a note telling your family how much you appreciate each of them.

Suggestion: If you have begun a *Princess Prayer Journal,* designate a section of that journal for praying God's favor over a family member each week. Put their name on the left side. On the right side place the week and year. For simplicity, mark down the week as: Week 1 through Week 52. Jot down a few notes regarding a specific prayer of favor you'll be praying for that family member. Designate one day, each week, that you intend to pray God's favor over specific areas of each family members' life.

Remember to enjoy some quiet time this week-just you and Jesus. Meditate on His goodness and all of the perfect provisions He presents you with, as He invites you to find refreshing for your soul, in Him.

THE DIRECTOR OF MY HEART'S JOURNEY

"May the Lord bring you into an even deeper understanding of
the love of God and the endurance that comes from Christ."
2 Thessalonians 3:5

Few Christian classics leave behind the indelible impression that Hannah Whitall Smith's timeless book, *The Christian's Secret Of A Happy Life,* leaves in the hearts of its readers. From a Quaker background, this simple woman of God continued, throughout her life, to captivate her audience. Hannah knew how to touch the heart of God. She was blessed with knowledge-the knowledge of a truly inexhaustible love that flows from God's heart, to ours. Hannah knew that, through the Holy Spirit, we would be brought to "...an even deeper understanding of the love of God..."

Hannah speaks of "...knowing the voice of the Good Shepherd...as to what really is His will concerning you." In the area of obedience, she pens her thoughts, "Your soul only needs to know the will of God in order to consent to it, then you surely cannot doubt His willingness to make His will known, and to guide you into the right paths."

2 Thessalonians 3:5, gives great insight into God's will for our lives. In this verse, we find that God's will is made clearly visible to a soul open to receiving instruction from Him. Hannah makes this observation, "... the way in which the Holy Spirit, therefore, usually works in a fully obedient soul, in regard to direct guidance, is to impress upon the mind a wish or desire to do or to leave undone certain things."

When we begin to ask the Lord to reveal His specific will for our life, it is His joy to respond to our request. Just a quick reminder: ask God for precise instructions before you take that first step. It is what Hannah refers to as "direct guidance".

Hannah expounds upon her reference regarding the chariots of God. She describes these chariots as being invisible and makes the observation that, "Everthing, then, becomes a chariot of salvation when God rides upon it." Interesting! We can purpose to "ride" toward the very heart of our God, knowing that His heart is always filled with His Forever Love for you, and for me. It is His intent to point you in the direction He has drawn, like a blueprint, for your journey. Just know that His heart motive is to spread His Never-Ending Love through us, to the unsaved, wherever our path may take us!

Heart Whispers...

Dear God, You are the God of Inexhaustible Love and Grace,

I thank You that, no matter what our odyssey looks like, Your intention, for each Princess, is that we spread the Good News of Your plan of Salvation and the amazing love You have for Your children! Please bless Your Princess with wisdom and insight, like You gave to Hannah Whitall Smith.

God, we ask for glimpses into Your heart so we can emulate Your Passion; Your desire to share with the world, through each of our personal testimonies, that You are the God of Awesome Wonders. Bless Your Princess with the gift of encouragement that will touch those You place in her life. In the name of the God whose "directional signals" are always perfect! Amen.

Bouquets of Grace-Filled Blessings...

"Let the Lord write the prescription for your life..mix the ingredients... write the instructions... Don't presume to direct your own life on your own terms... walking in that will...will be the most fulfilling thing that could...happen to you."

-Pastor Jack Hayford
Pursuing the Will Of God
Multnomah Publishers

Gems of Wisdom...

Psalm 16:11
Proverbs 3:5-6

Refreshing Hugs...

A fun week-end project can be to create an odyssey scrapbook. Fill it with a collage of pictures that have quotes containing faith-based sentiments. If you are really in a creative mood, you might consider a collage of family gatherings with photos and cute captions. Memories are gifts God has given us to add generous helpings of joy, and a heaping measure of fun, to our lives...

FORGIVENESS THAT LEADS TO SERENITY AND PEACE

"And when they had come to the place called Calvary, there they crucified Him, and the criminals, one on the right hand and the other on the left. Then Jesus said, "Father, forgive them, for they do not know what they do." Luke 23:33-34 NKJV

Perfect, unconditional forgiveness...It's what Christ, our beloved Savior, shed His precious blood on Calvary for...forgiveness for every believer, for all eternity. The depth of His forgiveness is incomprehensible. The Holy Spirit, our Revealer, gives us only what we can comprehend, as human beings, in our finite minds. It is only by the Spirit of God, that we can realize the full debt, paid by Jesus, in order for us to experience eternal life. We cannot, in our finite minds, imagine what the Kingdom of God will look like. We are only given a glimpse, by way of some word pictures, from His Word.

Gordon Lindsay, in his book series, *The Life And Teachings Of Christ,* paraphrases Jesus' last words on the cross, with this powerful impact, "With His parting breath, He would speak pardon to sinners." Lindsay proceeds to graphically paint a picture depicting the cruxifiction of the King of Glory, "There Jesus hung betwixt earth and heaven, a spectacle to men and angels, with tortures momentarily becoming ever more unendurable, ever more maddening as the minutes slowly passed."

Who among us can sense the agony our Savior experienced? Who can possibly imagine what the instant He was separated from the Father, could possibly have looked like? It was only an instant, but an instant, suspended in time, magnified by the shadow of death. None of us will ever know. But, Praise God, the Father raised His Son up from the horror of death; He raised Jesus up from the stench of Hades; He raised Him up to heaven, to be seated at His right hand. Jesus tasted death for all of us. He died, so that we might live an abundant life here on earth, and eternally, with Him.

Sometimes, we need to remind ourselves that forgiveness is always a choice. Forgiveness is also a gift. The unwillingness to forgive; the refusal to pardon an offense, will imprison us in deep bondage. It may also lead to bitterness, anger, or just plain borderline rage. The ultimate response, would be the desire to take revenge. Even if we have not crossed the line into any of these territories, we understand their ramifications. God commands us to forgive, just as Jesus forgave those who persecuted and crucified Him. He then states the consequences, should we refuse to do so.

Here's what we do know: Jesus' perpetrators choked the life out of the God of Glory, or so they thought. Yet, with His final breath, He asked the Father to forgive them because His perpetrators were not aware of who it was that they had persecuted, and who it was that they were about to crucify.

God's exhortation, to every believer, is that we learn to genuinely forgive those who have committed any offense against us. Unforgiveness leads to the absence of peace. Learning to exonerate those who have wounded us, on the other hand, will open the door to God's blessings. As we practice the necessary art of forgiving others, His serenity will enfold our hearts like a blanket of calming warmth, allowing the Holy Spirit to envelop our soul in tranquility, and give us His "Shalom", His Peace...

Heart Whispers...

Dear God, You are the Author of Serene Peace and Forever Forgiveness,

May we be ever mindful of Your incredible Mercy which forgives all our sins and removes them as far as the East is from the West... Thank You, God, that Your legacy to every believer is Eternal Life in Your Presence. And that gift, precious Daughter of our Abba Father, is free!

I ask, Lord, that You give Your Beautiful Princess, the desire to cultivate genuine courage, and the strength it will take, in order to forgive those who have wounded her. Thank You, Lord Jesus, for modeling authentic forgiveness. Thank You, God, that when she admits her sin, truly repents, and asks for Your forgiveness, You forgive her, instantaneously, and erase her sins forever from Your memory. In the name of the One who teaches us to abide in a spirit of forgiveness, and in the peaceful calm that forgiveness brings to our hearts, and our minds... Amen.

Bouquets of Grace-Filled Blessings...

"One of God's exhortations is that we learn to genuinely forgive those who have committed any offense or hurt against us. Unforgiveness can often lead to the absence of peace, and, may become the cause of a root of bitterness. Learning to exonerate those who have wounded us will open the door for God's blessings and favor to be poured over our lives..."

-Jan

Gems of Wisdom...

John 8:1-8
Acts 10:43
Colossians 1:13-14
Matthew 6:14-15

Refreshing Hugs...

Close your eyes. Now think about the most peaceful time or place that you can remember. Focus on that experience. Now, visualize Jesus sitting beside you. Keep that thought for as long as possible...Open your eyes slowly. Can you still sense His peace enveloping you? Repeat this exercise as often as you feel the need. And may the Shalom of God, be with you always.

GEE... IT'S KIND OF DUSTY AND DESOLATE HERE

"The Lord guided them by a pillar of cloud during the
day and a pillar of fire at night. That way they could travel
whether it was day or night. And the Lord did not remove
the pillar of cloud or the pillar of fire from their sight."
Exodus 13:21-22

Finally released from the hands of a persecuting Pharoah, God led His people on a desert road toward the Red Sea. Knowing that, if they went in any other direction, they would face the prospect of war, and might decide to return to Egypt. God knew, only too well, the hearts of His people.

As Moses led the Israelites, God provided protection in the form of a cloud to guide them on their way by day, and fire to give them light so they were able to travel by night. God's guidance, protection, and every provision we could possibly need, even in the middle of a parched wilderness, is always available. The Lord's supply is limitless; it is perfectly suited for every circumstance we might face in our lifetime on earth.

When God awakens memories of the Israelites going through the Red Sea experience, we can't help but be reminded of the awesome God we serve. He parted the waters so the Israelites could pass through safely. God still parts the waters today. No matter how gusty the wind becomes, no matter how fierce the tide, as it rushes the waves of water to the shore line... God is there. He puts His hedge of protection in place, so His people will be provided a way of escape from a dangerous scenario. After the Israelites were safely on the other side, Pharoah and his men attempted to cross the parted waters. We know how they met their demise. Pharoah and his troops were quickly swallowed up, horse and rider both, and the danger ended for God's people.

Daughter of the Living God, the Lord is able to part any "sea" you might find yourself engulfed in, because, He is the Great "I Am." He is the God of the "hard places" of your life. He is also the God of the "dry places" of your life. If you are in the midst of a "dry desert experience," wondering if God will provide water from His vast reservoir to quench your spiritual thirst, wonder no longer, He will! If you are wondering if God will ever fulfill the promises He has made to you in His Word...you can count on it, He will! Know that He is the God of "Yes and Amen." He is, even at this very moment, setting in motion everything necessary to pour His water on the parched soil of your heart.

I say to you, His Jewel, all you need to do is ask... Ask the Holy Spirit to give you His vision for your life. Ask Him to show you how things look from His perspective. Ask Him to increase your faith so that you can stand on His promises...every one of them... God wants to reassure you that He will bring every promise He makes, to pass.

Before I continue, I'd like to pose a question for you to ponder. Are you looking for God's perfect will for your life, or His permissive will? Trust in His promises...believe God for His "best" for your life. This may involve making some hard choices, at times. But the promises of God do not come to pass through easy choices. Don't shy away from trusting the Lord with complete trust, absolute trust. Just know that God always keeps His promises, always...

The result of your trust in the Lord will look something like this: He will part the "sea" for you. He will move "heaven and earth" for you. You may have to endure the wilderness just a little bit longer. So, I have a suggestion. While you are in that dry place, waiting for God to move on your behalf and instruct you on how to have His "best" for your life, praise Him. Praise Him because you love Him. Praise Him because He is the Great "I AM." Praise Him because He is God, and there is none other. Praise Him for every provision He has made in your life. Praise Him because He, alone, is worthy of all praise. Praise Him because His promises are "Yes and Amen." Praise Him for the mighty things He has done, and will continue to do, for you, His Devoted Princess.

Seek the guidance of the Spirit of God when you come face-to-face with making a hard decision. God never intended for you to make difficult choices on your own. Remember, He is the God for whom nothing... nothing... nothing... is impossible. Listen for His Whisper... Determine not to settle for His permissive will, when He wants you to have His very best!

Heart Whispers...

Dear God, You are the God of the "I WILLS..."

You have lovingly placed the "Red Sea" trials in each of our lives, in order to help us grow. You use each trial to develop and strengthen our character. Holy Spirit, it is You who re-direct our feet, should we head down the wrong path.

Thank You, Father God, for giving us wisdom and guidance to help us make our choices with deliberation and intentionality. Thank You, God, that You will use our response to each wilderness experience to lead us out of those difficult places, and into Your Perfect Will, for our lives. In the name of the God who walks with us through every "Red Sea" experience, pointing the way toward His Perfect Will for His Beloved Princess... Amen.

Bouquets of Grace-Filled Blessings...

"How many times do we pull away from making tough choices because we can see the crisis that choice will bring? ...then they say no to the very thing that God wants to use to take them out of the cycle of hopelessness and into the promise."

-Cathy Lechner
*I Hope God's Promises Come To Pass Before
My Body Parts Go South*
Creation House

Gems of Wisdom...

2 Corinthians 1:20
I Kings 8:56
Hebrews 11:13

Refreshing Hugs...

Have you found yourself in the midst of a dusty and desolate place recently? I encourage you, don't quit! Instead, add to your quiet time by reading God's Promises in His Word. Look up the scriptures that cite His "I Will" promises... Be patient while God is bringing you out of that desert experience and into His Presence... He can and He will!

HIS NAMESAKE

"Your words are what sustain me. They bring me great joy and are
my heart's delight, for I bear your name, O Lord God Almighty."
Jeremiah 15:16

Consumed with a burning desire for God's Word, Jeremiah longed to tell
the people, by way of the prophetic ministry given to him by the Lord, the
things that would soon come to pass. Jeremiah is sometimes referred to as
the "Weeping Prophet," but he spoke only the words God gave Him to speak.

Jeremiah was given a truly divine revelation of the God he served. Jeremiah
10:12-16 clearly indicates the prophet's concept of God as the Creator of all
existing things. Let's pause here for a moment and meditate upon some of the
names that bring God Glory...

"Creator God, Master, Lord, Savior, Kinsmen Redeemer,
Messiah, Protector, Defender, Prince of Peace, King of kings,
Lord of lords, God of Grace, Alpha and Omega, First and Last,
Eternal God, Ancient of Days, Good Shepherd, God of Healing,
God of Compassion, God of Glory, God our Reward, God Almighty,
God of Mercy, God our Comforter, God of
Israel, God our Righteousness..."

God does, in fact, meet every qualification for each of these titles, and
so many more! For Jeremiah, God's words provided all the nourishment his
soul would ever need... "Your words are what sustain me..." Search your heart,
Princess of the Living God. Are you so famished for the Word of God that
once you begin reading His Word, you could devour its contents without
being aware of how much time has passed? Are you so hungry for the things
of God that as the dawn awakens you, you begin to think about the things
that God is passionate about... and you desire to be passionate about, as well?

We serve a God of immeasurable Grace; His heart is His longing to make
us whole and complete, in Him. And, it is His passionate longing to do just
that, which will make all the difference in our lives. In order to accomplish
that, God offers us His Word... His Love... His Passion...His Promises...

The nourishment and sustenance God longs to give His Kids, is what I like to call: His "Mega Manna." That nourishment is, quite simply, amazing! My challenge to you, His Jewel, is that your heart begins to rejoice, knowing that your Papa God calls you by name, is always thinking about you, and knows the future plans He has set aside, expressly for you. You are His Namesake... Imagine that!

Heart Whispers...

Dear God, You know Your own and You call each Princess by Your special name for her,

As she searches Your Word daily, may she develop a deep desire to know You more, and never be satisfied with a mediocre relationship with You. May Your nourishment and refreshing be all she needs to water the garden of her soul, day by day. Lord, please bless her with a profound sense of Your Presence. Help her, Holy Spirit, to plunge into the depths of Your Word, so that she might experience the passion You have to bring revival to her spirit. Remind her often, God, that You know her by name. In fact, her soul is permanently imprinted on the palm of Your hand. In the name of the God who is Rav-Chesed... Abounding in Love... Amen.

Bouquets of Grace-Filled Blessings...

"Quite a thought... Your name on God's hand. Your name on God's lips... to think that your name is on God's hand and on God's lips... Spoken by His mouth. Whispered by His lips..."

-Max Lucado
When God Whispers Your Name
Word Publishing

Gems of Wisdom...

Isaiah 49:15-16
Isaiah 45:4
Isaiah 43:1

Refreshing Hugs...

Selah. Pause and think about it. Think about just how special you are to God. He knows you personally, "I have called you by your name..."You belong to Him, "You are Mine..." And, you are precious to Him... You are His Namesake... What awesome thoughts to carry you throughout your day!

CUSTOM DESIGNED FOR HIS GLORY

"I myself no longer live, but Christ lives in me. So I live
my life in this earthly body by trusting in the Son of
God, who loved me and gave Himself for me."
Galatians 2:20

In the previous segment, we were given a glimpse into the nourishment our Creator provides for our heart and soul, through the eyes of the prophet Jeremiah. We read of the passion Jeremiah had for the Word of God, and how His Word provides us with all the sustenance we could possibly need, from our Father God.

The Apostle Paul, in the above scripture reference, utters a profound truth; the nature of this truth is that while we are in this shell of an earthly body, we exist and function by putting our complete trust in the Son of God. Jesus not only loves us, but He allowed Himself to be tormented beyond what we could possibly imagine, in order to demonstrate the magnitude of the love His has for His children.

Since we, as Christians, are being conformed into the very likeness of God, our goal is to allow Christ to fulfill His purpose for our lives by inviting Him to live His life through us. I cannot remember the countless times I was challenged to get on my knees, or, if that was not possible at the time, to bow in my heart, and symbolically gaze into the face of Messiah Jesus.

Imagine the Lord uttering these words straight out of Isaiah 43:1, as they are phrased in the NKJV, "Fear not, for I have redeemed you; I have called you by your name; you are Mine." What reassurance! What affirmation! What grace!

If you have questioned your purpose, struggled with your identity, or simply wondered if you could possibly make a difference in the world, Isaiah 43:1, should answer that question for every Princess. He says, "Fear not..." Our Lord reassures us with these words, "...for I have redeemed you..." Our Papa God reiterates the fact that He knows each of us personally, "I have called you by your name..." And, with respect to our heritage, God reminds us that we belong to Him, "...you are Mine." We belong to God! He has His loving hand upon our lives. This solves the mystery of who we are, and what priceless value we have, in the eyes of our Messiah.

Here's the next part, and it has to do with our destiny... God has a perfect plan. Yes, I did say a perfect plan; He has a unique plan for your life, and for mine... The NIV version of Jeremiah 29:11, states it this way, "For I know the plans I have for you, declares the Lord, plans to prosper you...plans to give you hope and a future. Then you will call upon Me and come and pray to Me, and I will listen to you." Ahhh! The plans God has for you are awe inspiring, because, you have been custom designed by Him, for His Glory! Your purpose, and mine, is to bring God glory and honor and praise.

The NKJV of Isaiah 43:7, phrases the verse in these words, "Everyone who is called by My name, whom I have created for My glory, I have formed him...I have made him." Once again, God has custom designed us with the express purpose of bringing Him glory! To state it another way, we were designed for His pleasure. We were created for His Glory!

It's time to look up! It's time to proclaim, "I myself no longer live, but Christ lives in me." Say it with all the confidence of a Daughter of the King of kings. Now, with that kind of confidence, you can know that He takes great delight in walking beside you, and sharing every part of your day with you-all because He loves beautiful you.

Heart Whispers...

Dear God, You have given us a perfect place in Your Kingdom Design,

I do remember a time in my life, decades ago, when I really wasn't confident about where I fit in. I wondered what my place was, for Your Kingdom Purposes. All that changed when I discovered that You had a plan for my life-a plan that was intricately adjoined with the lives of many others, and so it is with every believer.

God, please re-affirm to Your Princess, who may have questions regarding her purpose, her value, her significance, that she is more precious to You than she can possibly imagine. Remind her that You will accomplish Your divine purposes through her life, as she yields her will to Yours, Lord. In the name of the God who patiently waits for us to share the moments of our life with Him, because He designed us for His good pleasure. Amen.

Bouquets of Grace-Filled Blessings...

"What a miracle it is to be able to claim the King of Glory as our own. We love Him, and He loves us. We have the sweet assurance that we belong to Him. Allow this truth to bless and comfort your heart today."

-Jamie Lash
A Kiss A Day
Ebed Publications

Gems of Wisdom...

Read Song of Songs, (also referred to as the Song of Solomon), in your favorite Bible version.

Refeshing Hugs...

Retreat to your quiet place. Slowly read Song of Songs. This book of the Bible captures the very essence of what it means to belong to the King of kings and Lord of lords; we are His Bride, not just in the present, but throughout all eternity... Doesn't that just leave you breathless? Ahhh, me too!

NOTHIN' BUT GRACE

"...Love mixed with faith be yours from God the Father and
from the Master, Jesus Christ. Pure grace and nothing but
grace be with all who love our Master, Jesus Christ."
Ephesians 6:23-24 MSG

"...Love mixed with faith... Pure grace and nothing but grace..." God desires His Love, in ever increasing measure, to flow through our lives. God the Father and our Master, Jesus Christ give "Pure grace and nothing but grace..." to every believer. When we grasp that kind of grace, bestowed upon "...all who love our Master, Jesus Christ," well, it can just be overwhelming.

God's Grace... His Unmerited Favor, is totally undeserved by us, and yet, God gives that pure grace freely. It is that kind of pure grace, totally underserved by us, that compels us to confess our sins and show God that we are truly repentant...sorry for our transgressions...and to ask Him for His forgiveness...His Grace... Now we must not only tell God, but show Him, by our words and our actions, that we will live intentionally, to please and honor Him. True repentance coupled with His forgiveness, will pave the way for living the healthy and abundant life God designed for every believer, to live.

Ephesians 6:24, poignantly finishes the chapter with these words, "May God's grace be upon all who love our Lord Jesus Christ with an undying love." Suffice it to say, we live in a world in desperate need of God's "...Love mixed with faith..." And that is the reason He appoints us, as His ambassadors, to help spread the Good News of His Gospel and to address the needs of others, as He equips us to do.

Elizabeth George, in her classic book, *A Woman After God's Own Heart*, refers to "a bountiful eye as being like the eyes of God." Elizabeth, with a firm call to action, exhorts us in this manner, "Whenever you see a person in need, be direct. Walk straight up to the wounded sheep and see what she needs and what you can do." Elizabeth then cautions us against waiting, with the hope that someone else might show up to take care of the matter, because, Elizabeth points out, "God has allowed you to find this person in need..." In other words, we are appointed by God, as His ambassadors, to witness to others by sharing His Gospel and are also appointed by Him to use a "bountiful eye" so we can recognize "...the wounded sheep..." see that she has a need, and offer to help. Each of us are, in fact, appointed to be ambassadors, and clothed in the compassion of Christ.

What a great privilege to serve our Master Jesus by extending a hand to serve anyone in need, wherever our odyssey path may take us. Colossians 3:11 says this, "In this new life... Christ is all that matters, and He lives in all of us."

Don't hesitate! Purpose to give Him the honor and the praise for which He, alone, is worthy. Give Him your love, faith, and trust. Give the Lord your time, finances, gifts, resources... all that He has so generously given to you. Give these back to your "Gift-Giver." Watch, now, as He miraculously uses the gifts He has given you, to begin unfolding His destiny promises for you, and for those He has placed you in a position to serve.

Heart Whispers...

Dear God, You model a Perfect Servant/Leader's Heart,

May Your Cherished Princess give back to You all that You have so generously given her. May she give You her agenda, her time, the spiritual gifts You have given her, Lord, to use as You desire. Please help her, Holy Spirit, to catch the vision of what it means to be a giver... and what it looks like to have a servant's heart like Yours. Bless her with Your Love and Pure Grace. In the name of the God who is the Master Gift Giver, and Pure Grace Provider... In the name of Messiah Jesus. Amen.

Bouquets of Grace-Filled Blessings...

"...Compassion is the heart's response to a person's need combined with a helping hand that offers mercy and grace."

-Carol Kent
Becoming A Woman of Influence
Navpress

Gems of Wisdom...

Matthew 6:3
Psalm 112:4-5
I Timothy 6:18
Galatians 6:10

Refreshing Hugs...

No matter where you find yourself, along your odyssey path, make yourself available for God to give you Divine Appointments, to bless others by meeting some needs they may have. Bless you, as you minister, through God's Love and Grace...

SPREADING WORDS OF LIGHT,
GRACE, AND ENCOURAGEMENT

"Jesus said to the people, "I am the light of the world. If you
follow Me, you won't be stumbling through the darkness,
because you will have the light that leads to life."
John 8:12

Rising at daybreak, to experience the beauty of rays of sunlight, in all of its splendor, coming down to overshadow the darkness of night, is a truly magnificent sight. Dawn is an incredible time of each new day. Yet, honestly, I am not your basic "morning person." It seems my biological clock causes me to function far more creatively late at night and into the early morning hours. I am making progress, by retiring a little earlier each night, and rising earlier in the morning, but not by sunrise. My friend, Diane, will testify to the fact that rising super early in the morning is still challenging for me. On one occasion, she left an interesting message as a wake-up call on my recorder. It sounded strangely similar to the tune of reveille, (a military term which means to awaken, or a signal to get up in the morning). Memories of this call from my wild French Cajun friend, has made me laugh, laugh, laugh... no matter what had transpired in my crazy life, the day before. You know, even if you are not an early riser, you can't help but love a fresh new morning.

James 1:17 causes us to reflect upon the fact that our God is the One "...who created all heaven's lights." God's equation of life and light, is a truly inspiring one, evoking a sense of awe and wonder. If we are walking with the Lord, His light is life. Darkness, when used in God's Word, is another word for "lack of knowledge." If someone does not have a personal relationship with the Lord, sadly, they are walking in darkness! The great news is that Jesus promises light, or knowledge of the Holy One, to those who follow Him...

Listen to how the Apostle Paul, in Romans 1:10-12, shares a portion of God's Good News, with great grace, encouragement, and blessing:

"One of the things I always pray for is the opportunity, God
willing, to come at last to see you. For I long to visit you so

222

I can share a spiritual blessing with you that will help you grow strong in the Lord. I'm eager to encourage you in your faith, but I also want to be encouraged by yours. In this way, each of us will be a blessing to the other."

An Invitation to His Cherished Princess...

Precious Princess...

You are invited to grasp the hand of your King. Greet each new day with anticipation as your Messiah is just waiting to lavish you with "Every good gift and every perfect gift..."

Ask the Holy Spirit to place opportunities, during the course of your day, to encourage the broken-hearted... Speak words of light, grace, and encouragement to someone who needs to experience the magnificent Grace of God....

Now, Princess, abide in His Matchless Grace!

Heart Whispers...

Dear God, You are the Father of Lights,

Help Your Precious Daughter, as she witnesses boldly to the lost, prays for those who are hurting, and is an encouragement provider for the discouraged... I pray that You give her words that are edifying and uplifting to those who need a fresh vision of You, God, and Your Never-Ending Love for her... In the name of El Oseh Phela, the God who Works Wonders. Amen.

Bouquets of Grace-Filled Blessings...

"...Lord, help my words be silver boxes. Silver boxes full of treasure, Precious gifts from God above; That all the people I encounter Might have a box of God's own love."

-Michael Bright

Adapted From: *Silver Boxes,*

The Gift of Encouragement

by

Florence Littaeuer

Word Publishing

Gems of Wisdom...

Colossians 1:10-12

Colossians 2:2-3

Romans 1:11-12

Ephesians 1:6

John 12:36

Ephesians 5:8

Refreshing Hugs...

You are so special. You have unique qualities unlike anyone else. Thank you for sharing your gifts, wherever your odyssey takes you. I celebrate you for all you have accomplished!

If one of your gifts is that of an encourager, the beautiful gift of encouragement is always a wonderful way of giving to someone you know, who may be needing that blessing...

A COVENANT OF UNENDING LOVE

"The Lord said to him, "I have heard your prayer and your request.
I have set apart this Temple you have built so that My name will be
honored there forever. I will always watch over it and care for it."

I Kings 9:3

When Soloman had finished building the Temple of the Lord, God spoke
to him for a second time. The Lord reminded Soloman that it was He who
"... set apart the Temple..."

Not only had God set apart the Temple that Soloman had built, but He
put His name there and it would be there forever. The Lord promised He
would always watch over the Temple and take care of it. This Temple became
a place from which the prayers of the Israelites would be heard; they would
be heard by the Lord whose "... eyes and... heart..." as it is worded in the
NKJV, would, "...be there perpetually." A Covenant of Love was established;
a covenant which became a bond between the Israelites and their God.

In the New Testament, God gives us a Covenant of Grace. And it is filled
with the promise of eternal life. It is a covenant that fills us with His Spirit.
It is an agreement which bonds His heart to the hearts of His people, both
Jews and Gentiles alike. God desires to shower His people with His Love, His
Promises, and His Protection. These promises are etched upon our souls, by
God, our Master Artisan, for all eternity.

May you, Princess of the Most High God, stand in awe of the eternal
promises He has made. May God fill the chapters of your life with page after page
of blessings. May you experience His Priceless Promises, throughout your odyssey,
as you add them daily to your treasure chest of hopes and dreams... Remember
to praise Him and give Him glory for the awesome provisions He gives you...

Heart Whispers...

Dear God, You are the Author of every Covenant Promise,

My prayer is that Your Princess will walk along her destiny pathway, with the
assurance of Romans 8:38-39, and can say what the Apostle Paul says, "...I

am convinced that nothing can ever separate us from His love. Death can't, and life can't. The angels can't, and the demons can't. Our fears for today, our worries about tomorrow, and even the powers of hell can't keep God's love away... nothing in all creation will ever be able to separate us from the love of God that is revealed in Christ Jesus our Lord."

God, I pray that Your Princess will live her life, basking in Your Promises and Your Presence. Thank You, Lord, for joining our hearts with Yours, in a covenant of Your Never-Ending Love Story... In the name of the God who is absolutely "love-struck" with His Beloved Bride. Amen.

Bouquets of Grace-Filled Blessings...

"Experiencing the incredible life of blessing that God has for you really isn't any more complicated than falling in love with the Almighty, and so letting Him do all for you that He intends..."

-Benny Hinn
The Biblical Road To Blessing
Thomas Nelson Publishers

Gems of Wisdom...

2 Peter 1:4
Deuteronomy 6:5
Hebrews 8:6-7, 10, 13
Ephesians 3:17-19

Refreshing Hugs...

Look up the Scriptures that pertain to God's covenant promises. Pray His promises over yourself, your family, your friends, your neighbors, your co-workers...

AHHH! GREAT GRACE

"And now, it has pleased You to bless me and my family so
that our dynasty will continue forever before you. For when
You grant a blessing, O Lord, it is an eternal blessing!"
I Chronicles 17:27

When my daughter, Danielle, was quite young, I would sit on her bed
at night while she would pray touching prayers like this one, "God, bless
this house and everyone here, and don't forget my animals, Lord!" Danielle,
along with her older brother, Adam, owned a veritable "Noah's Ark" chalked
full of stuffed animals, all of which snuggled with them in their beds each
night. Before falling asleep, they needed to say "nite nite" to every single one.
But, you know what, it is God's pleasure to bless the homes of His children,
including their pets, even if they are of the "stuffed" variety. And what a
magnificent promise, "For when You grant a blessing, O Lord, it is an eternal
blessing!"

Each day, I am reminded to thank the Lord for His abundant blessings.
And with each day that passes, I find more blessings than I could ever envision
having, even if I had a lifetime to give God thanks for every single one...

I am forever stressing the importance of alone time...just you and God. It
is in these quiet and reflective moments, that He is simply delighted to spend
time with you. It is in these quiet moments that you can ask your heavenly
Father to bless your home, your family, your work, your leisure time, your
friends and neighbors... And, I promise, I won't breathe a word to anyone, if
you should ask the King of the Universe to bless your very own entourage of
stuffed animals. Shhh!

I Peter 1:25 reminds us that, "... the word of the Lord will last forever."
In addition, we also have His Promise that He will bless us forever. As the
Lord blesses you in so many gracious ways, turn your focus to one in need of
God's favor upon their life. Share all of the good things God has bestowed
upon you with others. Some of our greatest blessings come when we are on
the giving end... Isn't God Good... all the time!

Heart Whispers...

Dear God, You are the Father of every Good and Perfect Gift,

You are the Perfect Gift-Giver. Please remind Your Princess to be generous and gracious to others, blessing them with the same spirit of generosity with which You bless her. Thank You, Lord, for every opportunity You give to Your Sweet Princess; the opportunity to bless others with great grace... I ask for Your richest, most abundant blessings to be continually present in her life, so she always has plenty to share. In the name of the God who gives, and gives, and gives... Amen.

Bouquets of Grace-Filled Blessings...

"Grace is stunning. It is breathtaking. It is more beautiful than Van Gogh's Irises. Grace finds us in our poverty and presents us with the gift of an inheritance we didn't deserve... the gift of grace."

-Patsy Clairmont
Devotion: *Pictures of Grace*
Adapted from *Extravagant Grace*
Zondervan Publishing House

Gems of Wisdom...

Psalm 84:11
Psalm 45:2
2 Corinthians 8:9

Refreshing Hugs...

Ask the Holy Spirit for some new creative ways to bless those God has placed on your heart. The Lord tells us in His Word that a gift ushers the giver into the Presence of the Great. Small blessings become multiplied to bless both the one on the receiving end, and the one on the giving end. Isn't His Grace truly awe-inspiring!

GETTING TO KNOW YOU...

"When Jesus had finished saying all these things, He looked up to
heaven and said, "Father, the time has come. Glorify Your Son so He
can give glory back to You. For You have given Him authority over
everyone in all the earth. He gives eternal life to each one You have
given Him. And this is the way to have eternal life-to know You, the
only true God and Jesus Christ, the one You sent to the earth."
John 17:1-3

James 4:8 says, "Draw close to God, and God will draw close to you." The
closer we draw to God, the better we will know Him. The closer we draw to
God, the more we will want to please Him. The closer we draw to God, the
more we will want to glorify Him by living the godly lifestyle He wants His
Kids to live. The closer we draw to God, the closer we will come to knowing
more about Him...

I'd like to share with you, by way of an example, just how transparency
served to enhance the quality of our marriage. Several Mondays of each month,
I seemed to have been confronted with another of those Lucy Days. I have
alluded to this dilemma previously. To expound... there are some Lucy Days
that look something like this: Everything that consists of at least one mechanical
part, decides to break down on a day that I have wall-to-wall coaching sessions,
or appointments I need to keep. There were times when the frustration level
would turn into a Southern Twang, particularly when Honey would ask me
how my day had gone... "Ohhh, I would whine, I've had a terrible day-a Lucy
Day Monday, multiplied by three. I would then proceed with a litany of wailing
sounds, until the tears would become floods, and the whines reached levels that
could impair even the best "trained" ear. Did I really just say that?

Well, I will not go on and on with the details of any more of my "Lucy
Day" reactions, as they occured decades ago. Suffice it to say, I might have
been given an Academy Award for the best Diva presentation. Of course,
I am just having a little fun with this "Lucy Day" stuff. Still, to this day, I
am perplexed at just how my husband's love could remain unchanged, no
matter how transparent I became. And that, Girlfriend, is how our Papa God
loves us-unconditionally! Isn't it just awesome to know that God's love never

changes, never, never, never... In Hebrews 13:8, as phrased in the NKJV, "Jesus Christ is the same yesterday, today, and forever."

Now, let's address the issue of integrity, as it relates to honesty with God, self, and others. God wants us to maintain the highest level of integrity possible. Since our number one priority is to become like Him, we must be willing to become totally accountable to Him. Accountability fosters integrity. In order to accomplish this goal, we must give God permission to permeate our heart and soul, with the truth, the whole truth, and nothin' but the truth, about ourselves. I like to call it "SELF 101". This takes lots of patience and practice. I am confident, however, that you will take up the challenge with earnestness and sincerity of heart!

Seriously, it really did take me what seemed like an inordinate amount of time to cultivate undisguised straightforwardness. This quality helps to promote healthy relationships because godly relationships must be based on the principle of honesty. Once we become honest with ourselves, it becomes easier to transfer that level of honesty into our safe relationships.

Here's my prayer for you, Beloved of God: I pray that you become so close to the Lord, that you allow yourself to crawl into His lap, put your arms around His neck, and just revel in His Lovingkindness. Practice placing trust in the One who so longs to bless you, and every relationship you hold dear. Should you ever experience a "Lucy Day", maybe you could try doing what I previously suggested. Ask the Lord to put some duck tape over your mouth, and some sugar in your spirit... That way, you'll be equipped to laugh your way through your "Lucy Day" experience.

Heart Whispers...

Dear God, You are the God of Never-Ending Patience,

Thank You for Your patience with me, as I continue to work at transparency in each of my safe relationships. Thank You, God, that I can be totally transparent, vulnerable, and genuine with You, Lord, because You love me, in spite of all my frailties-past, present, and future.

Thank You, Lord God, for teaching Your Princess that, it is in the shedding of masks, she becomes who You intended her to be... Your Beautiful Jewel. It just can't possibly get any better than that.

I pray, Father, that Your Beloved Princess will be able to drop her guard with trusted friends. In this way, she will be free to experience the joy of genuine friendships, without the fear of loss. Bless her in each of those relationships, God.

Bring wholeness to one who has been struggling with the inability to trust; that she may know, in the deepest recesses of her heart, that You are the God of all Truth. May she cultivate that closeness to You that will fill her heart with Your Love, Your Joy, and Your Peace. In the name of the God who is forever Faithful and True. Amen.

Bouquets of Grace-Filled Blessings...

"One problem with our self-protective false selves and misplaced dependencies is that our masks become our prisions... How sad to lose one's self, the self that God intended you to be-imperishable, indestructible... of eternal value in His sight..."

-David A. Seamands
Healing Grace
Scripture Press Publications

Gems of Wisdom...

Psalm 51:6
Psalm 15:1-2

Refreshing Hugs...

Consider setting a specific time each week for an hour of introspection. Are there masks you need to shed? If this is the case, hand then over to God. Then, trust Him to show you how to move toward a deeper level of transparency in every one of your closest relationships.

"...the power of this invisible kingdom...a place entered only by faith... in the invisible kingdom... We'll get new dreams of meaning and purpose... dreams that are full of the kind of hope that is far stronger than despair."

Nicole Johnson
Keeping a Princess Heart In a
Not-So-Fairy-Tale World
Published by W Publishing Group,
A Division of Thomas Nelson, Inc.

L'CHAIM TO LIFE!

"My advice to you is this: Go to God and present your
case to Him. For He does great works too marvelous to
understand. He performs miracles without number."
Job 5:8-9

The Gospel of John closes with the following scripture, "And I suppose that if all the other things Jesus did were written down, the whole world could not contain the books" John 21:25. We serve a miracle-working God. Yet, like the Pharisees and Sadducees of Jesus' time, we are constantly in search of signs and wonders.

Jesus is the God of miracles. All we have to do is look at His life, from the time of His supernatural birth, to the miracle of His resurrection. Talk about an amazing God! We learn about the miracle of Creation... the parting of the Red Sea... a God who turns water into wine... five loaves of bread and two fish into a banquet that feeds five thousand... a God who calls His dead friend Lazarus out of a cave, still dressed in his grave clothes... and the One who walks on water... How about a demon possessed man healed by a touch, a man blind from birth who can now see perfectly, a leper who is completely cleansed of the disease...

Each of the above mentioned miracles, including the supernatural healing Jesus performs on a demon possessed man, are miracles of physical healings; the exception is the miracle of God's Creation, as He takes a total void-absolutely nothing in existence, and turns it into the earth we now know as home to over seven billion inhabitants, and, of course, all of the animal life, sea creatures, the plant world... Let's take a closer look at how Jesus is able to transform emotional states, as well. As a point of reference, Isaiah 26:3, equates a state of "perfect peace" with our trust in God, and our thoughts and focus remaining solely on Him...

"You will keep in perfect peace all who
trust in You, whose thoughts are fixed
on You!"

It is the desire of God's heart to keep you in a perfect peaceful state, regardless of the stormy winds that may blow through your life. Let me state that another way: The God of your life wants you to live in perfect peace, despite the storms of doubt, despite the intense trials, despite the struggles that may shake you to the core. His will is that you maintain a demeanor of calmness, in spite of what is happening in your immediate world, because He has a handle on it all.

Dr. Archibald Hart, in his hope-inspiring book, *The Anxiety Cure,* affirms the power of meditation for the believer, "Christian meditation... Dr. Hart proposes, is "a powerful antidote for stress and anxiety..." Dr Hart expounds on the benefits of meditation and its' simultaneous effect of helping us "develop a worshipful lifestyle... "Christian meditation, designed to help your mind and body to become more tranquil... a spiritual discipline that can enhance your experience of God."

We began this segment with some advice given to Job by a friend. While our trials and troubles may not reach the magnitude of Job's crisis, sometimes, it might feel as though our immediate world is about to cave in. Dr. Hart highlights the benefits of Christian meditation as an Rx for anxiety and stress, and rightfully so. He also touts these benefits as being able to heighten our experience of God.

I have chosen a verse from Isaiah 54:5. Using the NKJV, as an example of a scripture to meditate on, because it cites four attributes of God:

"For your Maker is your husband, The Lord of Hosts
is His name; And your Redeemer is the Holy One of Israel;
He is called the God of the whole earth."

I chose that particular verse because it can inspire us to meditate on the many-faceted nature of our Messiah. Additionally, it can bring a sense of soothing calm to our sometimes parched soul. Let's begin by bringing that peace and calmness a Princess would really desire to have, when worrisome circumstances may be surrounding her. As Dr. Hart suggests, we can begin by meditating on God's Goodness... on His Covenant Promises to you, Treasured Princess...

Meditate on His Love... Meditate on His Perfect Peace... Meditate on His Grace... Meditate on His Miracles... Meditate on His Redemption... Meditate on His Holiness... Meditate on His Truth... Meditate on His Faithfulness... Meditate on His Forgiveness...

I encourage you to stand back and watch, in awe, as He works miracles in your heart, your mind, your emotions, your physical well-being, your relationships, your goals, your dreams, your aspirations. As you meditate on the Lord, each day becomes a Gorgeous Gift from your King. Each day is wrapped in His Grace and blanketed in His Incredible Love.

Discover your King in a way you have not experienced Him before. It is He "...who does works too marvelous to understand..." It is He "...who performs miracles without number." A heart that seeks God in an effort to draw closer and closer to Him, is a heart that finds Him. May God bless you with His serenity, His Soothing Calm, His Tranquility; from the dawning of each new day, until nightfall, when sleep enfolds you under a pavillion of His Sweet Peace... May God's Perfect Peace rest upon you as you meditate on His Word, focus on His Majesty, and think about His Loveliness, continually!

Heart Whispers...

Dear God, Your Loveliness is beyond comparison. Your Face is what we seek,

In this vast configuration that we call our universe, Your miraculous handiwork is so very real to us, as believers. But God, what about that skeptic; the one who is still shaking her head and thinking, "Can our creation truly be attributed to the hand of God?" How about that dear one, Lord?

You are such a Gracious God. You are Creator, You are Restorer, You are Redeemer, You are Healer, You are our Husband, You are our Savior, You are our Dream Weaver, You are our Heart Mender, You are our Master, You are our Lord and our King, You are our Messiah, our Everlasting Father. God, You are more than Amazing!

Father God, I pray for that Princess who may be questioning the purpose for which You created her. I ask, Lord Jesus, that Your Jehovah Rapha healing touch wash over her and heal her emotions, her worries, her anxious thoughts, her fears... May she begin each day, meditating on You... the very thing Dr.

Hart prescribes as "a powerful antidote for stress and anxiety." May she, throughout her day, meditate on the many names that describe who You are to Your people, Lord. May she pray for those who are perishing, "for lack of knowledge" of a Holy God. In the name of the God who is the Great "I AM."

Bouquets of Grace-Filled Blessings...

"Elohim is the Hebrew word for God... When we pray to Elohim, we remember that he is the one who began it all, creating the heavens and the earth... This ancient name for God contains the idea of God's creative power... his authority and sovereignty..."

-Ann Spangler
Praying the Names of God
Zondervan

Gems of Wisdom...

Psalm 19:14
Psalm 119:15
Psalm 23:3
Philippians 4:6
Psalm 107::9

Refreshing Hugs...

Reflect on the words of Psalm 139:1, 5-6. The Living Bible phrases it this way: "Lord, you have examined my heart and know everything about me... You both precede and follow me, and place Your hand of blessing on my head. This is too glorious, too wonderful to believe."

Let's purpose in our hearts to meditate on our Amazing Creator daily... to enjoy God and the precious life He's given us. Let's seek to emulate His Kindness, His Grace, His Everlasting Love, His Joy...

HONOR... IT'S THE RIGHT THING TO DO!

"Honor your father and mother. Then you will live a long,
full life in the land the Lord your God will give you."
Exodus 20:12

The breakdown of the family system in today's society... How often have we heard this type of phrase repeated? God, in creating His astonishing sociological structure, provides a healthy balance. He offers His Principles as a guide to creating healthy family relationships. One such principle deals with honor, as He gently admonishes children to honor their parents. The second part of this verse contains a promise, "Then you will live a long, full life in the land the Lord your God will give you."

Ephesians 6:1 reinforces the original commandment, "Children, obey your parents because you belong to the Lord, for this is the right thing to do." We are God's Kids, no matter our age. By learning how to submit and honor our parents, God teaches us how we need to be placed under their authority, as we are growing up. Once we reach adulthood, the umbrella of authority shifts from our parents to our Abba Father. Once we've reached that stage, hopefully we have already been groomed to honor and obey the Lord. While all of the above seems elementary, because many of us do learn the Ten Commandments, at an early age, there are those of us who have come from dysfunctional backgrounds. If this is the case, adhering to the "honor" and the "obedience" commandment, may not come so naturally...

In a world filled with open rebellion to nearly every authority figure, we need to return to the wisdom of our Abba Father, and listen... If we are parents, are we ever disappointed in the way our children behave sometimes? Of course we are. And, like some of you, who are parents, Honey and I have gone without adequate sleep, at times, because of our concern over some of the choices our children have made. Having said that, there are times when we learn God's Will from the unhealthy choices we make, like the Israelites were prone to doing... The very reason we need to stay focused on God's Wisdom, and not attempt to rely on our own, comes from the fact that His Wisdom is perfect; ours, however, definitely needs His thumbprint on it...

"Honor your father and mother. Then you will live a long life..." That's God's promise, and what a precious one it is. As far as the adequate sleep issue, well, the bible tells us this: "Our God, the God of Israel, never slumbers or sleeps..." [my paraphrase]. I have repeated that verse in another segment. Suffice it to say, God doesn't sleep because He doesn't need to... Instead, He watches over His Kids... 24/7.

So, "No worries," as my friend Heather puts it! Heather is a single mom to her teen-age son, Jaden. Heather is a talented jewelry artist and nail technician. She sometimes has to work long hours. But, Heather always knows exactly where Jaden is, at any given time. Jaden is a highly gifted young man, and his mom is very proud of him. Jaden is also a very responsible person. Nevertheless, Heather agrees that the best advice to offer a parent[s] of a teenager[s], is to keep close tabs on them, know who their friends are, and know that those friends are trustworthy. Several times I have heard Heather say, "Check-in, Jaden." As parents, it is our responsibility to pray over our children, and to daily entrust them into God's tender care.

In Psalm 3:5, God reassures us, through the Psalmist David, of His Loving Care...

"I lay down and slept. I woke up in safety,
for the Lord was watching over me."

In Psalm 4:8, David reiterates God's Promise of His Peace,

"I will lie down in peace and sleep, for
You alone, O Lord, will keep me safe."

REST WELL NOW...

Heart Whispers...

Dear God, You are our Papa God, and it is Your Good Pleasure to guide and protect us, and, to correct us, when we start to wander off in the wrong direction.

Thank You for Your guidance and direction that serve to empower us to follow Your Commandments. Ephesians 6:1 teaches us an important life lesson and the lesson is that, "...this is the right thing to do." Help those of us who are parents of pre-teens or teenagers, to pass Your legacy of Wisdom on to our children. Remind us to follow Your Word and Your example so that our children will pass them on to their children... In the name of the God who teaches His Kids to follow in His Footprints... Amen.

Bouquets of Grace-Filled Blessings...

"When children do not honor their father or mother... Identifying and destroying the idols of pride and selfishness through prayer can often be the key to breaking a child's rebellion.

-Stormie Omartian
The Power of a Praying Parent
Harvest House Publishers

Gems of Wisdom...

Exodus 20:12
I Samuel 1:27-28
Psalm 103:17-18
Proverbs 22:6

Refreshing Hugs...

The quote by Stormie Omartian clearly places the emphasis on the power of prayer. Prayer is the key to every issue that is challenging to us... including issues surrounding those challenges regarding raising our children.

If one or both of your parents are living, send them a card mentioning some of the ways you honor and appreciate them. If this is difficult for you to do, try writing a note but don't send it. God sees your heart's intent...

Continue to pray, asking for the Holy Spirit's creativity to help you process the "honor" principle...and how best to convey that honor to your parent(s).

A BEAUTIFUL PRAISE SONG

"...the Lord said to Israel: I have loved you, My people, with an everlasting love. With unfailing love I have drawn you to Myself."
Jeremiah 31:3

I say to you, Daughter of Elohim Chayim-The Living God, if you are experiencing a pervasive heaviness in your spirit; if you feel pressured by all of the responsibilies you may need to deal with on a daily basis; or if you are feeling just plain old "down in the dumps," I am speaking into your life right now. In a loud voice-I mean a really loud voice, shout your highest praise to your King!

Here's the thing, Adored Princess, it is simply not possible to remain despondent when you are giving God your highest praise! As you exalt Him, the things that are troubling you will begin to diminish in intensity; eventually they will begin to fade, because, He sends His angels to minister to those who are feeling overwhelmed, exhausted, or feel as if they have somehow failed. Sometimes, a Princess is just needing an extraordinary measure of JOY..."

Joy is exactly what we need when things begin to get "a little crazy," as our daughter, Anita, expresses it. A great example is Elijah, a prophet of the Lord. In I Kings 19:3-8, we find Elijah fearful for his life. He sits down underneath a broom tree and prays that God will take his life because he has, "...had enough." The man of God falls asleep. As Elijah sleeps, an angel touches him and tells him to "...get up and eat!" When Elijah looks, he sees some bread, or a cake, in one translation, that has been freshly baked. He also sees "...a jar of water..." The food sustained him for "forty days and forty nights..." God sent an angel to provide what the prophet needed, in order to continue to carry out the rest of God's call on his life.

Please listen now. While Elijah's situation is vastly different than ours may be, as is his response to those situations, what we do know is this: It is humanly impossible to focus upon two different things at the same time. If your focus is on Jesus, that focus will not be turned inward, but upward. Your focus will be directed on the Kings of kings, and the Lord over every one of your challenges. You have God's Promises to rely upon. Listen to the words of Isaiah 61:1-3, as it is phrased in the NLT,

"The Spirit of the Sovereign Lord is upon Me, because the Lord has appointed Me to bring good news to the poor. He has sent Me to comfort the brokenhearted and to announce that captives will be released and prisoners will be freed. He has sent Me to tell those who mourn that the time of the Lord's favor has come, and with it, the day of God's anger against their enemies. To all who mourn in Israel, He will give beauty for ashes, joy instead of mourning, praise instead of despair. For the Lord has planted them like strong and graceful oaks for His own glory."

So, His Priceless Treasure, "...the time of the Lord's favor has come..." Hold out your hands to receive beauty, joy, and a brand new praise song, just for God. Praise Him, for He says, "...I have loved you, My people, with an everlasting love. With unfailing love I have drawn you to Myself."

Heart Whispers...

Dear God, You are the original praise song Creator,

You are Mighty, Awesome, Powerful, Wonderful... Please cover Your Princess with Your Grace. Shower her heart with overflowing blessings. Give her a double portion of Your Presence, and Your Anointing, Holy Spirit, today, tomorrow, and straight into eternity... In the name of the God whose very name is Awe-Inspiring, and who is worthy of our highest praise! Amen.

Bouquets of Grace-Filled Blessings...

"Sometimes God puts a new song in our mouths-a hymn of praise to our God! Other times, He brings us back to an old song... No doubt about it, sometimes God wants to hear an old song from a new heart."

-Beth Moore
Beloved Disciple Bible Study
LifeWay Press

Gems of Wisdom...

Psalm 34:1-3
Judges 5:3
Jeremiah 17:14
Ephesians 5:19
Psalm 65:1

Refreshing Hugs...

Now would be a great time to start a new precedence. If you have not previously done so, consider beginning your daily devotional time with praise and worship. Psalms 136, 138, and 147-150, just for starters, are great joy boosters!

EXTENDING AN OLIVE BRANCH

"Never seek revenge or bear a grudge against anyone, but
love your neighbor as yourself. I am the Lord."
Leviticus 19:18

According to Leviticus 19:18, the love we demonstrate toward our neighbors is the same kind of love we should extend toward ourselves. When God finishes His sentence with the words, "I am the Lord," He should have our rapt attention-like immediately. The point is that we must learn to place great emphasis on each of our earthly relationships because God takes each one of them and makes them sacred.

God gently admonishes each and every one of His saints to learn from His chastening. In Hebrews 12:5-6, the Lord gives us this instruction, "And have you entirely forgotten the encouraging words God spoke to you, His children? He said, "My child, don't ignore it when the Lord disciplines you, and don't be discouraged when He corrects you. For the Lord disciplines those He loves, and He punishes those He accepts as His children." It was that very chastening that was teaching me to love, in spite of how I felt. I soon discovered, as God reminds us in His Word, that it is easy to love those who love us in return. But, oh, how difficult it sometimes becomes, to love those who have hurt or offended us.

The following is an example of how the Lord used His disciplinary method in order to teach me how to "love my neighbors" unconditionally. Many years ago, when my children were small, we lived on the other side of a duplex from a man who was a single dad. He was a traveling accountant who often came home in the middle of the night. He had his children living with him, part of the time. This family was disturbing our peace, and our rest.

I had to get up early in the morning, get my children ready for daycare, and get to work. I petitioned the Lord with a very compassionate prayer that went something like this: "Lord, You know all things. You know that we can't get proper rest with the level of noise on the other side of this duplex, especially, when it occurs, in the middle of the night. So, Lord Jesus, I ask that You either move our neighbors, or move us somewhere else." Needless to say, I was just a tad bit astonished when my prayer went unanswered. Imagine that!

On a serious note, I began to ask the Lord to change my heart toward our neighbors; something I really didn't want to do. So, I asked Him to give me a love for my neighbors that I did not feel!

Now, for the grand finale to the tale of a whining Princess... I asked the Lord to forgive me for the hardness of my heart. His answer came in a most unusual way. I felt the Lord prompting me to bake a cake for our neighbors. He reminded me of His instructions in Romans 12:20, "...If your enemies are hungry, feed them. If they are thirsty, give them something to drink, and they will be ashamed of what they have done to you." "Okay," I thought, "but our neighbors are not really our enemies, no matter how disruptive they are to our peace and quiet." God needed to do some major tenderizing upon the stubborn attitude that had decided to take up residency in my heart. I had to repent, because, I had allowed that to happen. Now that I think about it, I don't think He was suggesting using seasoning salt, either.

Just to make sure I was listening, God reminded me of Proverbs 16:7, which says this, "When the ways of people please the Lord, He makes even their enemies live at peace with them." The Lord was, indeed, softening my heart toward our neighbors. He showed me how to look past their inconsiderate behavior. He allowed me a glimpse into His heart-a heart filled with compassion for them because they didn't have a personal relationship with Him. To this day, I am still not sure that they came to know the One who absolutely adored this single dad and his children. But God knows, and that is all that really matters...

Heart Whispers...

Dear God, You are the Architect of Divine Appointments,

It's not always easy to love our neighbors, as You command. But, in my own life, in each instance, I have become a recipient of a blessing, through being obedient to You. It's good to know that a little thing like baking for someone, could open a door for sharing Your Goodness and Grace to a lost family. Thank You, God, for presenting us with that privilege.

I ask that You arrange divine appointments, for Your Precious Princess, to share Your unending Love and the message of Your Amazing Grace, with those You so strategically place in her life. In the name of the God who is the original Olive Branch Extender. Amen.

Bouquets of Grace-Filled Blessings...

"I have learned that when, at your lowest moment, you are gifted with grace and acceptance, you are given fresh grace for others, too."

-Shiela Walsh
Devotion: *Words of Grace*
Adapted from:
Extravagant Grace
Zondervan

Gems of Wisdom...

John 16:33
2 Corinthians 8:9

Refreshing Hugs...

Envision an Olive Branch in the form of a note addressed to God. Thank Him for all the Olive Branch prayers the Spirit of God has led you to pray. And thank Him for the way He graces your prayers with His never-ending thoughts toward you, His Beautiful Bride.

"I tell you, her sins-and they are many-have been forgiven, so she has shown
Me much love. But a person who is forgiven little shows only little love."
Luke 7:47

What? Dinner at that Pharisee's House? No way! Ahhh, let's examine
the verse, describing this event, in light of an earlier account found in Luke
7:36-39, "One of the Pharisees asked Jesus to come to his home for a meal,
so Jesus accepted the invitation and sat down to eat. A certain immoral
woman heard He was there and brought a beautiful jar filled with expensive
perfume. Then she knelt behind Him at His feet, weeping. Her tears fell on
His feet, and she wiped them off with her hair. Then she kept kissing His
feet and putting perfume on them..." The Pharisee, who was the dinner host,
proceeded to ostracize the Lord, saying that the incident proved that Jesus was
not a prophet. The Pharisee inferred that if He was a prophet, He would know
what kind of "woman" she was, and would never allow her to touch Him.

The "immoral woman" described in these verses, was a sinner whom God
chose to use as a prototype of all human beings. She needed the forgiveness
that only Jesus could give... So do we. Her sins were "many..." So are ours.
Her sacrifice was a genuine expression from her heart, stemming from the
privilege of being near her Lord. We want to be closer to Jesus, too. Jesus was
the only One who could wash away the stain of her sin forever. Jesus is the
only One who can wash away the stains of our sin forever, as well. It was His
tender forgiveness that she sought, and His Loving Presence that she longed
for. So it is with us. It was this woman, who, kneeling humbly at the feet of
her Lord, washed them with her tears...

This "immoral woman" kissed Jesus' feet and anointed them with
precious, costly perfume. But what we are not told is what this oil cost her in
terms of the emotional trauma often indicative of the life of a harlot... And,
that is what Mary was, before she encountered the transforming touch of
her Messiah's Forever Love. She experienced, first hand, the power of God's
forgiveness.

Not a shred of hypocrisy could be found in Mary; there was only
love and adoration for her Savior. Afterall, it was Jesus who was responsible

for setting her free. He set her free from the bondage her profession had branded, like a steaming hot iron, upon her soul. Only He could give her a new reputation before the eyes of the Pharisees. They had chastised her, and stamped her with the name "Sinner." But now, Mary had a new title, "Forgiven of God". Now she was free to share the incredible mercy of her Lord Jesus, for all future generations to embrace. Now, we, as believers, are free to share the incredible Mercy and Grace of our Savior, our Lord Jesus, for future generations to experience...

Many years ago, I was in a Christian bookstore browsing through some cards. A beautiful message was inscribed on one of those cards which reminded me of the lesson Jesus taught this woman. The words haunted my soul, in a melancholy kind of way, as these words drove home the same astounding love our Savior has for each of us:

> "Love trusts when nothing else seems sure,
> Love knows when pressing doubts endure
> Love stands when winds of turmoil blow,
> Love lifts when burdens bend us low;
> Love hopes when dreams seem sacrificed...
> Love endures when it begins with Christ."

As you allow the love of Jesus to flow through you, give all of it away that you can...

Heart Whispers...

Dear God, You are the God of Forever Forgiveness and Incomprehensible Grace,

Help us to be a lover of souls, just like You are, Lord Jesus. May we develop a heart that gives and gives and gives, without hesitation. May we strive, each day, to love much and to forgive every offense, just as You've forgiven our offenses...

May Your Precious Princess ask for Your forgiveness, and may she extend forgiveness to those who have hurt or offended her, so that she can become a living testimony of Your Tender Mercies and Your Extraordinary Grace. In the name of the God who has given us the example of His kind of Love: Love that trusts... Love that knows... Love that stands... Love that lifts... Love that hopes... Love that endures...when it begins with Christ. Amen.

Bouquets of Grace-Filled Blessings...

"I want my speech to be full of love even when I'm offering correction. Full of mercy and forgiveness, for God has had mercy upon me. Words fewer in number, but richer in truth and love."

-Joanna Weaver
Having a Mary Spirit
Waterbrook Press

Gems of Wisdom...

Luke 7:36-50

Refreshing Hugs...

Ask the Holy Spirit for an opportunity to "wash someone's feet." Through our ministry to a hurting world, we are given the privilege of showing our love for our Lord. I pray, loving Princess of Messiah Jesus, that I have blessed you in some way. Thank you for sharing a few moments of your time with me!

Remain full of His mercy, His forgiveness, and His never-ending grace... Extend these three to others, as generously as Jesus has poured His grace, mercy, and forgiveness over your life... And, may God bless your servant's heart!

GOD'S BEAUTIFUL "JEWEL"

"But the Lord said to Samuel, "Don't judge by his apprearance
or height, for I have rejected him. The Lord doesn't make
decisions the way you do! People judge by outward appearance,
but the Lord looks at a person's thoughts and intentions."
I Samuel 16:7

Obsessed with image-the outward appearance of what it calls "the beautiful person", today's society highlights beauty, in a physical sense, as something to be sought after. The end result is that we are constantly bombarded with advertisements touting products which will make us more appealing, prettier, ageless, handsome, more attractive, and on and on the promises go.

In His gentle voice, God speaks to each Princess about the beauty He sees when He looks at her. Precious Treasure of the King, your Master desires that when you look at yourself, you see what He sees: unmatched grace, a lovely disposition, a sweet spirit, tender compassion, the fruit of: love, joy, peace, patience, kindness, goodness, faithfulness, gentleness, and self-control.

So, does this sound like a litany of unattainable qualities we will never be able to grasp? Not true! These qualities are the embodiment of the fruit of the Spirit. Okay. So, does this mean that we should not give consideration to our appearance at all? It absolutely does not! If you are married, God wants you to be attractive to your husband, always thinking about ways to please him. Does God expect us to give little thought as to how we present ourselves to others, should we work in a professional office setting, for example? Again, the answer is no. Just as we should make every effort to eat healthy, get plenty of rest, and exercise on a regular basis-whatever that may look like for our particular lifestyle-we need to make an effort to look our best, as His ambassador.

The type of work we do will determine our attire. I meet coaching clients, occassionally, in a restaurant, coffee shop, or at their home. I always dress appropriately. I now do the majority of my coaching sessions by phone. The exception to that are the *Kool Kids Kitchen Klasses* I am planning, in our city, as well as outings to the market or grocery store to teach a younger Princess how to practice good stewardship, servanthood, selflessness, and sharing of their gifts and resources, etc.

If coaching by phone, I can wear whatever clothing is really comfortable. I love being able to work out of my home; regardless of the attire, however, the professional parameters are always in place. Once I walk into my office, I am all about that coaching client, and my passion to help her to realize her goals and dreams...

When all is said and done, what truly takes precedence is what is in our heart. What is a priority to God, are the "thoughts and intentions" of a pure heart. What truly matters is the substance of the heart of each Princess. I Peter 3:4 says, "You should be known for the beauty that comes from within, the unfading beauty of a gentle and quiet spirit, which is so precious to God."

And now, awesome Bride of Messiah, it's time to practice seeing yourself with the same qualities He chose to place in you from the beginning of your life story... As you grew, the custom designed qualities blossomed, as well. God loves you, and it is time for you to recognize that you hold a place of incredible value in His heart, because you do!

Last year, I had the blessing of attending an Extraordinary Women's Conference. From the very beginning of the week-end, to its conclusion, Julie Clinton, president of Extraordinary Women and host of E Women conferences held throughout the country, modeled, with grace, the role of an ambassador for God. Julie's enthusiasm and passion to partner with God in raising up extraordinary women, is truly inspiring. The messages given by great speakers, the awesome worship, and great fellowship, made the event truly special.

I have mentioned this point previously, but I strongly believe it bears repeating. We do not always stop to think about it, but, no matter where we are, no matter who we meet along our odyssey path, we are His ambassadors. We are not always aware of who is watching, so our behavior, our attitude, and our words, serve to form a mirror to the world, regardless of our geographical location.

"The fountain of beauty is the heart, and every generous thought illustrates the walls of your chamber." The author of that quote is unknown, but the sentiment is so lovely and filled with such truth, just thought I'd share it with you. Sometimes, God places something right in front of our eyes that fills our day with sunshine. I hope your day is filled with thoughts of loveliness and a heart that desires to give and give...

You are God's Jewel. You are absolutely lovely. And, as my forever friend Lenora says, oh, so eloquently, "You are Special." You are His Treasure. And may you always remember that God loves beautiful you!

Heart Whispers...

Dear God, You model Perfect Graciousness,

Holy Spirit, touch the spiritual eyes of Your Princess so that she may see herself as You see her-Your Jewel. It is You alone, Lord, who gives us our self-worth. In the name of the God who knows our hearts inside and out, and is pleased with what He sees! Amen.

Bouquets of Grace-Filled Blessings...

"... society has responded inadequately to rejection... we try to copy the... dress, ideas, and behavioral patterns of a particular group... to determine what is correct... turning to others for what only God can provide is a direct result of acceptance of Satan's lies..."

-Robert S. McGee
The Search For Significance
Rapha Publishing

Gems of Wisdom...

Colossians 2:8-10
Zechariah 9:9
Malachi 3:17

Refreshing Hugs...

If you struggle with feelings of rejection, there is an exercise that my friend, Pastor Elaine, introduced to me, and subsequently used, with a degree of success, when we were co-facilitating a support group.

On a blank sheet of paper, draw a line down the center. On the left side of the page, at the top, label the column: "What I Say About Myself When I Am Being Critical of Me." Now, list five or six criticisms you might have of yourself.

On the right side, at the top, label the column: What God Says About Me. List five or six Scriptures that are affirmations of what God has to say about you.

Read this page as often as you find necessary, until you are totally convinced that Satan is a liar, and the father of every lie! The really good news is that God is Truth. So, what He says about you is absolutely and unequivocably true!

A FOREVER AUDIENCE WITH THE KING

"Look! Here I stand at the door and knock. If you hear Me calling and open the door, I will come in, and we will share a meal as friends. I will invite everyone who is victorious to sit with Me on My throne, just as I was victorious and sat with My Father on His throne. Anyone who is willing to hear should listen to the Spirit and understand what the Spirit is saying..."
Revelation 3:20

This book was written to encourage you with hope-hope that your odyssey can have a new beginning. Hope that is intended to challenge you, Princess of Great Destiny, to allow the God of All Grace to teach you the deep truths of His Word. Hope that will help you grow in God's Wisdom. Come to Your Messiah. Only He can make it happen. Don't wait, don't hesitate another moment. Whatever you need, trust that God knows and will guide you in the direction He wants you to go. Find the treasures waiting for you in God's Word.

If possible, go to your quiet place. Once you have settled in, there are three words I'd like you to concentrate on: focus, discover, respond. Focus on your need. A personal relationship with Jesus is paramount. If your focus remains on the Lord, everything else will fall into place. His passion is to see every believer walking in step with the Holy Spirit...

Discover God's Provisions for meeting other needs you may have. Get the facts by discovering the biblical truths to support them. Once you have done this, you may want to explore an application bible that might help you apply God's Truth to your life.

Respond by way of action. Read Revelation 3:20. The last line calls for a response from His Bride saying, "Anyone who is willing to hear should listen to the Spirit and understand what the Spirit is saying..."

The joy God desires each of us to experience is expressed in I Peter 1:8-9, "You love Him even though you have never seen Him. Though you do not see Him, you trust Him; and even now you are happy with a glorious, inexpressible joy. Your reward for trusting Him will be the salvation of your souls." You know what, Princess, it just can't possibly get any better than that!

The author is unknown, but the following sentiment speaks volumes about our place in God's heart: "There will never be anyone like you. Allowing God to fulfill His purpose in you is the miracle for which you were created."

Heart Whispers,

Dear God, You are the God of Inexpressible Joy... and Soothing Comfort,

2 Corinthians 4:16, as The Message phrases it, reads, "Even though on the outside it often looks like things are falling apart on us, on the inside, where God is making new life, not a day goes by without his unfolding grace."

Lord, may Your Unmatched Grace and Your Unparalled Favor rest upon Your Princess. In the name of the God who comforts us and brings us joy in this present life, and invites us to spend Eternity in His Presence... Amen.

Bouquets of Grace-Filled Blessings...

"The person who has life with God is the person who confesses the nature of God as holy and who wants a relationship with the Holy One. That means holiness is esteemed, praised, and sought by those who live with and in God."

-Jim McGuiggan
The God of the Towel
Howard Publishing Co., Inc.

Gems of Wisdom...

Psalm 67:2
Romans 1:16-17
Titus 2:13-14
2 Corinthians 6:2
Isaiah 6:1-3
Romans 1:3-5
Acts 17:28

Refreshing Hugs...

Once you have received Jesus into your heart as your Lord and Savior, ask God to give you an opportunity to share your testimony with others. God is such a good God. Don't hesitate to give a testimony of what the Lord has done for you. It is the best one you have to share.

MAKING HIS PASSION... YOUR PASSION

"But Ruth replied, "Don't ask me to leave you and turn back.
I will go wherever you go and live wherever you live. Your
people will be my people, and your God will be my God."
Ruth 1:16

An object lesson in selflessness, Ruth's devotion to her mother-in-law, Naomi, teaches its reader a great deal about the characteristics of loyalty, steadfastness, faithfulness, and devotion. Eugenia Price writes about the love between Ruth and Naomi. I am uncertain as to the source of the quote, but, I like Eugenia's astute observation, "Love is not limited by the type of relationship between two people. Love is only limited by human self-concern..." She continues to expound upon this love, with tender insight, "Love itself is never limited by the circumstances of a relationship, because, God, Himself, is never limited-except by a closed heart."

When Naomi urges Ruth to go back to Moab, following the death of her husband, Ruth's response exemplifies her devotion and loyalty to her mother-in-law, just as Naomi had shown her own deep devotion and loyalty to her God. Ruth was blessed by her mother-in-law's example. What a beautiful witness Naomi was to Ruth. God desires a love relationship with His Precious Princess; that kind of devotion and love comes when we consciously choose, as Naomi did, to give our all to Him.

Rhetorical questions seem to work for me. There are times when I ask rhetorical type questions of my clients. There are also times I ask rhetorical questions of myself. An example: What else does God want me to do while I am working on re-kindling my relationship with Him? I began to study the relationships Jesus had with His disciples. I studied the relationships Jesus developed with those who needed healing. Messiah Jesus loved to fellowship. He loved to mingle with people while sharing a meal with them. I studied the prophets and Old Testament figures who seemed to have such an amazing depth to their relationship with God.

I began by reading books that were truly uplifting; books written by authors who were not only inspiring, but who challenged the reader to pursue God, to draw ever so close to Him, to brag about Him, to worship and praise

Him... It seemed like quite a while, but I began to notice a change in my prayer life. Contemplative prayer, reflective prayer, intercessory prayer-they all became instrumental in the changes I realized I had been looking to make.

If I am speaking to a Princess who desperately wants her relationship with the Lord to be an inspiring one, a passionate one, I have awesome news! The Spirit of God is waiting patiently for permission to lead you back into His arms. Don't hesitate; don't let circumstances or business stymie your passion for a closer walk with your God.

God is waiting to ignite in you, once again, a passion to draw ever so near to Him. And when that passion is ignited, He wants to bless you as you continue to grow in His image. He wants your relationships with friends to be rekindled. He wants you to partner with Him to become an encourager to those He so carefully chooses to place in your sphere of influence...

Heart Whispers...

Dear God, You are the God of every blessed relationship, beginning with our relationship with You,

Please give Your Princess many opportunities to share Your goodness, Your faithfulness, and Your Gift of Salvation, with the world. Protect her by placing Your angels around her. Protect her, Lord Jesus, from any attempt to interfere with Your destiny for her life that the enemy may be plotting to use...

Lord, increase her faith in Your awesome power to save and heal those who are living without that personal relationship You desire every soul to cultivate. In the name of the God whose heart is ablaze with a passion for every lost soul, and, for every Princess who desires to rekindle her relationship with You, first and foremost. Please help her to bring a refreshing to her relationships with close friends, and her desire to be an encouragement to them. In the name of the God whose passion for relationship is Awe-Inspiring. Amen.

Bouquets of Grace-Filled Blessings...

"How solemn, how almost overwhelming, is the thought that the Holy Spirit has no way of getting at the unsaved with His saving power except through the instrumentality of those of us who are already Christians. The Holy Spirit needs human lips to speak through. He needs yours."

-R.A. Torrey
Power Filled Living
Whitaker House

Gems of Wisdom...

Matthew 7:24
Jeremiah 1:9
The Book of Ruth in your favorite Bible version

Refreshing Hugs...

There are excellent sources on the how-to's of witnessing to the lost. Your local bookstore can be a great source for picking up some tracks to give away. Your local library can be another good resource of Christian books about or authored by Evangelists who travel the world spreading the Gospel of Good News.

May God bless every endeavor you make, to make His Passion-your passion.

AN EXCELLENT SPIRIT

"But when Daniel learned that the law had been signed, he
went home and knelt down as usual in his upstairs room, with
its windows open toward Jerusalem. He prayed three times a
day, just as he had always done, giving thanks to his God."
Daniel 6:10

Daniel was a young man whose faith in God was inspiring to behold.
He was a prophet living in exile in the middle of Babylon, one of the four
great empires of that era. The sixth chapter of the Book of Daniel speaks of
the reign of King Darius. It also heralds Daniel's appointment as one of three
governors:

"...Now Daniel so distinguished himself among the administrators... by his
exceptional qualities that the king planned to set him over the whole
kingdom..."
Daniel 6:1-10 NIV

In Daniel 6:10, we are told that Daniel got down on his knees not once,
but three times every day in order to give thanks to his God. That must
have worn out some tunics, huh? This scripture passage also gives us a clue
regarding the ammunition the satraps and govenors used to entrap Daniel,
and it came in the form of Daniel's devotion to serving His God and loving
Him with his whole heart.

When I first accepted Christ, many years ago, I remember hearing the
pastor speak on the importance of a "quiet time" with God. Some time later,
I began asking the Lord to bless my time alone with Him. That request led to
much circumspection and reflection regarding my attitudes and thoughts, some
of which desperately needed changing. Those times of quiet served to refresh
my spirit like a sweet comforting hug; a hug that ultimately led to a deeper
and far more comfortable relationship with God, than I ever thought possible.

Daniel learned early on that his "quiet time" with God brought victory
and deliverance. Not only was Daniel delivered from captivity, but he was
spared from a close encounter with the mouth of a hungry lion. His prayer

time with the Lord, as well as his faithfulness and obedience, resulted in glorious visions; a vision of the future for Israel and prophecy regarding the great empires of his time, all of which God imparted to him in those quiet moments that Daniel shared with his Messiah.

Daniel was also taught the amazing sovereignty of his Lord, after being asked to interpret a dream the king, Belshazzar, had experienced. Daniel 5:20-21, in the NIV, phrases it this way, Belshazzar, after he ... was driven away from people," because of his pride and his arrogancy, and was subsequently, "...given the mind of an animal... acknowledged that the Most High God is sovereign over the kingdoms of men and sets over them anyone he wishes." It is more than a strong implication. The truth is that it is God Almighty who appoints rulers, as He chooses. While we can't always comprehend His reasoning, we must respect the authority He places over us. In all circumstances, Daniel knew that his God reigns. It is a truth that should become permanently etched upon the walls of our hearts, as well.

Elizabeth George, in her inspiring and enlightening book entitled, *A Women's High Calling,* subtitled her book: 10 Essentials For Godly Living. Listen to Elizabeth's godly wisdom, as she points to the fact that if we merely seek to live a godly life and just seek to do the right thing, these things are still not enough to become the godly women that our Lord is calling us to become. She points directly, with vivid accuracy, to the type of character God expects us to develop, "...we must have God's image stamped upon our souls. Our hearts must belong to Him and beat along with His. Our desires must be His desires...our every deed marked by His presence..." We must also have "...a soul that is stamped by the image and superscription of God."

Let's purpose to become like Daniel. Let's make it our goal to become godly Princesses who exhibit the character of our Messiah Jesus. Let's strive to study His Word each and every day. Let's make it a top priority to spend quiet moments with our Abba Father. Let's determine to become a Daughter of the Most High God, who is devoted to much prayer, praise, spiritual discipline, generosity, and thanksgiving...

Let's commit, with intentionality, and with our whole heart, mind, soul, and strength, to serve the Lord out of hearts filled to overflowing with His Radiant Love, His Inspiring Encouragement, and His Matchless Grace...

Let's determine to pattern our set of core values with the same kind of "excellent spirit" that Daniel exemplified, no matter the consequences, throughout his life. Let's live purposely, to serve others who may be hurting.

May each of us tap into the treasures found in living a victorious life; a life that is meant to bring God Glory. And may we pass that legacy of an excellent spirit on to the next precious one, and the next, and the next... always giving honor to the Mighty God we serve!

Heart Whispers...

Dear God, You are the Master Artist of an Excellent Spirit,

May each of us become Beloved Princesses who seek after Your own heart. May we become devoted to much prayer, and time spent in Your Word, each and every day.

God, help Your Princess to turn over her schedule and plans to You. May she devote the first fruits of her time, each morning, listening to Your voice, and being obedient to the destiny road You have blueprinted for her life. Speak through Your Word, and through others that You place alongside her, as she travels along on her odyssey. May she empower others so they, too, will strive toward maintaining an excellent spirit that will bring glory and honor to You. In the name of the God who inspires us to develop an excellent spirit, and to serve others graciously, just as His servant Daniel did. Amen.

Bouquets of Grace-Filled Blessings...

"The secret of living a life of excellence is merely a matter of thinking thoughts of excellence... it's a matter of programming our minds with the kind of information that will set us free... to be all God meant us to be. Free to soar!"

-Charles Swindoll
Living Above the Level of Mediocity
A Commitment to Excellence
Inspirational Press, Published by
arrangement with Word, Inc.

Gems of Wisdom...

Daniel 5:12
Daniel 6:23
Romans 12:2

Refreshing Hugs...

Set aside ten or fifteen minutes this week to pray for anyone you may have recently met who has a need, or who may be feeling overwhelmed. Ask the Holy Spirit to give you ways to creatively minister to them. Be blessed for being a blessing!

PRAISE HIM! HONOR HIM! WORSHIP HIM!

"That is why I can never stop praising You; I
declare Your glory all day long."
Psalm 71:8

Attitude checks... ay yay yay yay yay! Or, however it's spelled ... Attitude checks are not the epitome of a boat load of fun. Nevertheless, they are necessary to get things put in the proper perspective, for a Princess of the King of kings. God calls us to establish, and maintain a posture of thanksgiving and a spirit of highest praise, to Him. Let's develop an attitude of genuine thanksgiving for our family, church family, friends, neighbors, country, and world... That's just a small sampling of a large list of attitudes God wants us to carbon copy...

Honey and I have a plaque in our home that personifies what we believe the attitude of our hearts should look like. It goes like this:

In This Home...

We Do Grace.
We Do Real.
We Do Mistakes.
We Do I'm Sorry.
We Do Loud Really Well.
We Do Hugs.
We Do Family.
We Do Love.

I particularly like these two: We Do Mistakes. We Do I'm Sorry.

I have a tendency to need to use these two often... uh, make that very often! The only three things I would add to this great list, by an unknown author, are:

We Do Personal Quiet Time With Jesus Daily.
We Keep Our "Stuff" Uncluttered, Organized, and Clean.

263

We Maintain An Attiude Of Respect For Other People's Possessions.

Now, for the "...I can never stop praising You..." part... the following is just a fraction of the multitude of things we can praise God for:

> *Praise God because He is Holy...*
> *Praise God because He is our Comforter through times of grief and loss...*
> *Praise God because He is our Messiah, our Savior, our King...*
> *Praise God because He fills us with blessings, beyond measure...*
> *Praise God because He is Sovereign...*
> *Praise God because He is our Defender...*
> *Praise God because He is our Redeemer...*
> *Praise God because He has written Words of Promise upon our hearts...*
> *Praise God because He has called us by our name and we belong to Him...*
> *Praise God because He has given us Eternal Life to spend with Him*
> *Praise God because He is the Rock of our salvation...*

Search His Word often, I encourage you, and you will find a lifetime of things to praise God for-beginning with this "Now Time" for your life. Psalm 119:24 says it so beautifully, "This is the day the Lord has made. We will rejoice and be glad in it."

Psalm 118:19-21, is a precious thank-you note to our Messiah, that we can express, just as the Psalmist David did when he penned these power-filled words,

> "Open for me the gates where the righteous enter, and I will go in and thank the Lord. Those gates lead to the presence of the Lord, and the godly enter there. I thank You for answering my prayer and saving me!"

Psalm 138:2, in the NIV, reminds us to worship and give thanks to Messiah Jesus...

"I will bow down toward Your holy temple and will praise
Your name for Your love and Your faithfulness..."

Heart Whispers...

Dear God, You fashion each day as a day for giving You our highest praise,

May our mouths be filled with praises to You as we rise in the morning and
lay down at night. May we fill our days with gratitude and joy because we
have been given the privilege and the pleasure of serving You, God. You are
mighty in power, Lord, and you set our spirits soaring. God, should there
be someone who needs a miracle in her life, please place Your soul-stirring
touch upon her in a new and life-refreshing way. And may she give You praise,
always. In the name of the One who is worthy of our highest praise... both
now and forever more! Amen.

Bouquets of Grace-Filled Blessings...

"...If you are singing praise songs to Jesus, or...thanking him for all the ways
he has changed your life... sitting quietly... as you listen to...praise and worship
songs...guess what? Jesus is there. With you. In the room. Worship Jesus. It's
time well spent."

-Karen Scalf Linamen
Just Hand Over the Chocolate and No One
Will Get Hurt
Fleming H. Revell

Gems of Wisdom...

Psalm 118:28-29
Psalm 119:47-48
Psalm 134:1-2
Psalm 135:1-3
Psalm 138:2

2 Corinthians 9:15
I Chronicles 16:29

Refreshing Hugs...

Consider treating yourself to an afternoon of R & R time, away from it all, just you and Jesus. Worship Him by singing your little heart out... That's it! Give the Lord your highest praise!

A FRESH BREATH OF EXPECTATION

"So I pray that God, who gives you hope, will keep you happy
and full of peace as you believe in Him. May you overflow
with hope through the power of the Holy Spirit."
Romans 15:13

Wonder-Working Power! That descriptive phrase alone, used to describe the Lord, could take your breath away-huh? Webster's dictionary defines a "wonder worker" as "a worker or performer of wonders or marvels." It defines the term "wonder" as "a remarkable or extraordinary phenomenon, deed, or event; marvel or miracle." We serve a God who can perform miracles in a heart that can, at times, be as obstinate and stubborn as a heart could be. We serve a God who can bring amazing change and stability to our emotions; emotions that can be as unpredictable as the prize in a box of Cracker Jacks...

Have you ever thought to yourself, "Is it really possible to be happy, filled with peace, and be overflowing with the kind of hope God promises? Each Princess needs a fresh breath of expectation from the Holy Spirit, to be breathed into that next important decision she is called to make... the next life transition that is just around the corner.. the next stepping stone infused with God's future destiny steps for the path He has designed, expressly for His Jewel. Only the God of Wonder-Working Power can make a promise like that! The Spirit of God wants to use that same powertank of hope, blended with joy, peace, and happiness, to bring blessings to every Cherished Princess...

Several times, throughout the bible, God speaks of pouring out His Spirit upon His people. The reference is found in Acts 2:17-20, which speaks of this outpouring, "... I will pour out My Spirit upon all people..." He closes this passage of scripture with Acts 2:21, containing God's Ultimate Promise, "And anyone who calls on the name of the Lord will be saved."

As you read those verses in the Book of Acts, keep at the forefront of your thoughts the Promise our Messiah has made. He promised to send the Spirit of God, who is our Helper, our Revealer, our Counselor... John 14:26 clarifies this promise, "But when the Father sends the Counselor as My representative-and by the Counselor I mean the Holy Spirit-He will teach you everything and will remind you of everything I Myself have told you." And to think, Precious Princess, all we need to do is ask.

The Holy Spirit is our Anointer. He wants to anoint and equip us with His Wonder-Working Power, so that we can help spread His light to others who may be needing assurance of His Love, His Help, His Hope, His Joy, His Promises...

So, ARISE, Beloved Princess! In the NIV of Isaiah 60:1-2, God calls us to, "Arise, shine, for your light has come, and the glory of the Lord rises upon you... His glory appears over you." God wants to use your story as a testimony! The process, as well as the progress of your own odyssey destiny, will draw people to Him and will display His Glory, His Purposes, His Plans for their personalized odyssey...

Arise and Shine for God! Now smile, Princess, for you have such a bright future ahead of you! Each time you are called on to give your testimony, may it touch, impact, and empower others to shine for Jesus, too!

Heart Whispers...

Dear God, You anoint Your Precious Daughter, for every act of service and good works, so that she may display Your Glory...

Fill her mouth, Father God, with holy laughter! May she delight in You forever! Use her, God, to empower others to walk in Your ways... May she spend her days giving You her highest praise, and bringing You all the Glory that You, alone, deserve! In the name of El Simchat Gili-God my exceeding joy! Amen.

Bouquets of Grace-Filled Blessings...

"...the wondrous world of privilege, blessing, victory, and conquest... is open to us. The same Spirit by which Jesus was anointed for service is at our disposal so that we may be anointed for service... The same Spirit... is here to teach us."

-R. A. Torrey
Power-Filled Living
Whitaker House

Gems of Wisdom...

Isaiah 61:1-3
2 Corinthians 1:21-22

Refreshing Hugs...

Visualize yourself as being filled to overflowing with the peace, joy, hope... of the Holy Spirit. Now, extend that vision to include His Power, as He works in you to accomplish His plan-a plan to use your testimony to inspire and empower others.

Can you see yourself as a vessel used by the Spirit of God to work in the area of health care? As an artist for Jesus? A musician? Or, maybe a marathon runner who contributes her donations for research to find a cure for a rare disease?

How about cooking for a local homeless shelter? As a guidance counselor? A mom that home schools?

Whatever call God has on your life, whatever odyssey He has in store for you, whatever purpose He has designated expressly for you, by His Grace, you can do it!

My prayer is that you receive a double portion of the blessing you are to others.

MY PRINCESS PRAYER ODYSSEY DAYBOOK

"May the Lord bless you and protect you.
May the Lord smile on you and be gracious to you.
May the Lord show you His favor and give you His peace."
Numbers 6:24-26

My Princess Prayer Odyssey Daybook is a preliminary guide, similar
to the one I use for my coaching clients. It is an easy way for you
to journal your prayers, and, encourage you to hand your agenda
over to God to help you prioritize your 1,440 minutes a day:

I cheerfully commit to giving God my agenda and my permission to
add, modify, or delete any items on that agenda that He desires...

&

I believe that by taking this important step, I will alleviate
much of the unhealthy stress levels in my overloaded, over-
committed, and, at times, overwhelming life...

&

By allowing God to prioritize my To Do list, I will be able to experience
more free time to devote to God's plan and direction for me in the areas
of: ministry opportunities, relationships, business, dreams, goals...

COMMITMENTS I WILL MAKE TO HELP
BRING BALANCE TO MY LIFE:

I will spend_____ time daily in Contemplative Prayer

I will spend_____ time daily in Meditative Prayer

I will spend _____ time daily in Intercessory Prayer

I will spend_____ time daily in Praise and Worship

I will spend_____ time daily in Leisure Time

I will spend _____ time daily devoted to Family, Friendships, and Fellowship

During your Selah Pause Breaks, this week, reflect on the following five qualities that were sent to me inside of a greeting card. The source is unknown, but the sentiments are filled with grace:

CARE...   *about others with passion and compassion...*

FIND...   *the true quality of contentment...*

GIVE...   *to others expecting nothing in return...*

HUG...   *a friend, especially your best friend...*

INSPIRE...   *someone to greatness by your example...*

DE-STRESSING AND DE-COMPRESSING THE LIFE OF A TREASURED PRINCESS:

The following are the first three, out of seven techniques, that I incorporate into some of my coaching sessions. My hope is that these will be of value to you as you plan your Selah Pause Breaks, and use these breaks as a time to begin de-stressing and de-compressing your life...

Always keep in mind the ultimate objective: To glorify God through creating an organized and well managed, yet flexible lifestyle; one that frees up extra time to devote to establishing a closer relationship with God, and the calling He has placed on your life.

These principles are best applied when working with a life coach whose niche is to help you develop your areas of spiritual giftedness... for example, motivational speaking, writing, expressing your artistic gift through painting or music, etc. And, whose niche includes helping you to recognize and define your strengths, and to develop those strengths so you are well on your way to successfully fulfilling those hopes and dreams you are longing to realize! Should you decide to select me as your life coach, here's a sample of where we would begin:

Technique #1: Learning to recognize and define your strengths emotionally, relationally, spiritually, occupationally... It will take time to get a handle on this process. We all have limitations, but working on this technique will help to emphasize your strengths so you can purpose to live out the calling God has designed exclusively for you.

Technique #2: The following exercise is one I formulated to use with some of my coaching clients who have a tendency to get "stuck" and have relationship issues because of some unrealistic expectations.

Take a sheet of paper. Draw a line down the center. Title the top left side: Unrealistic Expectations. Now, title the top right side: Realistic Expectations. Number the relationships on the left side, then place a first name next to the number. Begin #1 with yourself.

Do the same on the right side. Briefly state what you feel to be "Realistic Expectations." Repeat this process with each relationship.

Technique #3: The next step involves exploring a few of the unrealistic expectations you may have of yourself... It may take three or four sessions, but soon, we can begin to work on your expectations of others, which may need a little adjustment in your perspective. Please be mindful of the quality of grace. Remember to give yourself a little "grace room" so you can "lighten up" the room a bit. It won't be long before that "Unrealistic Expectations" column of yourself, and of others, will all but fade away...

BLESSINGS FROM JAN...

As your personal life coach, I look forward to encouraging and empowering you as you seek to clearly define your God-given goals, dreams, hopes and aspirations that are just waiting to be discovered. I want to inspire you to live an intentional life, focused on attaining the vision, placed on your heart by God, the Dream-Maker, who etched the blueprint for your destiny...

It would be a blessing to be your choice for the gift of life coaching sessions for your Mom, Sister, Aunt, Friend, Daughter, and Granddaughter... Gift Certificates available.

To contact me for speaking events, retreats,
coaching sessions, or signed book copies:

email: nanasugars777@gmail.com
Phone:1-702-807-5056

Jan Gantos
P.O. Box 36203
Las Vegas, NV 89133

My Princess Prayer Odyssey Daybook

Printed in the United States
By Bookmasters